Human–Computer Interaction

FASTTRACK

Human–Computer Interaction

Serengul Smith-Atakan

THOMSON™

Australia · Canada · Mexico · Singapore · Spain · United Kingdom · United States

THOMSON

Human–Computer Interaction

Serengul Smith-Atakan

Series Editors

Walaa Bakry, Middlesex University

Alan Murphy, Middlesex University

Middlesex
University
PRESS

Publishing Partner

Middlesex University Press

Publishing Director	**Commissioning Editor**	**Managing Editor**
John Yates	Gaynor Redvers-Mutton	Celia Cozens
Production Editor	**Manufacturing Manager**	**Marketing Manager**
Alissa Chappell	Helen Mason	Mark Lord
Production Controller	**Text Design**	**Cover Design**
Maeve Healy	Design Delux	Matthew Ollive
	Typesetter	**Printer**
	Keyline Consultancy	Zrinski, dd, Croatia

Contents

The FastTrack Series

Thomson Learning and Middlesex University Press have collaborated to produce a unique collection of textbooks which cover core, mainstream topics in an undergraduate computing curriculum. FastTrack titles are instructional, syllabus-driven books of high quality and utility. They are:

- **For students**: concise and relevant and written so that you should be able to get 100% value out of 100% of the book at an affordable price
- **For instructors**: classroom-tested, written to a tried and trusted pedagogy and market-assessed for mainstream and global syllabus offerings so as to provide you with confidence in the applicability of these books. The resources associated with each title are designed to make delivery of courses straightforward and linked to the text.

FastTrack books can be used for self-study or as directed reading by a tutor. They contain the essential reading necessary to complete a full understanding of the topic. They are augmented by resources and activities, some of which will be delivered online as indicated in the text.

How the series evolved

Rapid growth in communication technology means that learning can become a global activity. In collaboration, Global Campus, Middlesex University and Thomson Learning have produced materials to suit a diverse and innovating discipline and student cohort.

Global Campus at the School of Computing Science, Middlesex University, combines local support and tutors with CD Rom-based materials and the Internet to enable students and lecturers to work together across the world.

Middlesex University Press is a publishing house committed to providing high quality, innovative, learning solutions to organisations and individuals. The Press aims to provide leading-edge 'blended learning' solutions to meet the needs of its clients and customers. Partnership working is a major feature of the Press's activities.

Together with Middlesex University Press and Middlesex University's Centre for Learning Development, Global Campus developed FastTrack books using a sound and consistent pedagogic approach. The SCATE pedagogy is a learning framework that builds up as follows:

- **Scope:** Context and the learning outcomes
- **Content:** The bulk of the course: text, illustrations and examples
- **Activity:** Elements which will help students further understand the facts and concepts presented to them in the previous section. Promotes their active participation in their learning and in creating their understanding of the unit content
- **Thinking:** These elements give students the opportunity to reflect and share with their peers their experience of studying each unit. There are *review questions* so that the students can assess their own understanding and progress
- **Extra:** Further online study material and hyperlinks which may be supplemental, remedial or advanced.

x

Human–Computer Interaction

The aim of this module is to introduce you to the fundamental and exciting area of human–computer interaction (HCI) and to prepare you for more advanced reading on this subject. The aim is to understand better the designs that people need, and to understand the design processes better.

HCI is becoming very important, as a means of achieving more competitive designs, and as a growing field of employment for IT graduates and others. HCI focuses upon how best to design interactive systems that are both productive and as pleasurable to use as possible by their intended users, and is the study of how users interact with computer technology.

Throughout this module we will be looking at technology from the user's point of view: we are interested, for example, in whether a website allows the user to do what the user wants to do, quickly easily and efficiently.

The book covers the areas of:

- The user-centred system design (UCSD) process and user modelling
- Task analysis
- Requirements, design and prototyping
- Cognitive psychology: memory and perception
- Evaluation techniques
- Universal access and design for all.

Using this book

There are several devices which will help you in your studies and use of this book. **Activities** usually require you to try out aspects of the material which have just been explained, or invite you to consider something which is about to be discussed. In some cases, a response is provided as part of the text that follows – so it is important to work on the activity before you proceed! Usually, however, a formal answer will be provided in the final section of each chapter.

The **time bar** indicates *approximately* how long each activity will take:

short   < 10 minutes

medium 10-45 minutes

long   > 45 minutes

 Review questions are (usually) short questions at the end of each chapter to check you have remembered the main points of a chapter. They are a useful practical summary of the content, and can be used as a form of revision aid to ensure that you remain competent in each of the areas covered.

About the author

Serengul Smith-Atakan

Serengul is Senior Lecturer and a thread leader at the Collaborative International Research Centre for Universal Access (CIRCUA) at the School of Computing Science, Middlesex University. She holds a BSc in *Mathematical Engineering* from Istanbul Technical University in Turkey; an MSc in *Knowledge Engineering*; and a PhD in the *Application of Machine Learning Techniques in Web-based Information systems* at Middlesex University.

Visit the accompanying website at **www.thomsonlearning.co.uk/fasttrack** and click through to the appropriate booksite to find further teaching and learning material including:

For Students

- Activities
- Multiple-choice questions for each chapter
- Source code
- Tools & resources

For Lecturers

- Downloadable PowerPoint slides
- Questions (exam style) with outline answers and grading guidelines
- Discussion Topics

CHAPTER 1

Introduction

OVERVIEW

This chapter explains the basis of human–computer interaction (HCI): what it is, and why it is important. We look at several examples of interactive systems and analyse them from the user's point of view. We argue that most interactive systems are not designed with the user in mind. We discuss why this is and consider the consequences.

Learning outcomes	At the end of this chapter you should be able to:

- Discuss why HCI is a worthwhile study area

- Explain why it is difficult to 'engineer' for usability and why there is a problem measuring usability

- Describe the difference between 'useful' and 'usable'

- Identify and discuss how to resolve usability problems in existing systems.

1.1 Introduction

The aim of this book is to introduce you to the fundamental and exciting area of **human–computer interaction** (HCI) and to prepare you for more advanced reading on this subject. Theories about how to do computing remain of abstract interest only until they are brought forcibly into contact with the real people who will apply those theories in practice in real systems. HCI brings theory and practice together. The aim is to understand better the *designs that people need* and the *design processes* – so that people's needs will be met by new system designs in the future. The world of technology is becoming more competitive. It is no longer sufficient to use the functionality of the technology and to add as many features as possible. That is where HCI is becoming very important: both as a means of achieving more competitive designs, and also as a growing field of employment for IT graduates and others. HCI focuses upon how best to design interactive systems that are both productive and as pleasurable to use as possible by their intended users. In the past, we were limited by what the technology would allow us to do. We still see this influence in current system designs and upgrades.

It is still commonplace to believe that simply adding new features will ensure commercial success. We are all aware of systems which add new features with every new version. Such features may not relate well, if at all, to user needs. They are often added simply because they can be added. Adding new features can provide multiple options for carrying out tasks which are simply not needed. Furthermore, adding new features may alter the menu structure of an application, so that experienced users have to search around for their new location. New users are often unaware of many of the functions which an application can offer them. Many clever functions are never used by them. Paradoxically, adding new functionality can even disempower or confuse experienced users. New users may also become confused by the emerging complexity of an application and be discouraged from making the effort required to learn to use it properly and efficiently. It can look as if someone is trying to build up a lucrative training market for themselves! It seems as if there is actually a growing market for the provision of advice and guidance for people who have purchased new technology, but who cannot understand how to use it properly.

In the modern world, the focus is now on what people can do with the technology and that is what really counts. If so, we need to have a radically different approach to interactive system design and to the development of design skills. The starting point is not to consider what the technology can do. That can be considered somewhat later these days, since we can usually be confident that the power of modern computational systems will suffice to support the types of task that most people will want to do, most of the time. The power of the technology is often not a limiting factor. If we want to produce a product or service that will be useful and usable (see section 1.5 and Chapter 6 for a discussion of these concepts), then we must start with an appreciation of the potential users and the types of task they will need or want to do. For example, you may want to design a system which allows people to select a university programme online, or you may want to create a simple computer game for pre-school children. Clearly, you must identify the people for whom the system is to be designed. An initial consideration of your potential users may even lead to your deciding to appeal to a different set of user groups, if you find that the potential products would be unprofitable or unsuccessful. (Note that we are not assuming that profit is always a motive – in some cases, altruism may be the driving force. Developers may want to make a contribution or provide a worthwhile service.)

If the above arguments are correct, the starting point for an effective, user-centred design, has to be the users. Designers must have some insight into the needs of their users. This insight will vary from a simple appreciation of the preferences and interests of the users through to thorough 'user models' which capture the skills and abilities of the users.

A simple example of the former would be a simple 'recommender system' which recommends new websites to an individual on the basis of their stated interests and preferences. Perhaps you have an interest in football. Imagine that you have signed up for a simple recommender system which asks you about your interests and hobbies. When you go online next, the recommender system will point you to new websites or services which are relevant to football. If, on the other hand, you had expressed an interest in clothes, then the same system would point you to a different set of options.

As such systems become more powerful they may not need to rely completely on your own answers, but could infer your interests from your behaviour when searching on the Internet. For example, you may report interests in sociology and psychology, but spend a lot of your spare time looking at football-related sites. Such systems would conclude that, though unstated, football was one of your true interests. As a side thought, this type of system raises the ethical question 'Would you want your behaviour to be observed by a system which then tries to recommend or even sell you new services?'.

A more complex example of user modelling would be the development of a document production application for use by individuals with different disabilities at work. To customise the design for each individual would require that you have a complex model of the strengths and weaknesses of each.

In conclusion, there is a range of options: from simple accounts of a user's preferences (gathered by asking them) to the production of complex user models, which build up psychological profiles of the users. In addition, it is often important to be aware of the range and diversity within the user population.

There is a danger that we think only of the *typical* user and not of the *range* of users. If so, we may produce a product which is less attractive to this wider audience. We will return to the notions of user profiles and user models in later chapters. For now, simply note that HCI is important because it provides a framework in which to produce user-centred designs (based on user models) which may be more acceptable than traditional, technology-driven solutions.

As well as understanding the needs of the users, it is very important to appreciate the tasks that people want to carry out. There is no reason, other than for personal satisfaction, to produce a system that no one except you will want to use. Often, a new system design originates with a new idea thought up by a system designer. There is nothing wrong with that. However, it will not necessarily benefit anyone else if it does not reflect their requirements. It is usually important to produce a system for others. Sometimes, too, a new design starts with a realisation that existing systems have design or functional problems. That, too, can be a useful starting point, particularly if it leads you to have good ideas about possible solutions.

The danger here is that, in starting with other systems, you may tend to repeat the assumptions and errors of those designs. Good ideas are of potential value, but we run the risk of sticking to our own original thoughts even when our users would prefer other options. That is why it is vital that we go back to the actual tasks and objectives of our users, so that we get beyond other people's mistakes. In **user-centred system design** (UCSD), task analysis is an important and early component of the design process. Although a good designer will iterate through the different design components, task analysis is vital if we are to remain close to what users actually want or need to do. Task analysis takes many different forms. Learning to conduct a task analysis is important for you, so that you can become skilled in user-centred system design in particular and HCI in general. We will cover task analysis in further chapters. In fact we will focus on **hierarchical task analysis** (HTA), which is a specific version of task analysis. For now, simply note that HCI is important because it provides a clear focus on methods of task analysis which take us away from self-centred designs towards more user-centred system designs.

HCI is also important for theoretical reasons. It provides a field within which we can investigate and understand the psychology of users in a realistic and practical environment. It has variously been called: human–computer interaction (HCI), human factors, ergonomics, cognitive ergonomics, man machine interface etc.

There are, perhaps, problems with each of these labels. A better, descriptive label has been coined by Stephen Pinker (1997). He prefers to call the current approach to this area the study of 'natural computation', since this label refers to the natural activities of the human brain or mind, with or without external help, to process information and manipulate symbols.

In Pinker's words:

> 'The proper label for the study of mind informed by computers is not Artificial Intelligence but Natural Computation' (Pinker, 1997).

We all do mental computation – especially when we do not have computers or calculators to call on. Our actions reflect, in large part, our propensity to use language and symbols and to create artefacts or devices with which to support what we want to do. Such artefacts vary from the simple sling shot weapon to the most advanced interactive computer-based system. There is no need to liken the human brain to a computer, on this view.

Of course, computers process information too, but they do not have sole ownership of these processes – and there is growing evidence that people and computers deal with information in markedly different ways.

Though we refer to a computer analogy when discussing the human brain, it is perhaps more confusing than helpful: not only is this an unnecessary simplification, it also sounds as if we are reducing the human brain to no more than a pile of metal. Nothing could be further from the truth. Although we may draw inspiration from concepts of computing with which to understand the human mind, we look increasingly to the real world, including the human brain, as an inspiration for new systems design that draw upon the incredible power of new technology. It is a sobering thought that, although our technology seems incredible to us, it is as nothing when compared to the awesome power of even the average human brain.

The challenge of this book is to get you thinking critically and inventively about the ways in which people use interactive systems, such as computers, to support what they want to achieve. You will also learn effective design and evaluation methods. How can we make such systems as useful, usable and accessible as possible? To what extent could we achieve designs for all or move on to achieve universal access to such systems by any variety of means? Only time will tell, but the focus used to be on what the technology could do, since technical limitations and functionality seemed of paramount importance. Today, the prime focus is on what people can achieve when given advanced artefacts like interactive computer systems.

HCI is the study of how users interact with computer technology, and throughout this book we will be looking at technology from the user's point of view: that is to say, when we look at (for example) a website we are not really interested in the underlying technology. What we are interested in is whether the website allows the user to do what the user wants to do: quickly, easily and efficiently.

We will use the term 'interactive system' to refer to any technological system which requires interaction with users. So, a money-dispensing machine is an interactive system, as is a calculator, a word processor, a spreadsheet or a website.

Indeed, a modern washing machine or central heating control fits into this category, together with many of today's cars. Anything electronic that requires some sort of input from the user and gives some sort of output is considered to be an interactive system.

In summary, there are a number of reasons, both theoretical and practical, why HCI is a worthwhile field of study:

- It provides a context in which to consider user-centred system design methods. We often encounter systems that are badly designed, that do not consider the needs of users or which are difficult to use without substantial training. As users are becoming more selective in their choices of software, there is an increasing emphasis upon user requirements. UCSD methods also have important commercial implications. To appeal to a sufficient proportion of the potential market, it is vital that diverse groups of users take up and use the new systems on offer

- HCI provides a basis upon which we can evaluate design methods for their efficiency and effectiveness. The art of system design is more than just a collection of methods. It also needs systematic ways of evaluating those methods. HCI provides such ways of doing evaluations

- HCI provides a real-world environment in which to develop new theories of user psychology. It provides tests for existing theories, as well as the data for developing new ones. Finally, this field is one of the fastest-growing areas of employment in computing science.

1.2 A badly designed interactive system

Let's start with an example – a simulation of a ticket machine. You'll need to access these online.

Activity 1.1

Train ticket machine simulator

You will require computer and Internet access for this task, a simulation of a train ticket-booking machine as used in the south of England. This initial activity allows you to get used to the simulator and consider its actions.

Activity 1.2

Booking a ticket

You will require computer and Internet access for this task, which takes you through the ticket machine simulation again, this time carrying out specified tasks.

Imagine that, instead of using the ticket machine, you are buying your ticket from the booking office by asking a clerk for a ticket. How long will it take you? Typically, the conversation will go something like:

'Hello, sir. Can I help you?'

'Yes. Can I have a ticket from Welwyn North to New Southgate with a network gold card, please?'

'Certainly, sir. That will be £3.70.'

'Thank you.'

That took at most 15 seconds and there is no way that the customer can fail to book the ticket, unless they speak a different language to the booking clerk.

Now imagine, once more, that you are talking to a clerk in the booking office. This time you want a ticket to a station, near Alexandra Palace, where an auction house is:

'Hello, sir. Can I help you?'

'Yes. Can I have a ticket from Welwyn North to the station near Alexandra Palace where the auction house is?'

'Do you mean Hornsey, sir?'

'Hornsey! Yes, that's the one!'

'Do you have a network rail card?'

'Yes.'

'That will be £3.70.'

'Thank you.'

In this case, booking with the clerk allows you to complete a task that is impossible with the machine: you can't tell the machine that you want a ticket 'to the station near Alexandra Palace where the auction house is'. The machine needs to know *exactly* where you are going.

Let's now have a think about the ticket machine:

- It is slower than booking your ticket with a clerk
- It is possible to fail to be able to buy a ticket
- It is less 'flexible' than buying a ticket from the clerk (this means the machine only really allows you one way of booking a ticket)
- It does not 'speak the user's language': it is perfectly understandable for a passenger to forget the precise name of the station they wish to go to, and to make an imprecise description of the station. People are imprecise by nature – but the ticket machine forces its users to be precise
- If it typically takes computing science students two or three minutes to work out how to book a ticket, how long would it take a normal member of the public?

We have scratched the surface of what looks to be a fairly straightforward piece of technology and found that it actually is not all that helpful or easy to use.

1.3 Who designs interactive systems?

The ticket machine is badly designed, and therefore the interesting question is 'Why is it badly designed?'. If we can answer that question, then there is a good chance that we can go on to answer the more constructive question 'How can we make sure that interactive systems are better designed?'. Most of the problems we address in this course fall under these two headings:

- 'What is wrong with a system?'
- 'How can we redesign it to make it better?'.

It really does not take someone very highly skilled in HCI to see that the ticket machine has some fundamental usability problems. However, if *we* can notice those problems and the designers did not, why not?

The problem is not that designers are idiots; the designers are actually far too clever. Most designers of systems such as the ticket machine are computer experts and programmers: people familiar with computer systems, how they work and not really intimidated by them. The designers have not designed the ticket machine for normal members of the public; they have designed the ticket machine for themselves, in the mistaken belief that they are typical members of the public.

If we look at many interactive systems, we can see that they have been designed by computer programmers and software engineers on the false assumption that everyone else in the world understands (or should understand) computers as well as they do.

For many examples of poor or inefficient design, visit **www.baddesigns.com/ranges.html** from which both of these examples were taken.

Which knob (boxed, at the top) controls which hotplate?

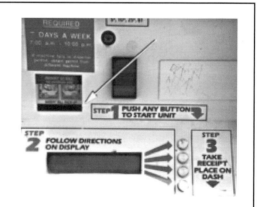

In this car park ticket machine, you need to 'push any button' before you can insert the money to the arrowed slot. Although it is logical to choose the requirement (number of hours, maybe) *before* making the payment, the visual sequencing here is not very helpful. Stand and observe people using a variety of ticket machines and see which designs require the least amount of 'study' time by users.

Figure 1.1: Poor design

1.4 Engineering

Most things that we use have been 'engineered'. This means that the designers have been through a fairly systematic process in order to arrive at a product that meets its requirements.

Consider building a bridge: nowadays we would not expect people to build a bridge by guesswork and trial and error. We would expect a long and thorough process of design before anything gets built at all. Engineers would work out the heaviest weight that bridge would be expected to take, what the maximum wind speed would be and then set about finding materials that are strong enough to take that maximum weight and wind speed without twisting or breaking. To do this, breaking strains of various materials would be measured and compared so that the most suitable material and design can be arrived at. On the way to arriving at a final design, several other designs will have been considered and rejected, maybe because they are too weak or too expensive.

The result of all this effort will be a bridge that the engineers *know* will not fall down, because they have engineered it not to.

So if we can engineer a bridge not to fall down (or an aircraft to take off, or a road not to melt in midsummer, or a building not to crush in an earthquake), is there an engineering process that we can follow to ensure that an interactive system is easy to use?

In later chapters we will look at just such a process, but there is a fundamental problem: that of 'measurement'. Note that in the above description of engineering a bridge all the factors we described that the engineers would deal with (maximum weight, wind speed, breaking strain) are all 'quantitative' – that is to say we can fix an explicit, objective number to them to measure them (1,500kg, 120kph, 800 Newtons per mm^2, for example). Therefore a bridge engineer can measure all the relevant factors, apply a calculation to them and arrive at a *yes* or *no* answer as to whether the bridge will fall down.

It is very difficult to define what 'ease of use' means, and show that one system is easier to use than another. This is because ease of use is 'qualitative' – it is not something that we can count, in the same way as we count how many kilos something weighs. There are lots of things in life that are qualitative, such as happiness, beauty or friendliness; they are important but cannot be measured. 'Ease of use' drops into this qualitative category: important, but difficult to measure. Because engineering is all about measuring things and making systematic decisions based on those measurements, it is very difficult to define an engineering process that ensures ease of use – because it cannot easily be measured.

This goes some way to explain why the ticket machine is not easy to use: because there is no (accepted) engineering process that engineers can apply to ensure its ease of use.

1.5 What is useful or usable?

For something to be **useful** means that the user can actually achieve the task they want to. For example, the user wants to write a letter; the system supports letter writing. Thus a useful system supports the objectives of the user.

For something to be **usable** it must allow the users to achieve the task they want to easily and enjoyably. For example, one letter production system might be easy and pleasant to use, while another might be difficult and frustrating to use. The point is that both systems support the objectives of the user – but do so in different ways.

So we can see that when we wanted to book a ticket from Welwyn North to New Southgate in North London we could use the ticket machine to do this, even though it may not have been easy. However, when we wanted to book a ticket from Welwyn North to a station we had forgotten the name of, then the task became impossible.

In the first case we say that the ticket machine is 'useful' but not 'usable'. In the second case we say that the machine is 'useless'. (Note that in both cases we can describe the clerk in the booking office as both useful and usable.)

So long as we are clear about what the task is, usefulness is quantifiable: we can say, objectively, that the user can – or cannot –achieve their task. However, usability is qualitative and therefore not possible to measure objectively.

Designers often confuse usefulness for usability: if a system can do something, then that is usually taken as sufficient for a good system. On help systems set up so that designers can give advice to users, you typically see or hear exchanges like this:

User: "I can't save my file as XML!"

Designer: "Yes you can. You select 'Properties' from the 'File' menu and then click on the 'Save' tab. Halfway down the dialogue box there is a drop down menu marked 'File type' which allows you to select the type of file you wish to save your work as. Select XML from that dialogue box and then click on 'Save preferences'. The system will then give you a confirmation box to ensure that you actually want to do this and you should click on 'Yes'. Then go to the file menu, select 'Save as' and save your file as you normally would."

In this case the system is clearly *useful*: the user *can* save their files as XML as they want to, and the designer is probably happy that the system does in fact allow the users to do what they want. But is it *usable*? The process they have to go through to do the saving is rather tortuous and clearly not obvious as the user has had to ask for help.

A third valuable concept is that of **accessibility**. A system might be both useful and acceptable for a typical user. But many users are not typical. We vary in the level of (for example) past experience, qualifications, strengths and weaknesses, disabilities, preferences or working conditions. A system can only be said to be accessible if the full range of our intended users can actually access it.

In conclusion, it is vitally important for system designers and HCI practitioners to distinguish between usefulness, usability and accessibility if they are to be as effective as possible in their work:

- **Useful** means that the system supports user objectives
- **Usable** means that it supports these objectives in easy-to-use ways
- **Accessible** means that it can be used by the full range of intended users.

1.6 The rest of this book

Hopefully we have now shown you that there are usability problems with most interactive systems that we come across. The rest of this book is about looking at what those problems are, why they occur and how to solve them.

A brief overview of the rest of the book is given here.

- **Chapter 2: Making interactive systems feel natural for users**

  Natural computing is what people do and also what information technology does. We share the common activity of processing information, though we may differ in other, equally interesting ways. Both people and technologies work with symbols to perform computations and calculations in everyday life. So if we are to do well in researching, designing, evaluating or customising interactive systems, then we should possess a grounding in natural computing.

- **Chapter 3: User modelling in user-centred system design (UCSD)**

  This chapter explains and explores the central notion of the user model and why it is important to user-centred system design.

- **Chapter 4: The user-centred design process**

  The 'user-centred design' process is an attempt to define an engineering process that ensures that systems are usable. We compare a UCSD process to more traditional ways of designing systems.

- **Chapter 5: Task analysis**

  The first part of a UCSD process is gaining a thorough understanding of existing systems. Task analysis is one way of doing this. We look at different ways of doing task analyses, concentrating on 'hierarchical task analysis'.

- **Chapter 6: Requirements gathering, storyboarding and prototyping**

  The middle three stages of the UCSD process go from deciding what the interactive system should do, to how it does it, and producing a working prototype which can be tested with users.

- **Chapter 7: Psychology: memory**

  This chapter looks at how cognitive psychology can inform the design of interactive systems. Psychology looks at how people understand, perceive and remember things. Knowing these properties, we can design systems that do not put undue strain on the user's capabilities.

- **Chapter 8: Cognitive psychology: perception**

  This chapter looks in depth at the key concepts of perception and attention. It introduces several important theoretical analyses and discusses their relevance to interface design.

- **Chapter 9: Evaluation**

  The final stage of the UCSD process is to test a prototype with users and see if the requirements are met and, if not, explain why not. Different evaluation techniques are explored with an emphasis on 'user observation'.

- **Chapter 10: UCSD and advanced technology**

  In this chapter we look at Don Norman's important book *The Invisible Computer* and discuss his arguments. It is argued that when technology becomes genuinely useful and usable it 'disappears' – users are no longer aware that they are interacting with it. What is 'invisible' information technology and can we design it?

- **Chapter 11: Universal access and 'design for all'**

  Universal access indicates system design that can be used by anyone, anytime, anywhere. It involves both suitable system designs and suitable means of access to the systems. 'Design for all' indicates a design or set of designs that can be used by all users, regardless of their strengths and weaknesses, their level of expertise, disabilities or environments. This chapter concentrates on these topics.

- **Chapter 12: Review**

  We bring together the various strands of HCI, and contextualise the learning from the book.

1.7 Summary

In this chapter, we introduced you to the basis of human–computer interaction (HCI): what it is, and why it is important. We have briefly looked at two examples of interactive systems and analysed them from the user's point of view. Our argument is that most interactive systems are not designed with the user in mind. We have briefly discussed the reasons for this – and the consequences.

References and further reading:

Pinker S, (1997), *How the mind works*, London: Penguin.

Preece J, Rogers Y & Sharp H, (2002), *Interaction Design: beyond human computer interaction*, J. Wiley.

Cooper A. (1999), *The Inmates Are Running the Asylum: Why High Tech Products Drive Us Crazy and How To Restore The Sanity*, SAMS.

Darnell MJ. (1996-2004), *Bad Human Factors Design* www.baddesigns.com/ranges.html

Norman D. (1999), *The invisible computer*, Cambridge, MA.: MIT Press.

1.8 Review questions

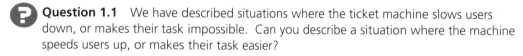 **Question 1.1**   We have described situations where the ticket machine slows users down, or makes their task impossible. Can you describe a situation where the machine speeds users up, or makes their task easier?

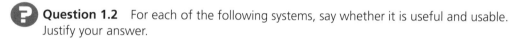 **Question 1.2**   For each of the following systems, say whether it is useful and usable. Justify your answer.

Your answer should be in the form: 'System X is (not) useful because... , system X is (not) usable because... .' Note that it is what you write after 'because' that is important, because this demonstrates the thinking behind your answer. In almost all questions in this book we will ask you to justify (or explain) your answer. This means that you should always say *why* you have answered the question in the way you have.

    a) An automated teller machine (ATM) for a user wanting to withdraw money

    b) An ATM for a visually impaired user wanting to withdraw money

    c) The amazon.com website for a user wanting to buy the book *Harry Potter and the Order of the Phoenix*

    d) The amazon.com website for a user wanting to buy a book containing the illustrations of Alfred Kubin, the German Expressionist artist

    e) The amazon.com website for a user wanting to buy a pet snake.

Question 1.3   Why is it very easy to find (from question 1.2) the Harry Potter book on Amazon, but not the Alfred Kubin book?

(Hint: think about the difference between getting a ticket to New Southgate and getting a ticket to a station of which you have forgotten the name.)

1.9 Answers to review questions

Answer to review question 1.1   One of the problems with the machine is that it is tricky to work out which buttons to press to get your ticket. However, if you travel regularly to the same station then you will quickly learn which buttons to press to get your ticket. In this case the machine becomes very quick to use. You just have to hope that the person in the queue in front of you is not booking a ticket for the first time!

Answer to review question 1.2   These are sample answers: your answers may be different.

a) The ATM is useful because the user can achieve their task: they can withdraw money. The ATM is usable for most users because it typically takes only a few seconds and a few obvious key presses to withdraw their money.

b) The ATM is useful because the user can achieve their task: they can withdraw money. The ATM is not very usable for visually impaired users because it is difficult for them to achieve their task. They typically need to see the screen to know which keys to press to get their money.

c) The website is useful because the user can achieve their task: they can buy the book. The website is also fairly usable assuming that the user has set up an account with Amazon. The book is easy to find: the user simply needs to type the title (or even just 'Harry Potter') in the search box and the book's details will be displayed. The process for ordering the book is fairly simple.

d) It is difficult to tell whether the site is useful, because it is difficult to know whether there are any books containing Alfred Kubin's artwork. There is a book written by Kubin, but does it contain his artwork? There are also a couple of books that seem to be about his work, but they do not have any product details, so you cannot tell whether they contain his artwork. The process you need to go through to find this out can be quite complex and time-consuming so the system is not very usable in this case.

e) The site is useless, because the user cannot achieve their task: Amazon do not sell pets. (If something is useless, then it must also be not usable.)

Answer to review question 1.3   The task of finding the Alfred Kubin book is imprecise – the user knows that they want a book containing Kubin's work, but they do not know the precise name of the book (in the same way that the ticket machine user knew that they wanted to go to an auction, but did not know the precise name of the station.)

Again we see an example of interactive systems relying on the user being precise: knowing exactly what book they want.

CHAPTER 2

Making interactive systems feel natural for users

OVERVIEW

The aim of this chapter is to provide you with an understanding of how natural computing can be applied in the context of the interactive system design. Natural computing is the study of how we process and store information, manipulate symbols, ascribe personal values to events, attribute cultural and emotive meanings, and use interactive artefacts to enhance our lifestyles. Natural computing is a powerful concept that has wide-reaching implications for our understanding of the needs of users and of the design of interactive systems.

Learning outcomes   At the end of this chapter, you should be able to:

- Define what natural computing is

- Explain the main principles of natural computing

- Explain the key concepts of user-centred system design (UCSD)

- Explain what interactive design is

- Evaluate the strengths and weaknesses of actual or proposed designs of interactive systems.

2.1 Introduction

Natural computing – or natural computation – is the study of how people process and store information, manipulate symbols, ascribe personal values to events, attribute cultural and emotive judgements and so on – and how we use interactive artefacts to enhance our lifestyles. Such artefacts include computer-based systems as well as other technologies such as interactive TV, mobile phones and embedded processors.

Natural computing is a powerful concept that enables us to consider systematically the requirements of users of new interactive systems. It also provides a framework to consider the methods by which designers can build systems that are more useful, usable and accessible. Hence it addresses both the user's and the designer's perspective.

The human brain as a computer

There is, however, one potential misunderstanding that we must avoid. Natural computing is not the same as using a computer analogy where the human brain is regarded as a computer. As technology has moved on, so the analogy has been applied to each new generation of computer product. Initially, the human brain was viewed as a simple, serial computer; eventually, it was viewed as a complex parallel processing machine.

The analogy can be useful for teaching purposes and, perhaps, for thinking about what properties the human brain must possess or even transcend. The problem is that it is limited to what current technology can do: it can limit our imagination. Today, we tend to think the other way around. We ask ourselves: what lessons can we learn from nature in general and from the design of the human brain in particular?

Moreover, the act of comparing the human brain to a computer can lead to a mechanistic and reductionistic way of thinking. It is as if we are saying that people's brains are just computers: physical structures with no souls, no imagination, and no social skills. It is very close to thinking of people as robots – and that conjures up the nightmare scenes of science fiction, as in the Terminator series of movies.

2.2 Natural computing

Information processing is just one of the capabilities of the human brain. The main idea of natural computing is that information processing is a natural process for us. It is how we have survived as a species. As a research and application area, natural computing draws from cognitive science, cognitive psychology, human-computer interaction, interaction design, sociology and anthropology.

Activity 2.1

What do we mean by 'natural computing'?

You will require Internet access for this activity. Use Google to find three websites concerned with 'natural computing'. Write brief reviews of the differing perspectives on this fascinating research area. What's included – and what's excluded?

How do those perspectives compare with the views expressed in this chapter?

The main idea of natural computing is that people are naturally capable of processing information. It is a natural process for us: it is how we have survived as a species. While the computers that we build may also process information, they do so in radically different ways from the methods that we humans use.

There are at least three linked aspects of natural computing:

- **The user perspective:** if we are to achieve user-centred system designs then, of course, we need to place the intended users at the centre of the process. One way to do so is through the creation of user models, simple or more powerful. Thus the concept of natural computing provides a conceptual framework within which to address the issues of user modelling

- **The designer's perspective:** as designers, we need to understand the intended users well enough to design well for them. If we can understand human information processing sufficiently, then we will have a better understanding of the sorts of designs that will support users in their activities

- **The sustainability perspective:** there is the necessity for well-designed systems. As a species, we have learned to make use of tools, artefacts and systems to boost our chances of survival. The need for well-designed systems is no mere luxury: it is a necessity. Thus the link between the user perspective and the designer perspective is motivated by the human need to create artefacts that support our strengths and weaknesses, our activities and the achievement of our objectives.

2.3 Natural computing and user-centred system design

A simple comparison

- **Natural computing:** the phrase 'natural computing' was coined by Stephen Pinker (1997) and was intended to supplant the older and possibly defunct term 'artificial intelligence'.

  Natural computing is what people do – and also what information and communication technologies do. We share the common activity of processing information, although we differ in lots of other interesting ways

- **User-centred system design (UCSD):** in the early days of computing, computers were very expensive and were extremely difficult to learn to use. They required significant effort from users, and opportunity for interaction was limited. Only specially trained people could work with them.

According to Ben Shneiderman, 'The old computing is about what computers can do, the new computing is what users can do.' (quoted in Preece, 2002). If this is so, then any consideration of the present and future of computing science should start with people. In particular, we should consider the people who are going to be the users of our systems.

Key features of user-centred system design

UCSD (sometimes called UCD: user-centred design) was developed at the University of California at San Diego; the key features include:

- A central focus on the people who will use the systems, on their preferences and requirements
- Building simple models of the users, the tasks and the technological systems
- An iterative process
- Prototyping and the evaluation of alternatives by users.

These elements are illustrated in figure 2.1.

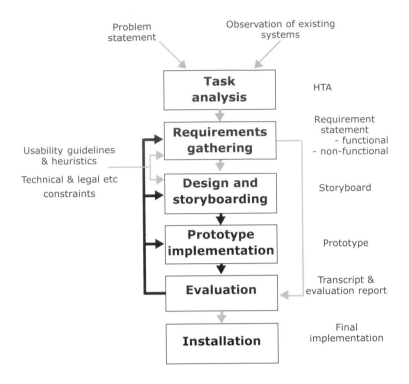

Figure 2.1: The user-centred system design process

Prototyping and the evaluation of alternative designs

UCSD forces designers to be explicit about decisions made, reviewing them through prototypes and storyboards with other members of the team and potential users.

The designer has a vast number of key decisions to make. Each screen, for example, may contain many individual items, each of which require design decisions about layout, use of colour, grouping, labelling of features and so on. This is more than a designer can realistically deal with at any one time.

During the process of design, it is natural to have in mind a few general principles from the usability requirements, together with some high-level ideas about proposed solutions. It is impossible, however, for a designer to keep in mind the presentation and dialogue design of the whole of the future system. Yet each of those individual design elements and features is critical to the usability of the eventual system.

Another point is that designers work with their own 'mental model' of a system. Over time, it is natural for them to develop and become familiar with their own terms to describe system concepts. In a sense, the designer is the person who is least able to stand back from the work and assess how a first-time user would react to it.

So, designers need ways of sharing design thinking by producing physical representations of design ideas. These could be working computer-based prototypes or something as simple as a pen-and-paper sketch. Either way, it means that the designer can see an idea taking form and is better able to assess it. Moreover, other members of the design team and potential users can share in the process, evaluating the design ideas and suggesting improvements.

'The user' or 'users'

But who are these 'users'? The term 'user' is a particularly clumsy one. It sounds as if there is nothing else of interest about a person than that they are a 'user' of the super, new system that I've designed. All of the psychological complexity that characterises us as persons – that makes us who we are – is disregarded: we become one-dimensional 'users'.

What do you think of when you read the phrase 'the user'?

Do you think of:

- Someone like yourself?
- A stereotype 'user'?
- A group of 'typical users'?

… or do you picture individuals, each with different skills and preferences, different priorities and objectives?

There is a temptation to undervalue the psychological issues involved in using IT. In general, people come to information technology with their own abilities, internalised socially mediated constructs, problems, priorities and objectives.

The term 'the user' is particularly clumsy and may lead us to think in terms of one typical user, rather than capturing the range and variety of different users and user groups. Differences are ignored or devalued.

The people who use our systems may come from different groups, with significantly different skills and preferences. It is better to stay in the plural, talk about 'users' rather than 'the user'.

Is UCSD sufficient?

Yet UCSD may not be enough. It may be impossible to understand and capture the needs or preferences of all your users in one design, even with variants. People may need the facility to:

- Customise a system
- Add assistive technology for extreme circumstances or disability
- Have adaptable systems that respond to the ways in which they are used or to a user's known profile.

Almost certainly we will need to talk more about 'design for all' or 'universal access': system designs that are usable by anyone, anytime, anywhere. For example, consider an adaptive web browser that translates websites into appropriate formats. The focus is on providing many paths to a well-designed system. UCSD may focus on 'the user', but overlook substantial diversity among the people who use the systems and the variety of solutions required.

Activity 2.2

Voice messaging at the 1984 Olympic Games

One of the first examples of a large-scale system developed using user-centred system design principles was that provided by IBM to support voice messaging for athletes at the 1984 Olympic Games in Los Angeles. The system was based on (then) novel technology, and was intended for use by athletes and their families.

How would you go about designing such a system? From what you know of UCSD so far, what practices would you deploy?

For instance, would you start with a set of scenarios or discussions with key stakeholders, including athletes?

Given that this was a high-profile system for use during a unique occasion, how would you test it beforehand?

2.4 Six principles of natural computing

We can identify six specific principles or elements of natural computing:

- **Natural computing**
- **What can users do?**
- **Modelling users**
- **Understanding the domain**
- **Understanding human learning**
- **Meaning, as a basis for practical action.**

Let's look at these in more detail.

- **Natural computing:** both people and technologies work with symbols to perform computations and calculations in everyday life. If we are to do well in researching, designing, evaluating or customising interactive systems, then those systems should be grounded in natural computing. Natural computing is a research and application area that draws from cognitive science, cognitive psychology, human–computer interaction, interaction design, sociology and anthropology

- **What can users do?** if our focus is on natural computing, then the second principle must be an emphasis upon what people can do. We need to understand better the people who use the systems we design and build. That is why Ben Shneiderman argues that today's burning issue is not what the technology can do, but rather what users can do. People drive technology to achieve their objectives, not the other way round.

    Human cognition is also one of the sources of inspiration for computing science:

    - in going beyond von Neumann machines (the design of most modern computers)

    - including fuzzy logic in our designs

    - producing adaptive and adaptable systems

    - developing fault-tolerant and self-repairing systems

- achieving approximations to universal access and design for all

- perhaps even providing software inspired by advances in human neurophysiology.

Don't worry if some of these phrases are unfamiliar right now; we will return to them later

- **Modelling users:** if we want to understand people better, then one way is to develop better models. Here you need a theory that is representative of the current state of the art, but is also capable of facilitating the design process.

   Our objective is to offer you a working model of human, natural computation. This is based upon the Simplex theory, described in the next chapter, which is presented as a:

   - concise, overall theory to guide good practice in system design

   - framework within which to capture current research findings.

   This is a definition of a simplistic theory (i.e. simple enough to guide best practice and complex enough to encompass current research issues)

- **Understanding the domain:** we also need to understand the domain in which we are working. Natural computing is best seen as a hybrid field of study, drawing upon a wide diversity of professions and disciplines

- **Understanding human learning:** given the centrality of the people who design or use new systems, we need to appreciate and apply principles of human learning

- **Meaning as a basis for practical action:** many texts seek to give students and designers sets of design principles and methods that can be applied without reference to the people for whom designs are made. In this chapter we aim to provide you with the vital links between theory and practice, to encourage the better understanding of both.

Activity 2.3

Designing a new ticket machine

You will require computer and Internet access for this activity, which builds on your experiences in Chapter 1, and helps you to consider improvements which could be made to the machine.

2.5 Core concepts

There are a number of core concepts that are common to both natural computing and user-centred system design. Here we focus on them and define them for you. This list is intended to introduce you to such concepts:

- **User model**
- **Universal access**
- **Design for all**
- **Inclusive design**
- **Task models**
- **Technological platform.**

The list above is not intended to be the final word: you should question whether we have omitted any important concepts. If we have, then please add your own working definitions of them. Let's now look at our list in a little more detail.

- **User model:** these can vary from a simple list of stated preferences right up to a full psychological profile covering the user's strengths, weaknesses, skills, interests, potential, disabilities, age, culture, experience and interests. Clearly, the more powerful the user model, the more useful it can be in system design. Conversely, the more powerful the model, the more time, expertise and money must be invested in developing it.

  There is thus a trade-off between the cost and the power of a user model. There is no point in having a useless, underpowered model. Likewise, an overpowered model can be an expensive luxury. Current HCI researchers and practitioners are looking for ways to develop powerful user models quickly.

  When considering user models, we tend to think of the typical or average user. We may even be tempted to think of ourselves as typical of the user population. However, when considering how to design for all, we must be able to take into account the diversity and complexity of our user population

- **Universal access:** universal access is the second key concept on our list. Universal access is the objective of making systems that are accessible anytime, anywhere and to anyone of the intended user population. It does not insist on one design, but provides different pathways for different users. For example, one person may use a web browser that converts the displayed information into a format that they can see with their limited vision. Adaptive interfaces will respond to the observed needs of the user. Universal access is defined by the goal of creating access for a diverse range of potential users

- **Design for all:** this is similar to 'universal access', but also promotes the notion of careful design and design standards, so that users with special needs are not excluded from the use of a system. A system should be designed to be as inclusive as possible. In practice, different designs may be needed for different user groups. Design for all is an important aspiration for designers and researchers. This applies if they are driven by ideology (e.g. a wish to include) or by commercial considerations (e.g. a wish to achieve greater market share)

- **Inclusive design:** although universal access and design for all are essentially qualitative in their approach, inclusive design can also be quantitative. The aim of inclusive design is to create mechanisms by which designers can calculate the numbers of users who are excluded by specific design features. Those features are related to the perceptual, cognitive and psychomotor abilities of the users. To the extent that certain design features require specific levels of ability, it then becomes possible to quantify the inclusiveness of such design features. The importance of this approach is that it brings together both user and commercial perspectives in a commonly understood language. Commercial designers are aware of both the costs of excluding potential customers and the costs associated with meeting their requirements. Conversely, groups of users with disabilities are equally aware of the experience of exclusion and the difficulties associated with achieving inclusion. Inclusive design is defined by the goal of understanding and quantifying the consequences of different design options for the diverse range of potential users

- **Task models:** this is the output of a task analysis. Nobody wants to design a system that people do not need or want. It is neither satisfying nor profitable to do so. Nor should we take our own ideas of what is wanted or copy the ideas of others. To achieve relevance, we must get back to the basic consideration of the task or tasks that would be supported by the system that we wish to produce. For example, if you want to produce an online system for purchasing a car, it is probably not good enough just to observe other online car buying systems. If you do, you may build in the mistakes and assumptions of others. You need to observe car buying in the real world, if you are to understand the actual requirements of the intended users. You must identify the key features of the task to be achieved – and recognise those aspects that must or can be changed. A task model captures these vital insights

- **Technological platform:** this relates to a model of the intended technological platform. In the earlier days of system design, technological considerations were paramount. In those days, available technology placed severe restrictions on the functionality of proposed systems, and great ingenuity was required to get around these restrictions.

  These days, technological options are less restrictive and, in general, we can expect our expectations to be fulfilled by the technology. Nevertheless, it is still part of the overall design process to consider the parameters of the proposed technology platform. Although we have powerful technology at our disposal, we increasingly attempt to pack more and more into less and less. Witness the development of the personal digital assistant (PDA) and the mobile phone's ever-increasing list of functions.

  It makes little sense to design a system without having some idea as to the technology upon which it will be based. The process of user-centred system design may be characterised as the development of user, task and technology models and, through an iterative process of design and improvement, bringing the three models together so that the maximum compatibility may be achieved between them.

What other concepts may be relevant here? Pause for a moment to think about this, and maybe make a few notes, before continuing.

2.6 Interactive design

The phrase 'interactive design' refers to both the process and the results of design. User-centred system design is itself an interactive process. Clearly, if you believe in creating interaction between the system and the user, then it makes sense to employ the same concept of interaction when the user is, in this case, the designer.

User-centred system design is essentially an interactive and iterative process. The main stages are:

- Task analysis
- Requirements specification
- Prototyping
- Evaluation.

Another view of UCSD is as the creation and reconciliation of three elements:

- User model
- Task model
- Technology model.

In either view, the designer must cycle through the design process a number of times, as they approximate towards a working design.

The designer cannot passively go through a number of stages in a linear manner, doing each stage once before signing it off and moving on. This would be more like the traditional 'Waterfall model' approach to systems design, which has been shown to be slow, expensive and inaccurate. That usually results in extensive rework at a later stage in a project. There is more on the 'Waterfall' technique in Chapter 4.

In UCSD, by contrast, the designer and the design process must both work interactively. The emphasis is more upon research, design and evaluation as an interactive cycle. Initial good ideas are revised in the light of experience and evaluation. Thus designers cannot become stuck with their initial ideas and assumptions, but must respond to data about what works and what does not.

The design results of UCSD are themselves interactive designs. A truly interactive system design supports the intended users in achieving their objectives. To do so, it provides a number of interactive features including:

- Choices of sub-function (e.g. I now want to format this text differently)
- Choices about the ways in which to carry out functions (e.g. I prefer to use commands rather than menu items)
- Alternative ways of working as users become more adept at using the system (i.e. shortcuts or accelerators for more experienced users)
- Effective help functions when users need additional help
- Customisation and adaptation to meet user preferences
- Systems which can self-adapt intelligently in response to user performance.

2.7 Strengths and weaknesses of interactive systems

We do not live in an ideal world, so there will always be trade-offs to be considered and decisions to be made. In this section, we summarise some of the strengths and weaknesses of interactive systems:

- **Modern interactive systems can be powerful** because they draw on powerful technology: when they are designed effectively and well, they harness that power. When they are not, they may squander that power to a greater or lesser extent
- **Interactive systems may provide useful functions:** usefulness is a strength of a well-designed system. Unfortunately, some systems are little more than toys designed for the enjoyment and entertainment of their designers. The lack of usefulness is a weakness of such systems
- **Interactive systems differ in the extent that they are usable:** there is no point in having useful functions that are difficult to use. Usability is a strength; the lack of it a weakness
- **Accessibility varies between good and poorly designed systems:** some systems seem to be designed for the typical user only, whereas better system design allows a range of intended users to access it. Good accessibility is a strength; poor accessibility is a weakness.

A powerful, interactive system will be relevant to its intended users, will support the tasks for which it is intended and make good use of the technology. Another strength is that users can select options and make choices according to their requirements and preferences. Further strengths are the potential to customise a system design or for it to be self-adapting to user needs.

Unfortunately, interactive systems can also possess weaknesses. For each of the strengths just discussed, there is a corresponding weakness – for example, the potential for customisation is a strength; the lack of it a weakness.

But there are further potential weaknesses. Designers are often tempted to add additional features, sometimes providing multiple ways to perform a sub-task. Adding new functions is not always a strength; particularly when existing users are confused and new users are discouraged from even starting.

What is the difference between an interactive system which has strengths and one which has many weaknesses and problems? A good system is designed in such a way that the power of the system is harnessed to support the maximum number of intended users to carry out the tasks that they want or need to do. A poorly designed system wastes that power in providing unnecessary functions presented in unfamiliar and confusing ways.

2.8 Summary

We have looked at how natural computing might be applied in the context of interactive system design.

One approach that is congruent with natural computing is user-centred system design (UCSD), which places the user, their goals, needs and activities at the centre of the design process. It involves a rethink of traditional development processes, which are often too sequential and rigid, minimising the needs of the users. Key aspects of this approach are evaluation and iteration. In practice, designers cannot adhere strictly to rigid and linear processes, and benefit from an approach that makes explicit the iterative nature of design. The resulting designs benefit too: an approach that recognises the requirements of the users, both as individuals with individual differences and as a group, tends to produce better designs.

Although the UCSD process focuses on the user, it often stops at groups of users and not the individual. Although it may not yet be feasible to design systems for individuals, good system design allows for the customisation of designs for individuals with special requirements. User-centred design needs to include not only the relevant group of users, but also subsections and individuals with special needs.

Natural computing provides a basis to begin to understand people and systems, and how people might use technology to good effect.

References and further reading

Gould JD, Boies S J, Levy S, Richards JT, Schoonard J (1987), The 1984 Olympic Message System: a test of behavioral principles of system design, *Communications of the ACM* September 1987, Volume 30 Issue 9.

Pinker S. (1997), *How the mind works,* London: Penguin.

Preece J, Rogers Y and Sharp H (2002), *Interaction Design: Beyond Human-Computer Interaction*, New York: John Wiley & Sons, ISBN: 0-471-49278-7. Chapter 10 discusses, in some detail, the novel UCSD approaches deployed during the development of the system .

Shneiderman B. (2002), *Leonardo's Laptop: Human Needs and the New Computing Technologies*, MIT Press.

University of Leiden, Center for Natural Computing: **www.lcnc.nl**

2.9 Review questions

 Question 2.1: Computers can be hard to use. Even today, the use of an unfamiliar system can be a 'hit and miss' process. The more functions there are in the system, the bigger the problem. Yet many of us are reluctant to admit to difficulties in using information and communication technology (ICT).

Discuss why this is true and explain what kinds of challenges the designers of modern computer systems must deal with.

Question 2.2: What makes something easy to use? What are the properties of an interactive system that make it easy to use? For example, your list might include:

- are the instructions clear?

- is the machine efficient (i.e. can you select what you want in less then four key-clicks or button presses)?

... and other similar questions.

- Draw up a list of about seven questions to evaluate the usability of the ticket machine you designed in activity 2.3

- If possible, exchange your list with someone else studying this material; then use the two lists to evaluate the imaginary ticket machine

- Do the two lists produce the same answer / score?

2.9 Answers to review questions

Answer to review question 2.1: One view is that ICT is the home of the expert. On this view, to admit to a problem with ICT is to admit to an apparent lack of expertise. Yet computers are often found to be difficult to use. Why?

It's possible that all the users who complain of ICT problems simply lack the necessary skills, but that seems unlikely. It is also typical for system vendors to assume that their customers are at fault.

There may, however, be other explanations than simply blaming the users.

Problems may be due to poor design or training. That is where we can think of HCI and user-centred design. If we design interactive systems, but ignore the needs and preferences of the user, then we risk creating difficult-to-use products.

Using a new computer package or a novel phone system is often like finding your way through a maze. Despite errors of omission and commission, you find your way through in the end. You memorise the sequence of instructions and ignore anything you don't need.

The designers of modern computer systems face a number of significant challenges, including:

- Great variation in use (PCs are expected to support a wide range of tasks)

- A range of different contexts (ranging from the office to the battlefield)

- Significantly different users (abilities, training, disabilities and objectives) and the difficulty of explaining how to use it to a diverse and often unknown audience

- A large number of different features and functions, often buried underneath layers of menus.

These challenges underline the importance of putting the user at the centre of the design process.

Vendors of PCs, phones and other appliances are committed to supporting a wide range of tasks in as many contexts as possible for a diverse and expanding range of users. Vendors appear to believe that the best way to attract and retain users is to offer more and more features.

Ironically, this surplus of features can cause real problems for the user: many technological purchases are difficult to use until a lucky guess (or an accidental key depression) supplies some missing information.

Perhaps designers would be better off placing more emphasis upon designing for the diversity of users in the real world and covering the tasks that they need and want. This is where user-centred design methods are potentially of greatest value.

Answer to review question 2.2   There is no right or wrong answer here. It is quite common for different usability checklists to produce widely different results. The larger point here is about design for a diverse user population.

2.10 Feedback on activities

Feedback on activity 2.1: What do we mean by 'natural computing'?   The aim of this activity is to get you thinking from the outset. It will be apparent that 'natural computing' is a much larger and more diffuse research area than we indicate in this chapter.   Here, we're concerned primarily with natural computing in the context of user-centred system design and human–computer interaction.

Typical of the websites you'll find is likely to be the homepage of the University of Leiden Center for Natural Computing at **www.lcnc.nl**

The definition of natural computing you will find there is:

Natural computing is a general term referring to computing going on in nature and computing inspired by nature.

They describe the scope of natural computing as:

When complex phenomena going on in nature are viewed as computational processes, our understanding of these phenomena and of the essence of computation is enhanced. In this way one gains valuable insights into both natural sciences and computer science. Characteristic for man-designed computing inspired by nature is the metaphorical use of concepts, principles and mechanisms underlying natural systems. Thus, evolutionary algorithms use the concepts of mutation, recombination and natural selection from biology; neural networks are inspired by the highly interconnected neural structures in the brain and the nervous system; molecular computing is based on paradigms from molecular biology; and quantum computing based on quantum physics exploits quantum parallelism….

Feedback on activity 2.2: Voice messaging at the 1984 Olympic Games   You probably listed some of the following:

- A set of scenarios

- Discussion with stakeholders and other interested parties

- Production and test of user guides

- Olympian athlete on design team

- Simulations of the user interface: faked speech

- Demonstrations and trials with non-US users and phone systems

- Interviews with users (especially athletes)

- Tours of the Olympic Village

- Field tests at other events

- Testing by 4000 IBM internal users

- A 'try-to-destroy-it' test where users are challenged to crash the system.

Have you used any of these approaches or tools on a project? Would you use one or more of them? Under what circumstances?   When would you not use them?

What are the benefits of such extensive user-centred design and evaluation? Three that come to mind are:

- Problems are fixed before the system is shipped, not after

- The development team focus on real problems, not imaginary ones

- The system in use is likely to be much more usable and useful.

CHAPTER 3

User modelling in user-centred system design (UCSD)

OVERVIEW

In this chapter, we will explain and explore the central notion of user modelling and why it is important to user-centred system design.

Learning outcomes	At the end of this chapter, you should be able to:

- Define a user model

- Describe how to develop a user model

- Describe various ways of creating user models

- Explain the main features of the Model Human Processor and Simplistic theory

- Explain and apply Simplex One model

- Explain and apply Nielsen's heuristics.

3.1 Introduction

This chapter explains and explores the central notion of the user model and why it is so important to user-centred system design (UCSD). This topic is relevant to both the usability expert and the designer of user-centred systems.

To understand UCSD, you first need to understand the people who will use your systems. One way to do so is through the concept of user modelling. In this chapter we define a user model as a psychologically valid way of depicting the people who will use the systems, and whose needs and preferences will be considered when designing those systems. Ideally, such a user model should be able to represent, in part, their psychological processes, individual differences, social context, internalised cultural factors and lifestyle, and task objectives.

How do you construct a user model? In this chapter, we show you several ways. Our aim is to provide a firm foundation for a detailed account of a group of people, specific user groups or individuals with special needs (e.g. people with disabilities or in extreme circumstances).

3.2 Types of user model

We will focus on the Simplex theory (Adams and Langdon, 2003) as representative of the current state of knowledge about user models. There are, however, several ways to create a useful user model.

Psychological theories as user models

One approach is to take a well-established psychological theory. In cognitive science, there are now a number of powerful models to capture key parameters of system users, including Broadbent's Maltese Cross (Broadbent, 1984), Barnard's Interacting Cognitive Subsystems (Barnard, May, Duke and Duce, 2000), Anderson's ACT series of models (Anderson 1983), SOAR (Laird, Newell and Rosenbloom, 1987) and Simplex One (Adams and Langdon, 2003).

Since human cognition is clearly very complex, the difficulty is that many of these models almost require their users to become cognitive psychologists. Designers and students find them inaccessible and intractable. To do full justice to such theories, you probably need to learn them in some depth. A PhD in cognitive psychology might be useful, too! It would clearly be inappropriate for every usability or interactive design expert to take time out to add to their qualifications, unless they really wanted to go into considerable depth or into research. Otherwise, to identify important implications of such models will require you to call in an expert every time. For the busy designer or computer scientist, this may not be a feasible option.

Task analysis for user models

A second approach would be to take a more strongly task-based analysis. The idea is that an evaluation of the core tasks can lead to consideration of how users will undertake these tasks. In one sense, this is rather like creating a new theory of the users from a consideration of how they do the tasks to be done. This approach seems to reinvent the wheel. Why create new theories when good ones already exist? Second, the task-analytic approach seems to lean (perhaps accidentally) towards an overly behaviouristic approach to understanding, a school of psychology that has largely been overtaken by cognitive science.

Cut-down psychological theories as user models

A third alternative is to create a cut-down psychological theory: one that can be used by designers and other computer scientists, but without the irrelevant complexities of a fully fledged theory. The Model Human Processor (MHP) (Card, Moran and Newell, 1983) is one such theory that deliberately takes this approach.

The MHP has the dual advantage of being simple enough to be applicable and of having been developed directly to solve IT design problems.

MHP provides a simple architecture of human cognition, including perceptual and response components, short-term and long-term memory plus cognitive processing. It was intended to capture the then current understanding of human cognition, but to be sufficiently simplified for use in practice by designers and students.

Over the years, the status of MHP as a psychological theory has been strongly criticised. Such criticisms have been due, in part, to a failure to appreciate that MHP was never intended as a full psychological theory, but rather as a guide to system design and evaluation.

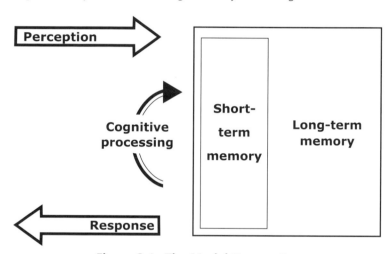

Figure 3.1: The Model Human Processor

However, it is perhaps true that MHP is past its sell-by date. A number of major paradigm shifts have occurred in system design and in the issues considered important in this field. So MHP is perhaps best seen as a brilliant trailblazer: one which should encourage us to develop new ways of dealing with interactive technology in all its forms, with user-supportive architectures and with adaptable and self-adaptive systems. As a teaching aid, it still has some value.

Moreover, MHP still inspires new approaches. For example, consider the inclusive design approach, which draws explicitly on MHP to construct the inclusion cube. This is a major component of their inclusive design theory.

Simplistic psychological theories as user models

Finally, there is what we call the simplistic model. Such a model seeks systematically to combine the benefits of the three methods just listed. It has two defining features.

- First, defined formally, a simplistic theory is intended to provide a powerful conceptual framework within which complex theories and research findings can be located
- Second, what is distinctive about simplistic theory is the ability to be repackaged to provide an

overall depiction that can be used by designers and practical computer scientists as a guide, without requiring them to become psychologists.

Simplex One as a simplistic theory

The model that we will be working with here is Simplex One (there is a more complex version called Simplex Two, which is considered in Chapter 7). It is chosen here to show one view of the current state of play in human cognitive research, and was developed by Adams and Langdon from the pioneering research of the then leading Cambridge psychologist, Dr Donald Broadbent – whose Maltese Cross model itself represents a significant advance on MHP. Broadbent recognised the need to postulate the flow of information in all possible directions in the system: MHP assumed that information flowed into the system to cause a response, but did not flow back in the opposite direction. This simplifying assumption turns out not to be tenable. Apart from this new axiom and the rather different architecture, Broadbent's model still acts as a simple memory store approach; such approaches are essentially like a von Neumann machine, with input, output, executive functions, memory and backup memory.

The Simplex One model responded to recent research and theorising by being constructed as five zones or modules of cognition, which are partially independent of each other. Each module possesses both memory and local processing capacity, each acting as a von Neumann machine, allowing the overall system a level of parallel processing and autonomous self-diagnosis. The result of this model building, together with further modelling work in neural networks, is a powerful framework that captures some of the current consensus about human cognition. It also provides a simple, yet elegant, framework for the interactive system designer or computer scientist to apply to the solution of real-world computing problems.

Simplex One looks like this:

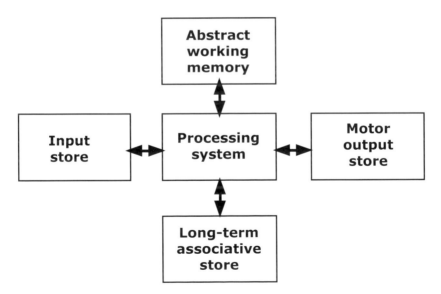

Figure 3.2: Simplex One

Simplex One, the overall architecture and functioning, plus its constituent modules is described in the next section.

3.3 User models and evaluation

Using design principles (heuristics) for evaluation

The HCI research literature and the Internet are full of design principles and heuristics which are intended to guide the evaluation (and hence the design) of an interactive system.

Design *rules* tend to give precise recommendations about specific design aspects, whereas design *guidelines* (and the design principles that they contain) are low in authority and are more general in their application.

Design rules are very prescriptive about specific areas of design. For example, a rule stating 'never use red text on a blue background' clearly tells you about what not do for a specific part of your design. Its authority comes from studies of the human eye that identified a likelihood that the two colours appeared blurred if used together.

Standards tend to be imposed by a regulatory body, such as a particular organisation or a regulatory body. For example, the International Standards Organisation (ISO) produces standards for industrial software. Quite often these standards are mandatory. It may be that they are a legal requirement, and the developers could be sued if they are not kept to. It may also be that they are part of the contract on which the developers are hired, so payment for the work may depend on compliance. Often they will refer to a specific type of system in a particular industry. So the coverage is not likely to be as wide as with guidelines or principles.

Hardware and software manufacturers produce commercial style guides, and corporate style guides are developed by companies for their own internal use. The advantage of using these guides is to enhance usability of a product through consistency. However, there are other reasons – for example, software developed for Microsoft, Apple Macintosh or IBM PC maintains its 'look and feel' across many product lines.

Many design style questions have to be addressed more specifically when developing corporate style guides. For example, how should dialogue windows be organised? Which styles, colour and fonts should be used?

Guidelines are not prescriptive in the way that rules are, but describe usability concepts that help us judge designs, and gain a stronger understanding of usability as a concept. They tend to be based on more general usability principles. Although they tend not to be specific in the same way as design rules, they cover a wide range of interface features and concepts. Let's now look at some of the well-known design principles:

- **Learnability:** as we will see in further discussion of human memory in Chapter 7, humans tend to learn systems through understanding and generalising about the system as a whole when they try new features. So the Principle of Learnability is very important

- **Predictability:** this interactive design principle requires a user's knowledge of interaction to be sufficient to work out what actions are possible at any point in interaction, and what the consequences of taking those options will be. The user needs to be aware of all the options that the system allows, and be able to work out which ones they will need for their desired action

- **Consistency:** consistency is essential and is probably one of the most widely applied design principles in user interface design. Consistency is discussed further under the *Heuristic evaluation* section

- **Flexibility:** flexibility in interactive design extends the way a user and the system exchange information. By applying flexibility principles to an interactive system design, designers aim to improve a system's usability.

- **Recoverability:** users tend to learn by exploration and they therefore need to be confident that mistakes are recoverable and not disastrous. Even experienced users may still make mistakes; they click or type the wrong action without checking what they are doing. So it is vital that they can undo actions and recover from mistakes
- **Responsiveness:** responsiveness is usually measured in terms of the rate of communication between the system and a user.

But which are the good heuristics – and how can you tell? They are often written in apparently easy-to-understand language, which, in practice, turns out to have hidden depths.

Writers of design principles can commit the 'expert knowledge fallacy' (i.e. when an expert designs a system or a set of guidelines, their creation will seem simple to them). So they are tempted to believe that everyone else will see it in the same way. That is where the fallacy arises. The expert has familiarity, experience and a depth of underlying knowledge to help them. When working with their system, they know where to look for key items such as hyperlinks, what to do when a problem occurs or simply what to do next without being told. The new user may have problems with all of these aspects and more!

The designers of heuristics face similar issues. Because heuristics seem to be written in simple language, readers are inclined to assume that they must indeed be simple to use. Recently, however, Ray Adams asked a class of twenty students to work alone to rate the clarity of Nielson's heuristics (detailed in section 3.4) on a ten-point scale (where 10 indicated total clarity and zero indicated a total lack of clarity). To his and their surprise, no one in the group was able to rate any heuristic as 10 (total clarity). The mean rating was 7.2, but that concealed quite a bit of variation. Overall, the students were relieved to hear that they were not the only ones to find some heuristics difficult to understand and thus interpret. Adams suspects that one of the problems that students (and some designers) face with heuristics is a lack of a conceptual basis with which to interpret them. Perhaps they would do better starting with the provision of a simple theory to understand users, tasks and systems.

Evaluating user requirements with Simplex One

The Simplex One theory is designed, in part, to meet the need of designers and students to understand better the key design issues in terms of the psychology of the user. To remind you, the formal definition of a simplistic theory requires that it be designed at two levels:

- It acts as a framework within which to understand current research findings and emergent sub-theories
- It may be presented in a simplified form to guide practical problem solving by practitioners.

The aim of Simplex One is to facilitate the design process. A key feature of the theory is that each cognitive module can take input from any other module in the system via the executive function. For example, the perceptual system takes in information from the senses, but it can also receive information from long-term memory when identifying and naming a newly perceived event.

Simplex One identifies five key aspects of human cognition or computation. They are:

- **Perception (input):** the ability to take in new information from the senses, to analyse and store that information and to relate currently held information to it
- **Response (output):** the ability to select, organise, time and implement appropriate responses
- **Abstract working memory:** to take, hold and process task-relevant memories while they are needed to support action. This is a limited capacity, time-limited, system
- **Long-term memory:** the warehouse of long-term associative memory, which stores the co-

occurrence of key events and symbols. Unlike working memory, long-term memory seems freer of many constraints, building inexorably over time as our experience grows. The main difficulties associated with long-term memory seem to be problems of the initial quality of input and errors of retrieval from memory.

It is generally agreed that long-term memory includes both *episodic* memory and *semantic* memory (where we remember the specific episodes together with the context in which they occurred).

- an example of an **episodic memory** would be : 'Last Tuesday I talked with Ben Shneiderman at a conference in Vienna.' There are four (or, arguably, five) discrete facts in this memory

- **semantic memory**, in contrast, is a store of our world knowledge where we have not retained the context. For example, I know that Vienna is a city in Austria, but I cannot remember where or when I learned that fact. There is also some indication that we build mental models of systems, which we keep in either working or long-term memory

- **Executive functions:** this is where information is switched between the foregoing four psychological modules of the theory, where sequences of such transfers are organised, where the functions of the different modules are mediated and where task requirements are organised and monitored.

Such a model can be used in at least two ways. First, it can be used to evaluate the strengths and weaknesses of the people who will be using a system. Here the focus is upon the profiles of the people who use the systems: we can formulate questions about them. Second, it can be applied to appraise a proposed design.

To illustrate how a practitioner could use such a theory, here are some typical questions that they might generate about the users, plus an explanation for each.

The point is that a system designer or evaluator can use their understanding of a simple theory such as Simplex to generate the most appropriate questions to meet their objectives. They are not stuck with the same old list of questions or principles.

- **Perception:** *what are the perceptual skills of the user groups likely to be?* What do we know about human perception in general to provide guidance? Are there any specific perceptual problems related to the users or subgroups of users (e.g. disabilities or extreme circumstances)? For example, how many of our users could have visual impairments or blindness? Do the symbols we have chosen make sense to the user groups or do they contain unwanted aspects / nuances of meaning that would be perceived differently by different groups of our users?

- **Responses:** *what are user responses likely to be like?* Again, are there any general, relevant, human factor principles to guide our expectations? Do our users have any specific problems with responding, for instance verbally or making psychomotor responses etc? Perhaps a system is intended for elderly users, where hand positioning may be poorly controlled. Alternatively, a person may be working in an extreme environment (e.g. a deep sea diver) where response options / methods must be designed carefully

- **Abstract working memory:** *what kind of memory capabilities do our users have?* We know that human working memory is limited in time, storage capacity and processing rates. We also know that different types of input from perception and from the other modules may differ in memorability. What can we expect from our users? Are they average members of the population? If not, what are their specific needs? What is their experience of earlier symbol systems of user interfaces? Is there anything in that experience that we can use to get the message across better? Anything that we should avoid? Do some user groups have significantly different memory resources from others? For example, consider individuals with learning difficulties or some older individuals

- **Long-term memory:** conversely, consider the long-term memory (LTM) abilities of our users. Almost certainly, they will use some of the contents of their long-term memory, deliberately or unconsciously, to make sense of their experience of a new system. But what can we know about these contents? At the least, human LTM appears, inter alia, to possess associative qualities. We learn what goes with what and how often. We build hierarchies of knowledge and one memory reminds us of other memories by association. Will the information presented by a new IT system make sense or will it perhaps seem unrelated to anything we have known before?

  Here, a dose of common sense, could guide our views. Perhaps some older users have significant amounts of information in long-term memory with which to inform their understanding of a new system. Judicious use of metaphor may link prior knowledge to the intuitive look and feel of a system. Inappropriate or inadequate metaphorical referents may confuse or just leave a user guessing. In contrast, if many of our users are very young, they may possess much less prior knowledge. They may be less open to metaphor as a way of referring to experience, though more amenable to new ways of organising what they need to know in convenient ways through analogy

- **Executive functions:** *finally, might our users vary in their executive functioning?* Some people are better at learning new tasks than others. In certain cases, greater task training will be necessary. Other people are not so good at monitoring and controlling their task performance once acquired and, if so, will require more feedback from a system in order to perform their tasks sufficiently well. Current research is exploring the potential of self-adapting systems that can adjust to the needs of users as indicated by their behaviour. Not all users can readily acquire new tasks and implement them with relative ease. Individuals with certain types of head injury (acquired through injury or illness) may show lack of insight into their cognitive deficits. They may also be relatively unaware of problems with their actual performance, not apparently noticing that they are performing badly. For example, individuals with injuries to the frontal lobes of the brain may demonstrate dramatic executive problems. They may be unable to acquire new tasks readily, they may perform disastrously badly without awareness of those problems and they may behave inappropriately in social settings. (Adams and Langdon, 2003). What are the abilities of our users to acquire new tasks with new systems? What kind and levels of feedback will they require to do well? Are there subgroups of users with special needs? Are there users who will benefit from additional help?

The better the designer understands the psychology of the users, the better the needs and requirements of these users can be respected and made central to the emerging design of a system. The use of a simplistic theory such as Simplex One, or others like it, might require some training time, but has the potential to help the designer in this way. However, that training time should be less onerous than that required by other, more complex theories. Individual designers must make up their own minds about the trade-off between the complexity and the accessibility of the theories that underpin user model building.

Evaluating design options with Simplex One

The second way in which Simplex One can be used is to evaluate the actual or proposed design of a system against the five main zones or modules of human cognition. Here the focus is on the systems, but the aim is to ensure that users can control the systems sufficiently well to achieve their objectives.

This time we can generate a different set of questions using the five modules of Simplex One. This time, we address the suitability of system design options. As before, however, the point is that a system designer or evaluator can use their understanding of a simple theory such as Simplex to generate the most appropriate questions to meet their objectives.

- **Perception:** to what extent does the proposed system design allow information to be delivered to the users in ways which will respect their sensory capabilities and perceptual skills so as to maximise their perceptual performance? Do system outputs facilitate users' abilities to take in new information from the senses, to analyse and store that information and to relate currently held information to it? For example, does the system cater for users with age-related or specific sensory and perceptual deficits?

- **Response:** what are the response options that the proposed system allows or provides for users? Do they allow the users to properly select, organise, time and implement appropriate responses? Is an adequate range of response media provided? What are users' requirements and preferences? Does the system provide adequate support for some users who have specific problems with verbal or psychomotor responses?

- **Abstract working memory:** since we know that working memory is a limited-capacity, time-limited and process-limited system, does the system design respect those limitations? Does a system design place inappropriate demands on users' working memory?

- **Long-term memory:** does the system design rely on unjustified assumptions about users' prior knowledge, the nature and quality of that knowledge, and their abilities to retrieve relevant knowledge at the right moment? Have we assumed that our own prior knowledge is representative of our users and treated them as if they know what we know?

- **Executive functions:** what demands do our system designs place upon the executive functions of our users? What new tasks do our designs require them to learn? Will they be required to perform familiar tasks in unfamiliar or even contradictory ways because we have radically redesigned our systems? Over and above these concerns, do any of our users require special features in the system design to enable them to perform adequately well? Have we added additional functions that make our systems more difficult to learn? Are we merely adding features for the sake of it – or because our users really want them?

In summary, it can be seen that theories such as Simplex One generate two types of question:

- The first type explores the *parameters of our users*
- The second type *challenges the proposed designs* we consider. In both cases, the aim is to empower the practitioner to formulate the relevant questions that they want answered, rather than to rely on second-hand questions.

Activity 3.1

Questions for the five modules of Simplex One

You will require computer and Internet access for this task, which again considers the ticket simulation machine, this time in the context of the Simplex One modules.

3.4 Heuristic evaluation

The word 'heuristic' means *search strategy*. All principles, such as the ones described in the list that follows, can be used as heuristics. The search that they are used for is a search for potential usability problems with a design. They cannot absolutely tell you what is right and wrong with a design. Standards for the use of colour can tell you specific things such as 'never use red text on a blue background'. By contrast, the use of heuristics involves making interpretations and judgements. The heuristic simply reminds you of the need to look for this.

Heuristics are normally used as a checklist of things to look for. This may range from relatively simple judgements (e.g. *is there an undo facility*) to harder judgements about the way that the system is designed. You will notice when you use the heuristics that sometimes it is hard to decide which heuristic best describes a problem that you have found. It is quite likely that you will find usability problems that can be classified in more than one category.

Several sets of heuristics have been proposed including Norman's seven principles (1988), Schneiderman's eight golden rules (1998), Tognazzini's interaction design principles (1992) and Neilsen's ten heuristics (2001).

The ten heuristics (rules) developed by Nielsen are :

1   Visibility of system status

2   Match between system and the real world

3   User control and freedom

4   Consistency and standards

5   Error prevention

6   Helping users recognise, diagnose and recover from errors

7   Recognition rather than recall

8   Flexibility and efficiency of use

9   Aesthetic and minimalist design

10   Help and documentation.

Let's look at these in more detail:

- **Visibility of system status:** *always keep the user informed about what is going on through providing appropriate feedback in a reasonable time.*

  This principle refers to the way that the system responds to each user action or to changes that the user will need to know about. This could be information such as a message telling the user that their file is being printed in response to their use of a 'print' menu option. But it does not have to be a message. The idea of 'feedback' also covers, for example, an object moving when it is dragged, or appearing in a new document after the user uses the 'paste' command. In modern systems, a lot of feedback is designed this way, but ensuring that it conveys the appropriate meaning takes very careful design.

  System output must be timely, visible, and meaningful: it is crucial that the system response is quick, as users will soon become concerned and distracted if their actions appear to have no effect. In addition, you must be careful that the system response will be visible. There is no value making a change that the user cannot see. But it is important that the system visibly changes in a way that allows the user to instantly assess the current state of interaction. Your user will be trying to achieve something using the system, and will have a notion of the end goal, what they have to do to achieve it and what the 'goal-state' (the completion of what they want to do) will look like. After each action the user will be monitoring progress towards this goal-state. The feedback from the system must give the user this information. This may not be a text message such as the printing example above, but simply a change in the image indicating what has happened

- **Match between system and the real world:** *speak the user's language, using words, phrases and concepts, rather than system-orientated terms.*

The system must look and behave in ways that are familiar to the user. This is particularly true when users are scanning the screen looking for features with which to perform actions. It is useful to think of users as searching for a match between what they are expecting and what is on the screen. The user will have an idea of what they are looking for. For example, a user looking to produce a diagram will have knowledge of pencil-and-paper drawing. These terms and concepts are useful to the designer because they can use words or icons that make sense to someone with knowledge of pencil-and-paper drawing. Part of the reason that we use task analysis is to learn about how our intended system users describe and think about the actions and objects that are part of the task. This is so that we can give them names, images and behaviour that they will recognise.

One important problem for designers and design teams is that they become very familiar with the system that they are designing and get used to talking about parts of the system in a computer professional's terms, or in what we call 'system-orientated' language. So there is a danger that our design will have features that are not understandable to users, because we have not presented them in a form that the user understands. Words such as 'cache', 'database' and 'compile' are meaningful to a computing professional, but they need translating into a language that the user can understand and would expect. So we use 'metaphors' that communicate the nature of the object and the possible actions to the user

- **User control and freedom:** *provide ways of allowing users to easily escape from places they unexpectedly find themselves, by using clearly marked 'emergency exits'.*

With many systems that we use, there is no single path for navigating through the system. Users tend to take different options either because they are exploring, or simply because they have made a mistake. Therefore, they must be able to recover when they find themselves in unfamiliar parts of the system. For example, if website users find themselves lost on an unfamiliar page (and it is designed well) they should be able to find links to the previous page and home page and perhaps also a trace of the pages visited. It is important that users feel confident to explore. This depends on them having confidence in their ability to undo actions and get back from places in the system that they explore

- **Consistency and standards:** *avoid making users wonder if different words, situations or actions mean the same thing.*

This principle is concerned with supporting the user's expectations and their attempts to learn as they use the system. When users use a new system, they are usually looking to understand how the system works. When they see one screen, or try an action, they are not only trying to achieve a goal, but also to learn how the whole system works.

It is useful to think of learning how to use the system as learning rules of operation. The user is not just trying to understand the current action, but to gain knowledge that can be reused as they use more of the system. The best a designer can do is to make sure that the number of rules that the user needs to learn is as small as possible. A good design is one that allows the user to use their early experience of using a few of its features again when they try more actions.

A bad design will force users to learn new rules for new situations when they could have let the user reuse something they had already learned. For example, changing text from *normal* to *bold* in Microsoft Word involves the following steps:

- place the cursor at the start or end of the text that you want to change

- drag the cursor so that the text becomes highlighted

- move the cursor to the button on the task bar or the menu item that represents bold

- click the button or menu item: the text changes.

Once the user has tried this, they will know how to do it next time. But they will also know – in principle – how to approach a number of similar things that they have not yet tried, including re-sizing text or italicisation. The general principle of 'identify text to be changed, then select the operation' can be reapplied. This makes systems easier and quicker to learn. It also means that users can learn by exploring, without much help and without having to look at instruction manuals. The same type of operation covers many features, so learning one helps the user to learn all similar features. Imagine, for example, that italicisation involved adding section breaks from the menu, above and below the text, before it can be selected. Users would have to learn a new rule just to use one feature. To make it worse, they would naturally try to use the rule that works for bold and for other features. So it is important that similar features behave in a similar, consistent way to help users explore, learn and become comfortable using the system.

Consistency in the way that screens are arranged and features positioned is also very important, as people tend to have good 'spatial' memory. This means that they learn and remember where objects or features are positioned, and use this to learn and use the system.

So it is important that features are positioned in a consistent way. For example, if your website has navigation buttons on the top under the page title on one page, your user will automatically look there for the same features on other pages. If you put them somewhere different on other pages, the user may not find them – and will certainly have their interaction made more difficult and confusing

- **Error prevention:** *where possible, prevent errors occurring in the first place.*
  On first reading, you may think that this principle is saying nothing that is not said by other principles. Surely good consistency and match between the system and the real world prevents errors? But there is an important distinction between this and other principles, and describing this distinction is useful in understanding the HCI view of user-system interaction. A user who falls victim to, for example, a poor match between the system and the real world, is led by the system to do something they did not want to do. Perhaps a menu option has been given a misleading name and has caused the user to click an option, which makes something happen that they didn't want. This is an error, *but from an HCI perspective;* it is not a user error. The user has done everything correctly. The user has worked out the feature that they want to use and looked for the best match with the options on display. The system is responsible for the error because it has not supported the rational behaviour of the user.

  The 'error prevention' principle has a different emphasis. It recognises that users are prone to certain types of error when they perform actions, and points to the need to cut down the chances of such errors. For example, we know that all users will sometimes make typographical or spelling errors. No matter how expert we are, it sometimes happens. So a good design should minimise the amount of text entry we need, or constrain it where possible. Something such as a drop-down menu can be used to save users the job of typing the name of a country, and eliminate the chance of incorrect text entry. Similarly, some text entry can be constrained, such as the entry for credit card expiry dates. The designer knows that there is a six-digit format and can limit the fields to this number. This does not guarantee error-free entry, but it cuts down the chances of an error. So this helps designers to check that they cut down the space of possible errors by the user

- **Helping users recognise, diagnose and recover from errors:** *use plain language to describe the nature of the problem and suggest some way of solving it.*

  Many error messages do not take into account the user's perspective. In particular, they do not take into account the terms that the user is likely to be familiar with or understand. Nor do they take account of what the user will need explained.

  This may result in the user failing to understand the current situation or being able to select a recovery action.

It is often possible to make a reasonable guess about the information that users will need once an error is made. For example, where forms are incorrectly filled in they will respond to the user pressing 'send' after completing the form by displaying the form again. The missing or incorrect information is highlighted in red with an explanation of the problem (e.g. invalid expiry date). This makes it easy for the user to identify and rectify the problem.   If the user is simply given a message that says 'form not accepted' they will have to press the back button or click the link to the form and fill it in again. They will not know what the problem is and may easily repeat the error

- **Recognition rather than recall:** *make objects, actions, and options visible.*
  Recognition is crucial to good, efficient, satisfying, user-system dialogue. It is the basis of display-based interaction and learning by exploration. It contrasts with the concept of recall, where the user has to make a conscious effort to remember.

  We use recognition when using computers and in everyday life generally. We are able to walk from one room to another because we recognise the door and the door handle, and understand the procedure for using them. Likewise, when we see familiar objects on the screen we associate them with their intended use and the procedure for using them. This is referred to as recognition-based interaction. If objects are labelled well, with text or icons, they can immediately be spotted by the user and matched with what they want to do. If information is visible to the user, they will not need to remember it as they go through the system.

  Recognition is based on the visibility of information and the familiarity of objects. For example, imagine an online catalogue showing furniture. Each item has a nine-digit code that must be entered on the order form. The order form is reached by clicking a link from the catalogue. When the order page appears, the name of the item and the code disappears. So a user wanting to order one chair will have to recall or write down the name and code in order to enter it on the form. Compare this to a website that gives the user a 'shopping basket' allowing them to monitor the items that they have selected, with details of product name, price and any code numbers. In the second example, a user would find it easier to select multiple items than to select even one with the former website. This is because all the important information remains visible when it is needed

- **Flexibility and efficiency of use:** *provide accelerators that are invisible to novice users, but allow more experienced users to carry out tasks more quickly.*
  It is very important that we design in a way that gives novice users every chance of quickly being able to use the system. However, there is a danger that making the system easy for a novice may make it slow and disturbingly awkward for expert users. So we need to take opportunities to make interaction faster for experts

- **Aesthetic and minimalist design:** *avoid using information that is irrelevant or rarely needed.*
  Designers are often tempted to fill the screen with eye-catching graphics or vivid colours. This often has the effect of cluttering up the screen, making it difficult to look at and, worst of all, hiding the important objects and information that the user needs. For example, many modern websites contain banner advertisements, flashing icons, and similar eye-catching items. Many of these grab user attention when really the user is looking for options to achieve their objective. The designer has the power to direct user attention by making important items prominent and clear. Equally, if a designer uses bright colours or other eye-catching techniques badly, it can direct users away from what they want to do and the features they want to find. It can also put the user off trying to interact with the system. This is a notable problem on business-to-customer (B2C) websites

- **Help and documentation:** *provide information that can be easily searched and provides help in a set of concrete steps that can easily be followed.*

Help systems are often difficult to use themselves and fail to address user needs. Frequently, they do not enable the user to find helpful information about features and merely waste users' time. Help can be evaluated by considering how likely a typical user is to find useful information that is relevant to what they are currently doing, rather than simply facts about the system. The same applies to the design of documentation. Documentation, such as the interface itself, must contain terms, concepts and images that the user can understand. There are many examples of documentation, for example using terms and descriptions that are appropriate for design experts talking to each other, but are not understandable for the novice.

Activity 3.2

Heuristic evaluation

Find a cinema booking website; apply two of Nielsen's heuristics (*User control and freedom*, and *Error prevention*) to it. You will need access to the Internet.

3.5 Summary

In this chapter, we explained and explored the central notion of the user model and why it is so important to UCSD. This topic is relevant to both the usability expert and the designer of user-centred systems.

We focused here on the Simplex theory (Adams and Langdon, 2003) since it is representative of the current state of knowledge about user models. As we have indicated, however, there are several ways to create a useful user model.

We also introduced Nielsen's heuristics, which will be revisited on many occasions throughout the rest of the book.

References and further reading

Adams, R, Langdon, P and Clarkson, PJ (2002), *A systematic basis for developing cognitive assessment methods for assistive technology*. In: Keates, S, Langdon, P, Clarkson PJ and Robinson, P (eds), *Universal Access and Assistive Technology*, London: Springer-Verlag

Anderson JR (1983), *The Architecture of Cognition*, Cambridge, Mass: Harvard University Press

Barnard, PJ, May, J, Duke, D and Duce, D (2000), Systems interactions macro-theory, Trans. *Human Computer Interface*, 7, 222-62

Broadbent, DE (1984), The Maltese Cross: a new simplistic model of memory, *Behavioural and Brain Sciences*, 7, 55-94

Card, SK, Moran, TP, and Newell, A. (1983), *The Psychology of Human–Computer Interaction*. Hillsdale, N.J.: Lawrence Erlbaum Associates.

Dix, A, Finlay, J, Abowd, GD, Beale, R (2004), *Human-Computer Interaction*, third edition, Harlow: Pearson Education; also www.hcibook.com

Laird, JE, Newell, A and Rosenbloom, P (1987), SOAR: an architecture for general intelligence, *Artificial Intelligence*, 33, 1-64

Nielsen, J. (1994), *Usability Engineering*, Academic Press

Nielsen, J. (2001), *Ten Usability Heuristics*. **www.useit.com/papers/heuristic**

Norman, DA (1988), *The Design of Everyday Things*. New York, Doubleday

Shneiderman, B. (1998), *Designing the User Interface*, 3rd edition, Addison-Wesley, Reading, Massachusetts

Tognazzini, B, 'Tog' (1992), *Tog on Interface*. Addison-Wesley, Reading, Mass
www.asktog.com/

3.6 Review questions

 **Question 3.1**   The Model Human Processor (MHP) theory has led to the development of a number of more advanced theories that provide an even better account of current research.

Simplex One is one such development. Explain each of the five components of Simplex One.

Question 3.2   How can you relate human memory to interactive system design?

Question 3.3   Design principles, such as design heuristics, are intended to cover all interactive systems. But can they be used in the same way for all designs? Could the same feature be a violation of a design principle in one system, but a good feature in a different one?   Can you think of any types of system that may need different heuristics from the ones that we have looked at?

3.7 Answers to review questions

Answer to question 3.1

1. An interactive system must provide input to users (input store) that they take in and remember.

2. A well-designed system requires user responses that are easy to remember and to implement.

3. The system will not require an excessive amount of information to be stored in working memory.

4. The system should provide the users with appropriate information for long-term memory use, in the correct form at the right time, and so that learning may be optimised. The system should also make good use of the prior knowledge of the people who use it.

5. Finally, the system should support the executive subsystem by ensuring that the tasks required by the system are not too complex to be mastered and maintained.

Answer to question 3.2

Input/perception

First, what input could systems provide to the people who use them? This question of perceptual input will be considered in more depth later. To answer this question, we first need a basic understanding of the human senses and perception. Initially, human perception was viewed as a simple set of input processes, rather such as those of a computer, based upon the deployment of a sequence of input analysers of increasing complexity.

However, there is growing evidence for the importance of memory influences in effective perception, including working memory, mental models in memory and long-term memory. We must store the results of perceptual analyses in memory while working and while integrating new information. In addition, we draw upon information in memory to recognise objects, symbols and people. Here we can distinguish between early and late stages of recognition.

In the early stages, key features are identified. In later stages, the description of an item is compared against information in memory and the item recognised. Perception is clearly not a simple, one-way process.

Output/response preparation

Second, any interactive system will require the people who use it to make appropriate responses. Ideally, response requirements should be well designed and not place undue pressures on memory. Where a sequence of responses must be held in short-term or working memory, that sequence should not be too long or too complex or responses may be unacceptably slow or inaccurate. Where such sequences must be committed to memory in the long term, then it is more important that they be well designed to reflect the experience and abilities of the people who must use them.

In addition, it is vital that response requirements match users' response capabilities. Legislation in the UK, the US and other countries provides a legal basis for provision for people with disabilities. Organisations must make all reasonable adaptations to the workplace, including work-based interactive systems. Individuals may have limitations to their psychomotor skills. Individuals with limited hand or arm movement may need assistive technology to support their responses.

Keyboards can be provided with larger keys. Keyboards also can be presented on screen. Pointing devices such as track balls, an eye mouse or a mouse with gravity-well responses and so on can be of help, since they are less demanding ways of responding. In the future, systems will be able to recognise gestures and respond appropriately. Furthermore, future technology will allow for the use of brain implants to enable people with physical disabilities to control external devices such as joysticks directly. Such developments are already at the prototype stage.

Using working memory

While conducting tasks with interactive systems, we often need to hold a lot of information in working memory. This information can take a number of forms, including perceived speech, speech production, spatial information, visual information.

Current theories of working memory postulate at least three components:

- a modality-free executive which controls attention and concentration (in Simplex this function is covered by the separate executive module)
- a store for speech-based information
- a visual sketch pad, which supports spatial or visual information.

Speech-based information may involve working memory and the output module in Simplex. Visual information could involve the perception module and working memory in Simplex. Spatial information would involve working memory in Simplex. The key quality of working memory is that it is seen to underpin the performance of a number of tasks which can be conducted with the help of interactive technology. If so, then systems should be designed to provide users with information for temporary use which does not exceed the capacity of working memory. It is important to note that some individuals with cognitive problems may have problems with working memory and may need a version of the task/system which places fewer burdens on memory.

Using long-term memory

Prior experience is a major factor in the effective use of an interactive system. A usable, accessible system will reflect the prior experience of its users. There are at least three types of information which can be stored in long-term memory, as follows:

- first, semantic memory contains an individual's knowledge about the external world and about the definition of concepts. For example, 'Paris is the capital of France' or 'a dog is a mammal'. Such facts are retained without reference to the contexts within which they have been learned. The design of the user interface of many systems, particularly the conventional graphical user interface (GUI), often relies on the individual's prior experience of such systems.
Typically, a GUI will make extensive use of icons, buttons and menus. The expectation is that all users will recognise them and know how to use them. This expectation relies on the general knowledge of users of such systems. Occasionally, you will experience a system in which your expectations are not met. For example, conventionally, the items in a menu stay in the same positions. Exceptionally, the menu items will change their positions. For example, the items on the 'Start' menu of MS Windows XP change according to your prior use of the available applications. New items may be added or the position of existing items may be changed. This may lead to your selecting the wrong item, by selecting the wrong location.

- second, episodic memory consists of personal memories. For example, you may remember that you found a new system difficult to use when you last used it on Friday. Such personal memories are related to specific contexts and events which occur in those contexts. Episodic memory can form the basis upon which you can build up your familiarity of a new system. The memory for specific episodes or events generalises into general knowledge, where contextual information is lost. In some cases, useful information can be inaccessible because it is limited to a specific context. It is a common experience of users that they only remember what to do when the system provides a suitable context. It is noticeable that some individuals with head injuries may experience problems with episodic memory. They may show lack of insight into their functional problems and may even display a lack of awareness

- third, when using a system such as the London Underground or a new computer package, we act as if we are developing and using a mental model of that system. When we wish to solve system-related problems, we seem to invoke such models, either held in LTM or created and held in working memory. In Simplex Two, discussed in Chapter 7, a separate module has been created for this type of memory.

Using executive functions

Although individual components of a system or subsystem may be well crafted, it is still possible to create an overall system or task which itself is too complex or contradictory to be mastered and maintained easily. When trying out systems with new users, it has sometimes been found that the overall task is simply too difficult to master, though sub-tasks were okay. This component of the Simplex model deals with the overall requirements of task learning and overall task implementation. A striking result of head injury where the frontal lobes of the brain are involved is the inability to deal with complex tasks even when the individual concerned can follow the specific instructions without error!

Answer to question 3.3 Systems have different objectives. For example, recognition-based interaction makes for quick interaction between users and websites. They can interact without working memory being burdened by worries about how to perform the next action. In a more safety-critical system, such as train signalling, it could be argued that engaging the user's working memory in thinking about the next action may be desirable. The objectives of such a system would be different to those of a website, and this affects our decision making about the way in which both the task and the user performing it should be supported.

3.8 Feedback on activities

Feedback on activity 3.2: Heuristic evaluation Clearly, the relevance of this feedback will depend on the site you are looking at.

User control and freedom The system should allow the users to recover from mistakes efficiently and painlessly. The users should have facilities that allow them to control how they navigate through the system. The system should not impose its own navigation on the users.

- Potential good point

  On every page, is there is a back button and a help button which are prominent and clearly labelled. If the user gets confused, can they easily 'exit' to the help system? If they have made a mistake (e.g. selected a film they did not want to see), can they apparently go backwards in the dialogue to correct that mistake? If these options are available on all pages, the user has control over their navigation through the site.

- Potential bad point

  A link labelled 'Back' may, in fact, take the user right back to the very beginning of the dialogue, not back one step as one would expect. Therefore the system enforces an unnecessary extra amount of work on the user. If they do press 'back', they will probably have to rework their way through several pages to get to where they actually wanted to be. Hence the back button, while on the surface supporting user control and freedom, actually does not because it does not behave in the expected way.

Error prevention   Users will make mistakes. It is best to identify what those mistakes may be and design the system to prevent them occurring, rather than allowing them to occur and tidying up the mess afterwards.

- Potential good point

  Drop-down menus used to the select the cinemas, times and films are good at preventing errors, as the user can only (for example) select a film that is showing. If the user were given a free text entry box instead of the drop-down menu to type in the film they wished to see, they may make errors. They may, for example, type in the name of a film that is not available or misspell one that is available.

- Potential bad point

  A text entry box for credit card details may allow users to type in any combination of letters, numbers or symbols they feel like.

  A credit card number must be four groups of four numbers, and the system should prevent the user typing in any text that does not fit that pattern. Having completed one batch of figures, does the cursor automatically move to the next group of four?

CHAPTER 4

The user-centred system design process

OVERVIEW

In previous chapters we introduced the fundamentals of human–computer interaction (HCI). In this chapter we look at how user-centred system design is deployed in the design process. We evaluate the reasons why traditional technology-focused design processes may result in unusable systems – and the consequences of those unusable or useless systems. This leads directly to a consideration of the different methodologies that go to make up a user-centred system design (UCSD) process.

Learning outcomes	At the end of this chapter, you should be able to:

- Identify weaknesses in traditional methods of software development

- Describe the individual methods that make up a user-centred system design process

- Apply user-centred system design methods in the development of interactive computer systems.

4.1 Introduction

In this chapter, we continue our exploration of user-centred system design (UCSD or UCD), an approach that is still evolving in both theory and practice.

We begin by looking at the traditional method of engineering computer systems: the Waterfall model. We discuss the limitations of this approach for engineering interactive systems. We also review the arguments that completely new design processes are required if users and their needs are to be central to the design process.

4.2 The Waterfall model

Traditional methods of engineering interactive systems have a 'technology' focus. The requirements, preferences and training needs of users are minimised, and the user interface is often designed around a technical view of how systems work. Why should this be so? Part of the problem, it could be argued, lies with the processes by which systems are developed.

The Waterfall model (as illustrated in Figure 4.1) is a common conceptualisation of this traditional approach to interactive systems design. For many years, this approach was seen as so obvious as to be common sense.

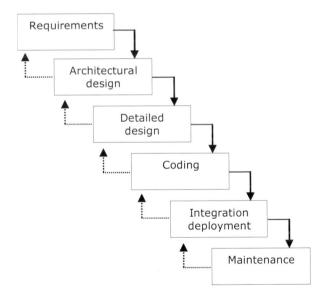

Figure 4.1: The Waterfall model

Weaknesses of the Waterfall model

What do you think could be the strengths and weaknesses of the Waterfall model of the software development life cycle? Think about this for a moment, before continuing.

Here are some of the weaknesses of the Waterfall model. Compare them with your own notes. Some are less obvious than others – so don't worry if you did not get them all. On the other hand, if you came up with some good points that are not here, you can congratulate yourself!

- Traditional methods such as these often focus on the technology or take a purely technical systems approach. The user is often ignored or given a minimal role. Users' preferences and abilities are often overlooked

- Such methods often reflect only the views of the designer rather than other important stakeholders (that is, anyone who has a significant interest in an enterprise or system). The designers will be tempted to try out a system themselves. It is easy for a designer to fall into the 'familiarity paradox' (i.e. the person who is most familiar with a system is often the least appropriate to evaluate it). They will find it relatively easy to use the system and may overlook critical design faults. There are at least three reasons why this happens:
  - when evaluating a system prototype, a designer may overlook an omission because they hold that information in their mind and automatically supply it. They may not even be aware that they are doing so
  - when an item of vital information is placed in a difficult-to-find location, the designer will not experience a problem since they know exactly where to look. A new user may be completely baffled
  - a process that is easy for the designer (who developed it and has used it many times) may prove to be very difficult for a new user

- The user interface is often designed around a technical view of how the system works. The designer may focus on technical issues: in particular, adding new functions at the expense of user needs. It is often easier to add new functions than to revamp a system design

- The problem lies partly with the processes by which systems are developed. For instance:
  - the processes are sequential. Do one design task, and then do the next without any opportunity to reconsider
  - they require the designer to 'get it right first time'
  - the Waterfall is a poor model of how designers actually work. Rather than completing each process in turn, designers often switch back and forth between processes, applying new insights and ideas
  - design may best be done iteratively, particularly for interactive system design
  - design should involve a significant level of design evaluation.

Nevertheless, the Waterfall model could be less restrictive if the various processes were conducted in parallel, with significant interactions between them. A parallel approach may, however, require a different set of processes.

Please note that we are *not* specifically advocating the use of the Waterfall model. Quite the contrary: it is presented here first so that you can appreciate the differences between it and user-centred system design.

4.3 Stages of the Waterfall model

As we saw in Figure 4.1, there are six discrete stages to the Waterfall model:

- **Requirements specification**
- **Architectural design**
- **Detailed design**
- **Coding and testing**
- **Integration and deployment**
- **Maintenance.**

Let's look at each of these in a little more detail.

- **Requirements specification:** this is the first stage in the Waterfall model and the most critical. For this reason, the outcome of this stage – the requirements specification – should be based upon a good understanding of the users and their needs.

  Pause for a moment to consider how you could obtain a good understanding of users and their needs. How would you do it?

  The most obvious way is to consult some representative users, but user research can be very expensive and time-consuming. It can also be done badly, with little attention given to subgroups of users, differences within user groups and atypical individuals – who , perhaps, may be significant customers.

  Nevertheless, one of the benefits to designers of conducting user research is the accumulation of design knowledge and expertise. On the other hand, some designers may consider that they have acquired sufficient understanding through their everyday experience. The former are likely to have gained valuable insights; the latter, unfortunately, may be working on the basis of untested assumptions and stereotypes.

  Key issues

  Key issues in requirements specification are:

  - what data do you need to collect to learn about requirements?
  - you will need to explore requirements iteratively. Your first attempt will not always be right!
  - poorly defined requirements are one of the main reasons for project failure.

  There are different types of requirement:

  - **functional requirements:** specify what functions are needed. For example, provide a means of undoing an action
  - **data requirements:** specify the data inputs and outputs of the system. For example, in a car rental system, if the user inputs the type of car and when it is required, the system indicates the cost of rental
  - **environmental requirements:** specify the environment or context required. For example, the system must run on the Linux operating system
  - **user requirements:** define the user population, but this may need to be defined at several levels. For example: the typical user, significant subgroups and important exceptions
  - **usability requirements:** specify the usability measures of a system. For example, the system must provide clear instructions.

  Task analysis is an important set of techniques during requirements specification and is covered in a later chapter.

- **Architectural design:** requirements focus upon what is required: architectural design is focused on how it can be achieved. The overall architectural design identifies the main components and sets out the relationships between them.

  Designers commonly use a range of methods to develop an architectural design from a specification of requirements, particularly from the functional requirements. Object-orientation (OO), for example, is a conceptually powerful approach to high-level architectural and detailed program design. It is relatively easy to identify most of the relevant objects in a given domain, along with their relationships and actions, and hence to rapidly build up an impressive-looking system model. The danger in OO design, however, is that other types of requirement are easily overlooked: for instance, user needs.

- **Detailed design:** the detailed design is developed from the architectural design, selecting between available options. Careful documentation of the options available – and the rationale for choosing among them – is important. Object-oriented designs, for example, benefit from a detailed specification of the classes, objects, methods and data required. Overall, the design needs to be elaborated in sufficient detail to enable the development of software using suitable programming languages.

  Again, there is a danger that the psychological compatibility between users, designers and programmers could be neglected.

- **Coding and testing:** given a detailed design, the next step is to produce software and to test it thoroughly. Bugs that impair functionality are easily spotted; assumptions built into the original design may, however, go unchallenged.

  Proponents of formal methods claim that it is possible to transform designs into software automatically – the argument being that since both the detailed design and the software are mathematical representations, the one can be transformed into the other.

  Before you move on, pause for a moment to consider what you think about the concept of transforming detailed design into a mathematical representation. Is it realistic?

  Whichever approach is adopted, the software components are implemented and tested individually before moving on to the next stage.

- **Integration and deployment:** at this stage, the individual components are integrated according to the overall architectural design.

  Relationships between the different components are evaluated. You should ask yourself if they communicate well, and if they are sharing resources effectively.

  Testing may also include asking users to test the system or to evaluate it against design heuristics and external standards.

- **Maintenance:** finally, there is 'maintenance'. This is when the system is in use: strictly speaking, it is not part of the design process. At this stage, practical use of the system often identifies further errors in the code or the design.

  There is a classic project manager's sketch of a small construction project where the Waterfall model was used. It is reproduced on the next page. Pause for a moment and consider how this could have related to a project in which you were, or are, involved.

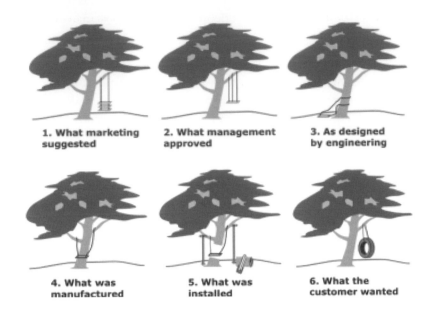

Figure 4.2: The stages of the Waterfall model

4.4 User-centred system design

Now that we have reviewed the flaws in the Waterfall model, let's look in more detail at the used-centred system design (UCSD) process, which is the design process we concentrate on in this book.

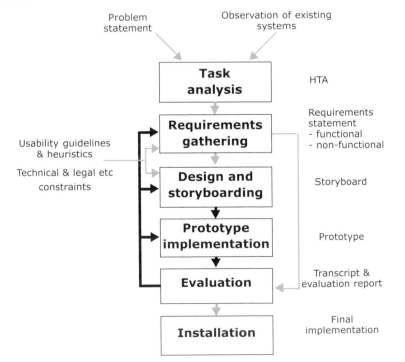

Figure 4.3: The UCSD approach

Central to the UCSD approach, as illustrated in Figure 4.3, are three key themes:

- **Analyse users and their world**
- **Evaluate ideas,** ideally with potential users
- **Test to be sure the design works well** with users, and iterate!

The boxes show activities. On the right-hand side are the elements (artefacts) or documents produced in each activity. Grey lines show the flow of information; and the solid lines show the ordering of activities. Central to this model are the design, prototyping and evaluation activities, which form an iterative cycle. Users are involved at every stage; designers are encouraged to revisit earlier stages if worthwhile improvements can be made.

4.5 Key activities of user-centred system design

We shall now work through all of the stages involved in the UCSD process, as depicted in Figure 4.3.

The starting point in user-centred system design is a statement of a problem to be solved, combined with an awareness of current solutions and their inadequacies.

Task analysis

We need to consider the task or tasks for which the new or revised system is to be used. Is it a diary management system? Is it for online shopping? Alternatively, do you want a system that records your favourite recipes and plans your shopping? Whatever the tasks involved, you need to understand them well and analyse them systematically and impartially.

- **Inputs to task analysis**

  Problem statement

  Observations of existing systems

  Analysis of user population

- **Outputs of task analysis**

  Hierarchical task analysis (or an analysis based on another structure, for example a matrix)

- **Why do a task analysis?**

  It provides a clear understanding of what clients want

  It gives a clearer understanding of what users want

  It is rare for something completely new to be designed: usually something existing is redesigned.

By doing a task analysis, you can gain a deeper understanding of the tasks to be done, of the existing system's strengths and weaknesses and, often, some initial ideas for design. The inputs consist of the problem statement, observations of existing systems and an analysis of your users. The output is a hierarchical task analysis (HTA) – although analyses are sometimes based on other structures: a matrix, for example.

The example which follows is based upon using a cash machine to withdraw cash.

0. Withdraw cash
1. Check machine will work
    1.1. Look at status indicator
    1.2. Look for card logo
2. Insert card
3. Enter PIN number
4. Initiate withdrawal transaction
    4.1. Select 'withdraw cash'
    4.2. Enter amount
5. Complete transaction
    5.1. Take card
    5.2. Take cash

The overall task is given the number zero (0). It is then divided it into five main sub-tasks, which are numbered 1, 2, 3, 4 and 5.

Where necessary, the main sub-tasks (in this case 1, 4 and 5) are divided into further sub-tasks. Indentations are used to make the overall structure more visible. Minor details and peripheral activities such as 'take card out of pocket' or 'spend the money' are omitted.

Activity 4.1

Hierarchical task analysis

Perform a hierarchical task analysis for the process of buying a cinema ticket in person at a cinema.

Requirements gathering

In the Waterfall model, it is assumed that a definitive list of requirements can be gathered, agreed and signed off by the project sponsor at the start of the project. In the UCSD approach, this is seen as problematic: requirements emerge through an iterative process of information gathering and user research, design, prototyping and evaluation. Over many iterations, a rich picture slowly emerges: it is in essence a learning process.

Task analysis is an important stage in UCSD, but it is not the complete picture. A hierarchical task analysis will tell you about the tasks that the system needs to support. Equally important is an analysis of the abilities, skills and preferences of your users.

For example, you may be producing a system for the general public. Alternatively, you may be working for specific subgroups such as individuals with visual disabilities or learning difficulties. Donald Norman makes an important point about the personal computer (PC): he argues that the PC supports many tasks for many different people, but does not suit anyone particularly well. The approach is 'one solution fits all'.

This focus on the user points to the importance of appreciating the requirements that the system must meet. The user-centred design process is not always as user-centred as the name implies: the process focuses on the typical user, rather than the individual.

Perhaps this comment strikes you as being too demanding. It is, however, an obvious point that any user group is made up of individuals. While it may not be possible to design systems for an individual, it may be possible to customise systems for specific needs.

- **Inputs to requirements gathering**

  Hierarchical task analysis

  Design heuristics

  Relevant user models

  Usability principles

  Other constraints (e.g. external standards, hardware platform)

- **Outputs of requirements gathering**

  A statement of requirements

- **Why do we need a statement of requirements?**

  It provides an explicit, testable description of what is wanted of the system

  It describes what the system should do without worrying too much about how it does it.

Overall, the output of this phase will be a statement of requirements, divided into 'functional' (task-related) and 'non-functional' (usability) requirements. Requirements are also subject to legal and ethical constraints, and to the capability of available technology.

Design and storyboarding

Design will be influenced by both task analysis and requirements gathering. In some cases, the task analysis may need to be revisited if the design stage proves to be too difficult to realise. Perhaps more clarification is required – or a more modest set of requirements accepted.

Storyboards provide designers with an opportunity to visualise their design and to test them, quickly and cost-effectively. Moreover, other members of the design team and potential users can share in the process, evaluating the design ideas and suggesting improvements.

Storyboards do not need to be complicated: they can be as simple as a pen-and-paper sketch.

Inputs to this phase include the requirements statement, usability principles and heuristics, other constraints and the evaluation of previous iterations. Outputs include one or more storyboards: an agreed design of how the system is to work and what it looks like; and a justification: why the system is going to be the way it is.

- **Inputs to design and storyboarding**

  Statement of requirements

  Usability principles, heuristics

  Other constraints (e.g. standards)

  Evaluations from previous iterations

- **Outputs of design and storyboarding**

  A storyboard design

  System justification: why the system is going to be the way it is

  A first-draft design of how the system works and what it looks like

  A stakeholder needs analysis

- **Why do we need a design and storyboarding phase?**

  It provides designers with an opportunity to visualise their design and to review it, quickly and cost-effectively with users.

Prototype implementation

Designers and users often find it difficult to hold in mind all the critical details of a proposed new system. A prototype provides an early opportunity to evaluate the strengths and weaknesses of the proposed system, and to identify any unexpected emergent properties.

Prototypes are simulations of the live system rather than pen-and-paper sketches. They are closer approximations to the proposed system. Inputs to the prototyping phase include an agreed storyboard design, as well as evaluations from previous iterations.

- **Inputs to prototype implementation**

  A storyboard design

  Evaluations from previous iterations

- **Outputs of prototype implementation**

  A working, testable prototype

- **Why do we need to prototype our designs?**

  It provides a relatively low-cost implementation that real users can usefully test.

During this phase, the team may iterate through a number of different types of prototype including:

- **Wizard of Oz:** where the prototype is controlled by the designer 'behind the scenes'
- **Horizontal prototype:** which simulates the user-interface only, with no functionality
- **Vertical prototype:** which has full functionality, but for a limited vertical slice of the proposed system
- **Full prototype:** which has complete functionality, but low performance.

Evaluation

User-centred system design is based on the belief that usable systems evolve through an iterative process of generating, representing, testing and refining ideas. In other words, they are developed through an iterated process of requirements gathering, prototyping and evaluation.

- **Inputs to the evaluation process**

  A working prototype

  The statement of requirements

- **Outputs of the evaluation process**

  Transcripts of the evaluation: what was said or done during the evaluation

  The evaluation report (Are the requirements met? If not, why not?)

- **Why do an evaluation?**

  It provides tangible evidence of how a system is actually used.

Heuristic evaluation

Heuristic evaluation is one of the most common approaches to usability evaluation. It is relatively quick and cost-effective.

Heuristic evaluation is usually done by teams of around five evaluators (it is generally considered that five evaluators are sufficient to find most of the usability problems in a system). Each of them inspects the system or prototype independently, noting any features that seem to be problematic.

For example, an evaluator might note:

- 'Help link on screen 3 hard to spot'

or

- 'Navigation buttons on screen 3 inconsistent.'

The team then discusses its findings.

User scenarios are often used to assist the evaluators in understanding ways in which typical users would use the system. This may be a list of tasks or sub-tasks derived from the initial task analysis.

Evaluators may also include references to the usability principles that have been transgressed, and an estimation of the error's severity.

Installation

Finally comes installation. By this stage, we have a fully featured prototype that has been through extensive evaluation. Unlike 'maintenance' in the Waterfall model, UCSD recognises explicitly that systems continue to evolve. Post-installation, our experience of the ways in which a system is used provides valuable feedback for yet further iterations of the UCSD process.

- **Inputs to installation**

  A fully featured 'prototype'

- **Outputs of installation**

  An acceptable evaluation

  The 'finished' system.

Activity 4.2

Comparing Waterfall and UCSD models

Carry out an analysis of the relative strengths and weaknesses of the Waterfall and the UCSD models.

Activity 4.3

Using UCSD

You will require computer access for this activity, where you are asked to try out (briefly) the UCSD approach to designing an application. Please note that the emphasis is on the *methods*. A fully-featured application is not required!

4.6 Summary

We have seen that traditional development methods often disregard users' needs and are too inflexible and rigid.

User-centred system design places the user, their goals, needs and activities at the heart of the design process. Key aspects of the UCSD approach are iteration and evaluation. In practice, designers cannot adhere strictly to rigid and linear processes.

As systems get bigger and more complex, development teams increasingly work in parallel, bringing together components based on common design standards.

Although the UCSD process focuses on the user, it often stops short at groups of users, rather than individual users. Although it may not yet be possible to design systems for individuals, good system design should at least allow for the customisation of systems for individuals with special needs.

References and further reading

Nielsen J (1994), *Usability Engineering*, London: Academic Press

Norman, DA (1988), *The Design of Everyday Things*. New York: Doubleday

Preece, J., Rogers, Y. and Sharp, H. (2002), *Interaction Design: Beyond Human–Computer Interactio*n, New York: John Wiley & Sons

Royce, WW (1970), "Managing the Development of Large Software Systems", *Proceedings of IEEE WESCON*, August 1970.

4.7 Review questions

 **Question 4.1**   List and critically describe the individual methods that make up a user-centred system design process.

 **Question 4.2**   Is the UCSD approach really user-centred?

4.8 Answers to review questions

Answer to review question 4.1   Typical phases in a UCSD approach are: task analysis, requirements gathering, design and storyboarding, prototype implementation, evaluation and installation. The phases of requirements gathering, design and storyboarding, prototyping and evaluation are often revisited many times. We made the point that: 'Over many iterations, a rich picture slowly emerges: it is in essence a learning process.'

Answer to review question 4.2   User-centred design process is not necessarily as user-centred as the name implies: the process tends to be focused on typical users or groups of users, rather than users as individuals. While it may not be possible to design systems for an individual, it may be possible to customise systems for specific needs: for instance, those with a visual impairment, by offering a 'text to speech' facility.

Another example of customisation for individual users is the popular '*my website*' approach. For instance, *My Yahoo* or *My Amazon*, where the web pages presented on your screen are customised to the preferences of individual users.

4.9 Feedback on activities

Feedback on activity 4.1: Hierarchical task analysis   Needless to say, the focus group discussion was not a success, and the resulting information was not at all in depth!

The hierarchical task analysis (HTA) below was constructed after further discussions.

HTA for buying a cinema ticket manually

0: Buying a cinema ticket manually

1. Choose cinema
   1.1. Gather info about available cinemas
      1.1.1. Draw upon previous knowledge
      1.1.2. Look in local papers for cinema listings
      1.1.3. Ask others
   1.2. Decide on which cinema
      1.2.1. Based on individual preference
      1.2.2. Based on group preference

2. Go to the cinema
   2.1. Choose time of travel
   2.2. Choose travel method
   2.3. Travel to cinema

3. Choose film showing
   3.1. Read the list of film titles
      3.1.1. Look at display board
      3.1.2. Look at leaflets
      3.1.3. Look at trailers on mini screen
   3.2. Read the list of times for the films
   3.3. Choose film showing
      2.3.1. Based on individual preference
      3.3.2. Based on group preference

4. Check seat availability
   4.1. Look on display board
   4.2. Ask staff

5. Buy ticket
   5.1. Initiate ticket purchase
      5.1.1. Give film details
         5.1.1.1. Give film name
         5.1.1.2. Give film time
      5.1.2. Give ticket(s) details
         5.1.2.1. Give ticket type(s)
         5.1.2.2. Give ticket count of each type
   5.2. Pay for tickets
      5.2.1. Find out amount due
      5.2.2. Tender payment
         5.2.2.1. Offer any proof needed for concessions
         5.2.2.2. Pay by cash
         5.2.2.3. Pay by credit / debit card
         5.2.2.4. Pay by voucher
      5.2.3. Collect tickets

Feedback on activity 4.2: Comparing Waterfall and UCSD models   You will likely find it quite easy to list several weaknesses of the Waterfall model – and several strengths of the UCSD approach. If in doubt, revisit sections 4.2 and 4.5 in this chapter

You may find it more difficult to find many strengths of the Waterfall model – or weaknesses of the UCSD approach. You may find it helpful to place yourself in the role of someone who is a supporter of the Waterfall model: the business sponsor of a project, for instance. What needs of theirs does the Waterfall model appear to satisfy? A need for certainty or reassurance, perhaps?

Chapter 6 looks again at this issue.

Feedback on activity 4.3: Using UCSD   Remember that the UCSD approach is iterative. In this activity you will probably work through the UCSD *Requirements Gathering - Design and Storyboarding - Prototyping - Evaluation* loop several times.

If you can, ask any fellow students for feedback on your design: what usability heuristics did they use?

Are some of them more constructive in their evaluations than others? In this book, we show you how to undertake practical systems development and encourage you to develop critical reasoning skills based on a sound appreciation of theoretical principles.

CHAPTER 5

Task analysis

OVERVIEW

Our earlier work, on the component methodologies that make up a user-centred system design (UCSD) process, identified the central importance of task analysis, and we identified hierarchical task analysis (HTA) as a useful method in many, if not all, settings. In this chapter, we look more closely at HTA.

Learning outcomes	At the end of this chapter you should be able to:

- Describe HTA and its features

- Explain the purpose of task analysis and modelling

- Describe where task analysis sits in a UCSD process

- Distinguish between different types of task analysis

- Carry out an HTA on an existing system

- Explain and show how the results of an HTA can be used to improve the usability of a proposed interactive system.

5.1 Introduction

In the last chapter, we worked through the UCSD (user-centred system design) process. We identified task analysis as an important part of system design. In this chapter, we will explore how best to use it in **system design** and **evaluation**.

5.2 Task analysis

The result of a task analysis is a description of the tasks that users undertake when interacting with a system. It also involves considering how individuals carry out these tasks. The typical use of a task analysis is to describe an existing system or task before serious design work starts on a new system to replace it.

The aim of task analysis is to find out what the old system enables users to do, so that the designers can understand what is required of the new system. A description of existing user tasks enables the designers to review those tasks – and hence to redesign, re-implement or remove them from the new system.

Note that the analysis should inform, but not constrain, the development of the new system. Following a development method is not a substitute for innovation.

Task analysis is very useful when it comes to designing 'walk-up-and-use' systems such as a ticket booking or a new telephone system. For 'walk up and use' systems you do not want to have to retrain the public to use your new system: it should be as natural to use as possible. It is therefore crucial to understand what tasks users carry out and how they carry out those tasks with the old system. The main failure of the ticket booking system we looked at in Chapter 1 was that it imposed an unnatural task structure on its users and did not support some subtle, but very important, tasks that users engage in when booking tickets with a human.

In this chapter, we will look in detail at how to gather the appropriate information to conduct a task analysis, and at notations for recording the results of a task analysis.

5.3 What is task analysis?

Task analysis provides a means of analysing and describing the jobs and tasks that people do so that they can be supported by interactive computer systems. Task analysis provides both a method of analysis and notation to capture the results. The focus is on people's goals and the actions they carry out to achieve those goals. The task is broken down into a set of related actions. The analysis includes the skills and abilities that people need to have to perform a task and the things that they act on while doing so. Different types of structure are available in the notation, which may be employed to relate each task's activities to another. The most commonly used structure is a hierarchy, though user structures (such as matrices or grids) are sometimes more appropriate.

5.4 Purposes of task analysis

The purpose of a task analysis is to help designers to understand existing systems, tasks, necessary skills encountered and people's existing jobs. The aim is to contribute to a better understanding of the requirements that users have of a system. In this way, task analysis can be very useful in evaluating the design of an existing system or in developing the design of a new system.

It may also trigger insights into how to do the task better. For example, before the development of the spreadsheet, Dan Bricklin, studying at Harvard Business School, wanted a system for performing large, complex financial calculations without having to write a new program or re-entering the data each time. His first idea was for a specialised item of hardware like an advanced calculator with a heads-up display as in a jet fighter. It was to be a combination of business tool plus computer game. Unfortunately, the necessary technology had not yet been invented. Then he saw how the Harvard professors wrote out their data in rows and columns on blackboards. If data in one cell needed to be changed, all the related cells had to be changed manually. He hit upon the idea of a system based upon rows and columns, but one where equations could be built in. Change one cell and, at a stroke, the equations could update all the related cells. In other words, he identified the task and produced the software solution that went on to sell millions of copies.

Note that the result of a task analysis is written in relatively simple descriptive language and is not intended to provide a deep psychological account of what people do. An example of an action or procedure in a task analysis might be 'Locate the main menu'. A deeper description might be: 'Process (perceive) the items in the main menu and select the one which appears (in your judgement) to take you nearer to your desired destination'. This latter item might relate more closely to the psychological processes of the users, but would be more difficult to produce. A good task analysis should cover both the tasks and the users.

5.5 Approaches to task analysis

There are several approaches to task analysis. We are focusing here on one type of task analysis, namely hierarchical task analysis (HTA) (Annett and Duncan 1967). But remember, some task structures may not be hierarchical in form – so do not force all tasks into the same shape!. The procedural task analysis is another form of task analysis which involves following a sequence of activities to achieve a goal. In a procedural task analysis, all activities are executed in a step-by-step, linear and sequential manner. Its directional flow has a start and an end; a proceeding task must be completed before beginning a new task. A procedural task analysis can easily be represented in the form of a flowchart diagram.

Generally, task analysis involves a focus on:

- The goals and actions (procedures or methods) that users carry out
- What users know about their work and tasks
- The psychological processes such as perception and memory
- Objects and entities on which users act
- Objects and attributes – and how they are related.

As already mentioned there are other, more complex types of task analysis, but they are beyond the scope of the present chapter. Examples include knowledge-based (KB) analysis and entity-relationship (ER) analysis.

Inputs-to-task analysis

What are the inputs of task analysis? They consist of:

- The problem statement
- Observations of existing systems
- An analysis of your users.

What is the output of task analysis?

- A 'hierarchical task analysis'
- Task analysis based upon other structures (e.g. a matrix)
- The problem statement: this is the first element required. For example, 'Design a new system for online shopping'
- Observation of existing systems: find an existing online diary system and write down the good and bad points of the system design. Include some of the good points in your design and exclude the bad points. Evaluate this existing system design using Jakob Nielson's heuristics
- Analyse and profile the user population: you need to identify the people who will use your system. In the real world, great care is needed to identify and evaluate the needs and preferences of the user population.

There are a number of issues to consider:

- **Who are the users?** Can you produce a profile of the group of people who will be your users?
- **How diverse is your user population?** Are you inadvertently excluding some? How would you know?
- **How could you improve your design so as to provide universal access?** How can your designs be inclusive?
- **Why don't people use the system?** Ask them why they don't use it. What changes would make them want to use a new version? What do they do? What do they really do?
- **Observe goals as well as tasks.**

Review your design with regard to the accessibility needs of people with sensory, cognitive or psychomotor disabilities or who are working in extreme conditions (e.g. a train driver).

Data collection

You do, of course, need to collect some data. Collecting data about the tasks people perform may be more difficult than is apparent at first sight. You are dealing with human psychology and that itself is complex. This is perhaps another reason why some designers would really rather not involve themselves in user research.

How can we find out about what people do? There is a spectrum of methods from which to choose. At one end, simply asking them may be sufficient. At the other end of the spectrum, experimental studies can explore the psychological resources that your users bring to the task.

Each method of data collection has its strengths and weaknesses. Moreover, your objectives and values – and ethical considerations – will influence your choice of methods, as well as practical considerations of what is possible. The larger your repertoire of methods, the more flexible you can be.

Methods you might consider for data collection include:

- Observe users working
- Talk to them informally, in focus groups or interviews
- Read available documentation or training materials
- Do the task yourselves
- Familiarise yourselves with existing systems
- Analyse real tasks
- Develop abstractions of real tasks

- Conduct experiments
- Use ethnographic methods, social probes, conduct surveys etc
- 'Contextual enquiries' (i.e. explore the context in which tasks are done).

Asking people assumes that they will have adequate insight and awareness of the issues you raise. They may not. In addition, for a variety of reasons people may not always tell the truth when asked. Conversely, exploring what people do in well-controlled tasks may overcome problems with lack of awareness and honesty, but necessitate a less natural or laboratory setting. Objectivity may increase, but relevance may decrease. This issue is currently an active research question and so cannot generate easy answers. A rough rule of thumb is that the more care and effort that you invest, the better the results are likely to be.

If you use more than one method and their results agree, then you can be more confident about them.

At the end of the day, it is vital to conduct genuine studies of what real users do in the workplace so as to gather and analyse real and relevant data. In essence, task analysis is not about speculation (though that has a place), but about gathering and analysing reliable data.

5.6 Hierarchical task analysis

Hierarchical task analysis (HTA) is one of the most common forms of task analysis. It involves identifying the goals that users want to achieve, breaking down (decomposing) goals into tasks, further decomposing into sub-tasks and repeating this decomposition until you reach the level of actions. The level of detail can be subjective, but it is usually clear in practice. The fundamental rule is that the task can be depicted naturally as a hierarchy.

HTA example: Withdrawing cash from an ATM

Withdrawing cash from an ATM requires the user to conduct some tasks. What are those tasks? Here is an example: you will see that it captures the sub-tasks and their overall relationships to each other. It is also in a fairly formal notation, which you should try to learn. When you have studied this example, try to write a new hierarchical task analysis for a different task, for example food shopping or cooking a meal. Make sure that it is in the same format as the example below.

Textual presentation

0 Withdraw cash

1 Check machine will work
   1.1 Look at status indicator
   1.2 Look for card logo

2 Insert card

3 Enter PIN number

4 Initiate withdrawal transaction
   4.1 Select 'withdraw cash'
   4.2 Enter amount

5 Complete transaction
   5.1 Take card
   5.2 Take cash

Adding plans

The textual notation just shown specifies the sub-tasks that are part of the main task. However, it does not specify how the sub-tasks are carried out. This is the role of the plan (or strategy), which describes:

- How sub-tasks are combined
- The order in which they are used
- Conditional or optional sub-tasks
- Optimum ways of using the sub-tasks
- Any repetition required or involved.

Plans

A plan is needed for each decomposed task. For example, examine the following carefully:

> Plan 0: do 1; if possible do 2; repeat 3 until PIN correctly entered; do 4; do 5.
>
> Plan 1: do 1.1, 1.2 in any order.
>
> Plan 4: do 4.1; then do 4.2.
>
> Plan 5: wait until card available; do 5.1; wait until cash available; do 5.2.

An HTA is not complete without a set of plans to guide the implementation of the sub-tasks.

Another example of an HTA

An analyst has studied a user (Alice) who is a do-it-yourself (DIY) enthusiast. Alice collects magazines in order to plan her projects, both short term and longer term. The analyst has produced the following informal description of how she uses the DIY magazines:

> Alice creates a small library of DIY magazines in her study. When she has time, she reads through them looking for useful ideas for her latest project, for example doing up the kitchen. (She only has one such project at a time.) When she finds something useful, she writes the details on a Post-it note, which she keeps on her desk. If she finds something of possible use in the future, she writes a note on a bookmark and places it in the magazine.

HTA Text

Given this informal description of how Alice uses her DIY magazines, we can now 'translate' it into the following HTA:

```
0. Using magazines
1. Browse items in magazine
    1.1   Browse for relevance to next project
    1.2   Browse for long-term relevance
        1.2.1   Browse in study
        1.2.2   Browse in bed
        1.2.3   Browse when watching TV
        1.2.4   Browse in bath
2. Mark items
    2.1   Details on Post-it note to go on desk
    2.2   Write on bookmark to go in magazine
```

Plans
Plan 0: do 1, then 2 if item found.
Plan 1: do 1.1 and 1.2.
Plan 1.2: do 1.2.1 or 1.2.2 or 1.2.3 or 1.2.4.
Plan 2: do 2.1 or 2.2.

Activity 5.1: Practise task analysis

Here is a representation of a system to organise a sports day at a school. Consider the task analysis, evaluate it and suggest any improvements.

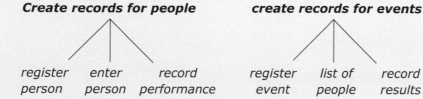

Questions about HTA

How can we improve these task analyses? What do the foregoing examples tell us about hierarchical task analysis and the user-centred system design process?

Clearly, in most cases we will need to create a flexible and interactive system. Portability is often an important requirement, in terms of both location and hardware.

The example about magazines requires different browsing criteria. This is a common feature of a flexible, interactive system. You may also have suggested that there is a need to improve the system for marking and recording selected items. These issues would be passed as requirements to the design cycle.

In summary, key features of an interactive system based on HTA include (in no particular order):

- Flexibility
- Interactivity
- Portability (location and hardware)
- Flexible browsing capability
- Suitable functionality (e.g. a system for storing selected items in the magazine example).

Note that functionality details are not the only key feature, nor are they necessarily the most important.

Use of HTA in design

Identifying requirements is a critical activity that comes out of the HTA, but it goes beyond simply supporting requirements. It is vital that an analysis of a task or system should identify the goals that need to be supported. This extends beyond task goals to social and cultural objectives.

Most design involves developing a system to facilitate carrying out an existing job or task. In other words, we are trying to model some important tasks in an existing workplace. Then we are better able to design changes to the work that improve either the task implementation, the task's support system or both. On that basis, we can usually produce a new task model that supports better work and system performance. Thus, we are led to design a new or improved system to support our changed task.

Designing dialogues

A critical aspect of design is the specification of the dialogues that will take place between both the person using the system and the system itself. We need to understand what will happen, why and when.

Consider, too, the information requirements of both parties. What information needs to be made available? Why and when does it need to be available and accessible? What actions can be carried out – and in which contexts can they be performed? What are the dependencies of the system? For example, does moving on to the next stage of a task depend upon having valid user identification? What will users expect to happen and under what circumstances?

Task analysis also provides a basis upon which to create new system documentation and user training materials. Too often user training manuals and guides are developed as afterthoughts and do not support users in achieving their objectives. For this reason, we always need to explore what users need to know and what skills they need to possess in order to carry out the task.

In addition, task analysis can be used to customise the system design for a user with special needs. Consider a user who has psychomotor limitations due to a road traffic accident. A task analysis can provide a powerful and practical evaluation of their needs and how systems can be customised for them.

Two different approaches

As we have seen, there are several different approaches to task analysis.

Here is an example of a **matrix form** of task analysis:

In order to cook	You need to obtain			
A boiled egg	an egg	water	pan	heat
A fried egg	an egg	oil	pan	heat
Chinese meal	ingredients*	oil	wok	heat
	*Chinese cabbage, spring onions, rice, noodles			

Figure 5.1: HTA based on matrix representation

Hierarchical task analysis is perhaps the best known, though system designers often act as if they have heard of none. Here is a representation of a hierarchical task analysis:

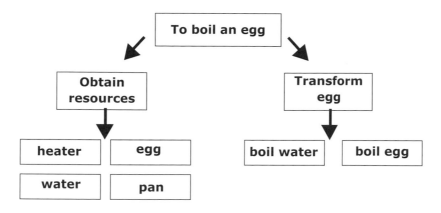

Figure 5.2: HTA for boiling an egg

You have now seen two types of task analysis. The first was based on a hierarchy (hierarchical task analysis or HTA) whereas the second was based on a matrix.

A hierarchical task analysis works best when each action gives two or more sub-actions and when these sub-actions are different for each action. In Figure 5.1, 'Obtain resources' and 'Transform egg' involve different sub-actions. A hierarchical task analysis seems to be suitable.

When the tasks share common items, as in the cooking example and when the actions are simple, a matrix would seem to be more suitable. Note that an HTA takes no account of concurrent actions – those which are shared with other tasks.

For example, the following task could be depicted as either a hierarchy or a matrix:

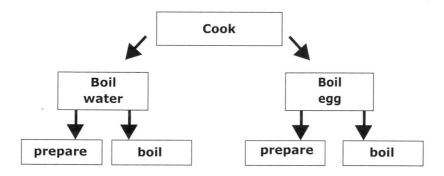

Figure 5.3: HTA for cooking items

You will see how the lowest-level tasks are repeated in both halves, but this is not acknowledged by the structure in any way. The questions remain: what is the most natural and accurate way to represent the tasks and are they the most useful? At a conceptual level, which is the most accurate representation of how we think?

Activity 5.2: Different task analyses

You are organising a book-sharing club and you want to design a computer-based system to keep simple records. There are ten members of the book club. The basic idea is that every member purchases up to ten books per year. Before making a purchase, each member must find one other member who agrees that it is a good idea to buy the book. This is to encourage the purchase of books of interest to the club. The member who buys the book retains ownership of it. Any member can request to borrow a book from another member for up to four weeks.

You want to have a system that records book purchases, who bought each book, who supported its purchase, who is currently borrowing it and when they are due to return it.

Your first step is to set up a card system with a card for every member and for every book.

Conduct a task analysis of this task.

How would this task analysis help you with subsequent stages of development if you were using the UCSD process?

One of your (respected) colleagues is concerned about errors in a computer system and suggests that any new data should be input twice so as to avoid errors. (There have been fierce rows in the past about ownership and possession of books.) What is your opinion of this idea? How would this design feature change the system?

It is important to realise that a hierarchical task analysis depends upon the task involved having at least a reasonable resemblance to a hierarchical structure. You are now required to design two tasks: one with, and one without, a hierarchical structure.

Activity 5.3: Different task representations

Consider the two examples of hierarchically and non-hierarchically structured tasks given earlier, and then think of two similar tasks. Design your own tasks and portray them in your own way, trying to be as original as possible in the selection, design and portrayal of your two tasks.

When you have designed your two tasks, write a brief discussion of how you would conduct an HTA for each of your two tasks (but don't yet carry out the HTA). Is it, in fact, possible to conduct an HTA for both tasks? What are the merits and problems of doing an HTA on your first task? What are the merits and problems of doing an HTA on your second task?

Activity 5.4: Conducting a task analysis

Now use your two tasks to conduct an HTA on each, even though the second task is not hierarchical in design. Set out the textual description of the sub-tasks and the sets of plans to guide their use. Evaluate your two HTAs, identify their strengths and weaknesses, then decide which is the better (if any) and why.

Activity 5.5: Evaluating task analyses

Building upon activities 5.3 and 5.4, now carry out a SWOT analysis of each of your TAs. Follow the four headings defined below:

- **Strengths:** what are the good points of this TA?
- **Weaknesses:** what are the weak points of this TA?
- **Opportunities:** how would this TA provide a good basis for system design?
- **Threats:** what problems do you anticipate in using this TA as a basis for system design?

Now compare the two TAs. Decide which, if either, is more suitable.

Activity 5.6: User-centred system design and task analysis

Explain how task analysis contributes to the stages of the UCD process.

5.7 Summary

We have seen that task analysis is important in systems design for a number of reasons. Establishing requirements is one key aspect. We need to understand what goals our users want to achieve, not only as a population of people, but also in teams and as individuals. Task analysis establishes a baseline from which to work.

We looked at a current system to see how it would work and what effect changes would have upon it and the users in practice. This work provides the foundation for the development of an informed and detailed system design. On this basis, too, we can begin to identify what information is needed and when.

Task analysis can be used for a number of other purposes as well as systems design. System design is perhaps the most prominent activity where human–computer interaction experts can contribute. However, we can also look at existing tasks. We can explore a number of additional questions. For example, can this system support a new version of the task? How well would it be supported? What usability problems would be encountered? What errors may arise in performing this new task?

References and further reading

Annett, J, & Duncan, KD, (1967), "Task analysis and training design", *Journal of Occupational Psychology*, 41, 211-221

Dix, A, Finlay, JE, Abowd, GA and Beale, R. et al (2004). *Human Computer Interaction* (3rd Edition). Harlow: FT Prentice Hall.

Procedural Task Analysis: **http://classweb.gmu.edu/ndabbagh/Resources/Resources2/ procedural_analysis.htm**

5.8 Review questions

 **Question 5.1** Discuss the importance of task analysis in the UCD process.

Question 5.2 Is it possible and feasible to conduct an HTA on a task that is not truly hierarchical?

Question 5.3 Discuss the best ways to conduct data collection in a task analysis in the UCD process.

5.9 Answers to review questions

Answer to question 5.1 Task analysis is essentially the first formal stage of UCD and influences every subsequent stage. It will often be necessary to revisit the task analysis to seek further clarification, to answer new questions and to challenge the task analysis with emerging, new considerations. Task analysis should also include consideration of what users will do and of suitable user models.

Answer to question 5.2 Yes, it is, but you might want to ensure that your task analysis captures the true structure of the task and how your users think about that task. Sometimes, imposing a hierarchical structure will create duplication, as we have seen earlier. However, the more levels that are required, the more that a hierarchical task analysis is convenient in order to describe a useful level of detail.

Answer to question 5.3 They are a wide variety of methods to collect data; including asking users, case studies of specific users and circumstances, observational studies and experiments. You should select your methods on the basis of at least three factors: your objectives, practical limitations and your repertoire of methods.

5.10 Feedback on activities

Feedback on activity 5.1: Practise task analyses Logically, this analysis seems fine. You have two classes of objects, namely people and events. You have actions for each. The problem is that this approach generates duplicate data. If you consider 'records for people', this contains the full set of data. The same data are repeated under 'records for sports events'.

You could do without either. The problem is that if your records are based upon people, it will be difficult to ask questions about events. For example, what was the fastest time in the egg-and-spoon race? Conversely, if you base your system on sports events, questions about people might pose a problem. For example, how did Fred do in the marathon?

Perhaps the task could be depicted in a different way? If so, what do you suggest?

Feedback on activity 5.2: Different task analyses   To create a hierarchical task analysis for this system, you need to realise that you are dealing with two classes of objects: people and books. You would then need to carry out activities on the information about each person and each book. For example, for person AB, propose to buy book XY etc; for book YZ, being read by AC etc.

When you consider building a computer-based version of this system, would you need / want to enter information twice?

If you take this approach, then you may well have to enter every item of information twice: once for the person and once for the event. If you wish to enter data only once, you could have automatic transfer of data from books to people or vice versa. Alternatively, you could organise your system by people only. You would then need to have a method of dealing with queries about books!

Feedback on activity 5.3: Different task representations   You may see distinct differences between your two tasks. What are those differences – and what are their implications for subsequent task analyses? A hierarchy allows different tasks to be broken down into different sub-tasks. A matrix or grid expects cross-references to occur over the rows and columns. Can a hierarchy depict a task based on a matrix? The answer, surprisingly, is yes, but the hierarchy effectively ignores the occurrence of the same sub-tasks in different tasks. They are set out as separate tasks.

Feedback on activity 5.4: Conducting a task analysis   You are probably getting better now at conducting task analyses. You may have found that it is possible to do an HTA on both tasks. (That is why HTA is so popular.) However, you will almost certainly find it more difficult to do a matrix analysis on both tasks.

Hierarchies can depict most structures. In your view, is it better to depict a task by a hierarchy or by its most natural form? Do you have a natural preference for one type of structure over another? Should we match the form of the task analysis to the forms preferred by users?

Feedback on activity 5.5: Evaluating task analyses   Try to be as impartial as you can in this activity. Don't be protective of your work (not easy, as many designers demonstrate).

All else being equal, you may have found the first task analysis (based on a hierarchy) to be easier to do. The second (based on some other structure) may have been more difficult. Try to distinguish problems due to the structure of the task from those due to other factors. For example, one of your tasks may have been a more complicated structure. Perhaps the practice on the earlier made the second one easier to do.

Decide, if you can, which of the TAs was the better and why. Finally, explore briefly some of the other methods of task analysis mentioned in this chapter.

Feedback on activity 5.6: User-centred system design and task analysis Task analysis is the first main stage of UCSD. It will influence all subsequent stages. The danger of task analysis is that it may focus too much on the task and pay less than sufficient attention to users' psychological resources and preferences.

Design will be influenced by both task analysis and requirements gathering. In some cases, the task analysis may need to be revisited if the design stage proves to be too difficult to realise. Perhaps more clarification is required or a more modest set of requirements accepted. The creation of a storyboard scenario will reflect or challenge the output of the task analysis. System evaluation will be informed, in part, by the task analysis. If problems are identified at this stage or during maintenance, the task analysis may help to clarify what can be done about it.

CHAPTER 6

Requirements gathering, storyboarding and prototyping

OVERVIEW

Our earlier work focused on the component methodologies that go to make up a user-centred system design (UCSD) process and identified the importance of task analysis. In this chapter we move on to the activities involved in the design of interactive systems, namely requirements gathering, storyboarding and prototyping. Please note that, since this is a rather broadly defined chapter, you will be expected to read up on its specific topics in more depth than you would for other chapters in this book.

Learning outcomes	At the end of this chapter you should be able to:

- Discuss the purpose of requirements gathering

- Distinguish between functional and non-functional requirements

- Relate requirements gathering to user-centred system design

- Develop a storyboard design

- Explain and apply various prototyping methods.

6.1 Introduction

This chapter follows earlier discussion to look at the requirements gathering, design and prototyping stages of the user-centred system design (UCSD) process. Given that task analysis provides us with some information as to what a new interactive system should do, we look at other sources of information about what such systems should, can or cannot do. In particular, we look at constraints that are put on system designs by their users or the technology with which they are implemented.

Given all these sources of requirements and constraints, we can compile a statement of requirements. The statement of requirements is divided broadly into functional requirements, which describe objectively what the system should and should not do, and usability requirements, which are more subjective but describe the manner in which the system operates. Recall from Chapter 1 the distinction between usefulness and usability; the distinction between functional and usability requirements is analogous. Typically, functional requirements describe what the system needs to do to be useful, and usability requirements describe what, how and by whom the system needs to be usable.

We look at how to design a system by storyboard. A storyboard is a hand-drawn mock-up of the system to be designed. A crucial part of this design stage is to present an argument that the system that has been mocked up clearly fulfils the requirements listed in the statement of requirements.

We also look at how prototypes can be generated from the storyboards, and briefly look at tools for rapid prototyping.

6.2 Waterfall versus UCSD

Typically in projects that reflect the Waterfall approach (introduced in Chapter 4), the costs up to the point of product release are lower than when a user-centred approach is used. It could also be argued that time management may be easier up to this point as the schedule is relatively stable (no repeated or corrective activities are accommodated in the Waterfall approach). These are both relatively modest advantages, however, and are outweighed by the advantages of UCSD after release.

Usually, any company that develops software commits to post-release maintenance. For example, if it is office software for an accounts department, the accounts people will report any problems, summoning the designers to help with difficulties. The software development team find themselves having to redesign numerous parts of the system, creating responses to user problems and complaints in an unstructured ad hoc way. These typically involve problems of poor match between the software and the working goals of the user, or software that is hard or slow to operate. As a result, projects incur spiralling costs. It is estimated that with the Waterfall approach, a very high proportion of overall costs are incurred after release.

The main problem with traditional 'Waterfall' design thinking is that it ignores key aspects of the 'tool' that is being designed. An interactive system is a tool that helps a user to achieve a goal. The overall aim of system design is to create the best way of supporting that user goal.

- Getting to that stage involves an in-depth understanding of the task (hence we use **task analysis**) and users' individual views of tasks (hence we use **requirements elicitation techniques**). This understanding requires validation from users and a shared understanding between users and design team members (hence we use **prototyping and evaluation methods**)

- **Architectural design:** having specified the functional requirements (essentially, a wish list of features written in plain language), this is processed into the specification of system components. These either come from a software library or are created anew. Typically the designers will have an idea of what to put in for users, but nothing about how to design interactivity

- **Detailed design/coding and unit testing:** some components of the program may require further description to be integrated in a suitable programming language (detailed design). The program is then put into machine code. This is then tested for robustness and completeness. This would not test any usability component, but tests for bugs or its ability to cope with the volume of transactions

- **Integration and testing:** components of the design are integrated into the unified program. The program is then tested against requirements. This is largely against functionality. No attention is paid to usability issues

- **Maintenance:** 'maintenance' may suggest a narrower range of activities than is typical in this phase. Maintenance suggests the routine upkeep of a working system. In reality, there is often more chaos and difficulty than that. It is usual for systems developed by the Waterfall approach to need a lot of corrective attention. This is usually to do either with the system's failure to support a key aspect of the task or user difficulties in performing tasks. In the former case, the early closure of the requirements activity may have caused requirements to be missed.

For example, a system may meet a functional requirement to support a secretary producing a weekly list of most productive staff. This requirement could have come from an interview in which a manager stated that this was important. However, the users (the secretaries) find themselves unable to compile the list because they cannot access staff records in the way that they need to. Or perhaps they can, but a short paper-based task has been replaced by a long awkward data-mining task. Had the designers properly understood the secretaries' job and better understood the interdependencies between individual tasks, the problem could have been avoided.

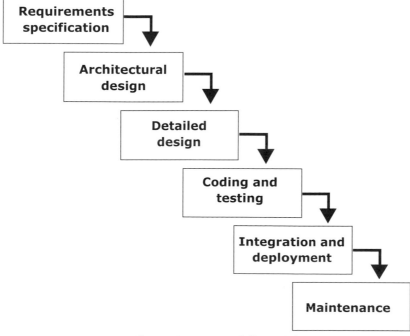

Figure 6.1: Waterfall model

The user-centred approach

Let's now remind ourselves of the UCSD model, as introduced in Chapter 4.

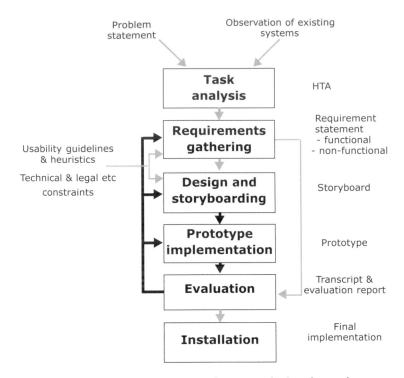

Figure 6.2: User-centred system design (UCSD)

The user-centred approach differs from the Waterfall model in two key philosophical and practical aspects:

- It takes the position that the user and consideration of user needs should be at the centre of the design process
- There is the belief that systems evolve through a process of iterative refinement, rather than simply being developed through a linear process.

On a practical note, it introduces two key concepts not present in traditional approaches: formative evaluation and design iteration.

- Formative evaluation: here we are referring to the evaluation of design ideas and the thinking that they embody. It may be an idea embodied in a prototype or simply submitted as an idea. The key aim is to learn more about factors that impinge on design, such as knowledge of the task-space, of users' abilities and needs and about requirements. Each developmental stage in the user-centred approach is accompanied by an evaluation

- Design iteration: this addresses a key problem in using traditional methods, such as the Waterfall method. User-centred system design builds on the use of formative evaluation by allowing for the revisiting and refinement of any phase of the design. For example, an evaluation of a prototype may reveal that a user may like a facility that compiles data into a particular presentation format. The user may only mention this requirement on inspecting the system and envisioning its actual use in real situations. As a result of this new information, the designers can modify the requirements statement.

6.3 Three phases of the UCSD process

Traditional methods of design tend to have a system or technology focus, rather than a *user* focus. The user interface is often designed around a technical view of how the system works. For example, the developers of an online marketplace might see technical aspects of designing software to handle complex transactions as the central design challenge. So many systems are designed with capabilities that users are unable to exploit – either because they cannot understand how to operate it, or it operates in such a way that they are unable to use it.

The next three sections consider three aspects of UCSD:

- **Requirements gathering**
- **Design and storyboarding**
- **Prototyping.**

6.4 Requirements gathering

Requirements gathering is the phase in which we find out what the proposed system needs to do. This involves gathering information by probing potential users and the environment in which the system will be used. It may involve a combination of interviews with management, workplace observation, user surveys and analysis of existing manual systems. The product of this (the requirements statement) will be information about the nature of the task, the intended user group and the intended circumstances of use. During this phase, we are not concerned with the details of how a future system will support the task or with what the system will look like: we are simply gaining a deeper understanding of the target that we are aiming for when we come to consider design options.

Whereas, in the Waterfall model, requirements are agreed and signed off by the project sponsor, in the UCSD view of the world this is seen as problematic. It assumes, for instance, that an accurate specification of requirements can be finalised at the start of a project. There are a number of reasons why this is unlikely to be the case.

One reason is that the client may be lacking in technical sophistication. They may not be asking for things because they do not know they are possible. As we saw in our analysis of tasks, requirements depend on a rich and accurate picture of the task from many perspectives – as well as rich knowledge of the user group. This picture often emerges slowly as the team learn more about the domain and the design problem. When (as in the Waterfall approach) the requirements statement is already signed off, this knowledge cannot be refined or developed.

The purpose of requirements gathering is to describe what the proposed system should do, but not how it should do it or what it should look like. The output from this activity is the requirements statement, which is divided into 'functional' and 'usability' requirements. This requirements statement lists what is required of the system. For each requirement, you specify what it is, what its justification is (where it came from) and (if possible) a metric that shows how the system can be measured against the requirement.

A 'metric' is simply a way of measuring the requirements. Metrics can be direct or indirect, quantitative or qualitative. For example, weighing a physical object such as a brick is a direct metric. Measuring the volume and density and subsequently calculating the mass is an indirect metric. Most HCI metrics are indirect. They can be quantitative (for example, response time, key presses, number of errors) or qualitative (for example, user satisfaction or user enjoyment). None measures usability directly.

Here is an example of a requirement:

- Requirement: the system should be readily learnable
- Justification: the system will be used by people with little, if any, previous experience of IT systems
- Metric: a novice user should be able to complete the task in 20 seconds.

Sources for requirements

The hierarchical task analysis (HTA) is one source for functional requirements. The HTA should tell you all the tasks that the system needs to support. Usability principles and the heuristics (the agreed 'set of rules') are a source for usability requirements. Other sources include technical and legal constraints.

Where hierarchical task analysis is used, the functional requirements list will have a close correspondence to the sub-tasks of the HTA. Some sub-tasks will be identical if it is simply a case of automating them. Other sub-tasks may not become functional requirements because they will be unnecessary following automation of the overall task. For example, an HTA for sending a letter by post would include sub-tasks that would be redundant in the e-mail equivalent (e.g. 'attach stamp to envelope'). There may also be sub-tasks in a manual system that simply can't be done by a computerised system. For example, a task analysis of somebody hiring a car manually would include an inspection of the vehicle prior to transaction. This sub-task cannot be supported in an online car hire system. Although such a system could offer pictures, video or webcam, they would not fully substitute for a personal, visual inspection.

Usability requirements will typically refer to such things as learnability. Usually, they will be accompanied by an explanation of how and why such principles should apply to the system in question.

Requirements are also subject to factors such as the limits to technology and legal issues. It is often the case that clients don't know the potential capabilities of new technology and that a restructuring of the task is possible and would make the task more efficient. Legal and ethical issues also affect requirements. For example, designers of a system that holds people's sensitive personal details would need to ensure that it complied with laws on data protection and limit access to the databases.

There is increasing activity in the area of standards so that different systems can communicate and exchange information, and to ensure that applications and online systems are accessible to users with special needs, including those with disabilities.

Types of requirement

We will consider the following types of requirement:

- **Functional:** as you might expect, functional requirements specify the functions that your system will need. For example, there might be a need to be able to return to the home screen directly from any screen
- **Data:** data requirements focus on the types of input and output required. For example, the system might require you to input a password in the form of a combination of numbers and letters. It might be required to output responses to users in the form of easy-to-understand sentences
- **Environmental:** environmental requirements set out the environment in which the system will be used (technical and non-technical). For example, the system might work under the UNIX operating system (technical) and be used in an office setting only

- **User:** the user requirement defines the user group (e.g. qualified lawyers)
- **Usability:** finally, usability requirements identify key usability issues, for example that the system is capable of being used by inexperienced users or those with visual impairments. Usability could also include learnability, flexibility and consistency.

The distinction between *useful* and *usable* is relevant here and worth exploring:

- **Useful** means that the system can do the task. Functional requirements are what make the system useful. Functional requirements are typically quantitative. They are there or not there, for example, 'The system should allow the user to enter credit card details and debit the user's account accordingly'. It is clear whether the system does or does not do this
- **Usable** means that using the system makes the task easy to do. Usability requirements are what make the system usable, and are more subjective, usually qualitative. It might not always be very clear how to measure whether a system fulfils its usability requirements, so a metric is needed to assess the system against requirements in as systematic and rigorous a way as possible.

Consider the following example, which is similar to that of Alice, the DIY expert in Chapter 5:

Gill keeps a stack of new shopping catalogues in a corner of her kitchen. When she is preparing dinner, she can flip through a catalogue to see what's new or on sale or what strikes her interest. In the evening she may pick out five or six catalogues to look at while the family is watching TV. She may even take a few to bed, or to the bath.

She generally browses through the pictures, reading descriptions only when the pictures look interesting. When she finds something interesting, she may fold down ('dog-ear') the corner of the page, draw a circle round it or mark the page with a sticky note. She keeps catalogues with marked pictures around until she wants to make a purchase.

HTA Text
0. Using catalogues
1. Browse items
    1.1. Browse by what's new
    1.2. Browse by sales
    1.3. Browse by items that interest
    1.4. Browse by catalogues
        1.4.1. Browse in kitchen
        1.4.2. Browse while watching TV
        1.4.3. Browse in bed
2. Mark items
    2.1. Circle item
    2.2. Mark page
        2.2.1. Dog-ear page
        2.2.2. Sticky on page

HTA plans
    The source doesn't say much about how the tasks are done, but...
Plan 0: do 1, then 2 if item found.
Plan 1: do 1.1 or 1.2 or 1.3 or 1.4.
Plan 2: do 2.1 or 2.2.
Functional requirements
The user must be able to browse items in the catalogues
Browse by what's new

Browse by sales
Browse by items that interest
Browse by catalogues

Justification: Sub-task 1 from HTA
The user must be able to mark items for later recall.

Justification: Sub-task 2 from HTA
But note that the HTA showed that the ways of marking things in the catalogue was problematic. Therefore stronger justification is needed here.

Usability
Requirement: the system should be flexible
Justification: the HTA shows that the user fits the task of browsing around other tasks. Therefore the system should be flexible to accommodate this
Metric: it should be possible to pause the system at any point without causing errors.

Activity 6.1: Functional requirements specification

Below is a hierarchical task analysis (HTA) description and related plans of someone buying a cinema ticket manually.

Based on the HTA and plans, formulate a requirements specification for a new online cinema ticket selling system. For each requirement you should give a thorough justification linking it to the HTA and you should also, if possible, describe metrics for the requirements.

Hierarchical task analysis (HTA)

    0: Buying a cinema ticket manually
    1. Choose cinema
        1.1. Gather info about available cinemas
            1.1.1. Draw upon previous knowledge
            1.1.2. Look in local papers for cinema listings
            1.1.3. Ask others
        1.2. Decide on which cinema
            1.2.1. Based on individual preference
            1.2.2. Based on group preference
    2. Go to the cinema
        2.1. Choose time of travel
        2.2. Choose travel method
        2.3. Travel to cinema
    3. Choose film showing
        3.1. Read the list of film titles
            3.1.1. Look at display board
            3.1.2. Look at leaflets
            3.1.3. Look at trailers on mini-screen
        3.2. Read the list of times for the films
        3.3. Choose film showing
            2.3.1. Based on individual preference
            3.3.2. Based on group preference
    4. Check seat availability
        4.1. Look on display board
        4.2. Ask staff

.../continued

5. Buy ticket
    5.1. Initiate ticket purchase
        5.1.1. Give film details
            5.1.1.1. Give film name
            5.1.1.2. Give film time
        5.1.2. Give ticket(s) details
            5.1.2.1. Give ticket type(s)
            5.1.2.2. Give ticket count of each type
    5.2. Pay for tickets
        5.2.1. Find out amount due
        5.2.2. Tender payment
            5.2.2.1. Offer any proof needed for concessions
            5.2.2.2. Pay by cash
            5.2.2.3. Pay by credit / debit card
            5.2.2.4. Pay by voucher
        5.2.3. Collect tickets.
Plan
Plan 0: Do 1, then do 2, then do 3, until satisfied.
    If not satisfied, then start at 1 again or stop.
    If satisfied do 4.
            If available, do 5.
            If not available, do 3 or start at 1 again or stop.
The user will choose a cinema, go to it and then choose a film. If a film they want to see is not showing, then they may either choose another cinema, or give up. If a film they want to see is showing, then they check seat availability and buy a ticket. If there are no seats available, they may choose another cinema, choose another film or give up.

Plan 1: Do 1.1, then 1.2.
    Users will find out about different cinemas, then choose one.
Plan 2: Do 2.1 and 2.2 in any order, then 2.3.
    To get to the cinema, users choose a time for travel and a method, then travel.
Plan 3: Do 3.1 and 3.2 in any order, then 3.3.
    To choose a film, users read the list of films available and times, and then make a decision.
Plan 4: Do either 4.1 or 4.2 or both.
    To check seat availability, the users can either look at the notice board or ask cinema staff.
Plan 5: Do 5.1 then 5.2.
    Users must first inform the cinema staff of which tickets they want, before paying for them.

Plan 1.1: Do 1.1.1 and/or 1.1.2 and/or 1.1.3 in any order.
There is no prescriptive order to how users find out about cinemas.

Activity 6.2: Other requirements

Based on the hierarchical task analysis (HTA) description and related plans presented in the previous activity, define the usability requirements for the new online cinema ticket selling system.

For each requirement you should give a thorough justification linking it to the HTA and you should also, if possible, describe metrics for the requirements.

6.5 Design and storyboarding

Design rationale

The space of possible designs is vast for any given design problem. The process of getting from an initial requirements statement to a usable system involves narrowing down this 'design space', eliminating unsuitable options through stages of design prototyping and evaluation. Design rationale allows designers to consider and document the thinking and reasoning behind the design options that they are proposing at any stage of the process. This serves both to help designers check their own thinking, and to record the development of ideas over the course of a project. A complete record of design decisions on a project offers insights into which alternatives were investigated and reasons for the choices made. Therefore, design teams are able to gain a shared understanding of the prototypes produced and the approach they embody. This knowledge is potentially useful beyond the current project. Analysed design ideas from one project can be reused as a solution to a new design problem, even if it was rejected on the current project.

Part of the thinking behind design rationale is that no single design idea will be completely right, and that designers will at times need to select between options, or merge multiple solutions, and also to rethink assumptions that may have gone into their production.

Design space analysis

Design space analysis is the best-known and most-used example of design rationale. It uses the QOC notation (question, option, criteria) to describe the issues raised in design meetings or wherever design thinking emerges. The analysis begins with carefully chosen questions, intended to explore the main design issues. The set of questions can be altered to capture the emerging issues and insights of the design. This leads the developers to the design options to be considered. These options are assessed according to a set of agreed criteria to determine the best options.

- **Question:** this refers to any design question that has been addressed on the project. For example, a question could be: 'How do you support database query formulation for novices?' This question may not have specifically been articulated at any meeting or in prior documentation, but has emerged as a theme
- **Option:** alternative design solutions may be compared or analysed in relation to the question that they are addressing. So for our database example the options could be as follows:

  Query by pointing from displayed lists

  Query via a virtual reality library metaphor

Query by structured list-based entry.

Each represents an alternative way of addressing the stated design question.

- **Criteria:** criteria would typically be derived from usability principles, but given a more specific description to address the specific question. For example, a criterion derived from 'speak the user's language' could be given specific focus with the description 'hide the complexities of SQL from novice users'.

For each question, the team uses scenarios to examine the robustness of the design thinking. An example comment could be: 'So if I'm a user from Myanmar would I really be able to recognise those icons on the toolbar?' The team is then able to discuss the likely success of interaction in the scenario described.

Design representation language

Decision representation language is another version of design space analysis. The aim is again to structure the design space, though this time with a language that has formal semantics.

Psychological design rationale

Psychological design rationale attempts to consider the psychological issues (for example, usefulness, usability and accessibility) that underpin good design. Questions that might be posed include:

- What can I do? What are the possible operations or functions that this system allows?
- What do the different functions do exactly?
- How can I use the different operations available?

For each type of question, the designer produces a scenario that captures important aspects of the behaviours of the system and the people who use it. For example, a scenario might describe how someone uses the help facility of an application to deal with specific queries. The key feature is to force the designer to document the rationale for the design options adopted and therefore the overall system design.

Essentially, a good design process forces the designer to be explicit about decisions made. It stops trial-and-error approaches – it stops designers throwing mud against a wall to see what sticks!

When producing a new system design, you should be able to justify the chosen design options in terms of your identified requirements. The design needs to argue that all the requirements are met, or (equally importantly) that the requirements are unreasonable and need adjusting (and how).

Design principles in the requirements need to relate to design rules in the design. The use of prototypes is central to the UCSD method. A useful prototype is something that can be tested on real users. It should enable you to elicit information on the functionality, operational sequences, user support and the look and feel of the proposed system solution.

Prototypes should be 'cheap' – easy, and quick to change. Typically, the prototype consists of pictures of the proposed interface with limited interaction and animation.

Storyboarding

Having to be explicit promotes better design decisions. It is important to add that the design rationale must relate design to requirements. One key feature is to make use of storyboards. These provide rough sketches of what the system will look like and are good for predominantly graphical interfaces and websites. They are cheap to produce and easy to change. You will find that you will also need a 'map' showing how the 'narrative' of the storyboard runs. Storyboard narratives should be produced that show how the sketches relate to one another.

As already indicated, the term 'prototype' does not even need to mean a piece of software. Storyboarding is an example of prototyping done using pen-and-paper sketches. The idea comes originally from drama design in TV and theatre. A writer would express an idea for a scene by showing a series of drawings depicting the characters, a set, and a sequence of verbal dialogue and physical movement. This simple paper-based expression of ideas could encompass a number of issues on dialogue, set design, costume, choreography and so on without committing any physical resources.

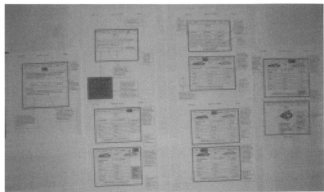

Figure 6.3: Storyboarding design

It is, therefore, a cheap and rich way of expressing an idea. Likewise, this approach helps system designers to demonstrate design ideas without even the need for a simple throwaway prototype. Despite being paper-based, aspects of navigation, screen design, feedback and feature representation can all be analysed with this technique.

The production of usable systems is dependent on a sound design process. In particular, UCSD forces designers to be explicit about decisions made, reviewing them through prototypes and storyboards, and presenting them to other members of the team and potential users. The designer has a vast number of key decisions to make. Each screen contains a number of individual items, all of which require decision making about layout, use of colour, groupings, labelling of features and so on. This is more than a designer can realistically deal with by simply producing and implementing a system. When one contemplates design, it is natural to have in mind a few general principles (from the usability requirements) and some high-level ideas about possible solutions. But it is impossible at this stage for a designer to imagine the whole of the presentation and dialogue design in the future system. Yet each of those individual design features and elements is potentially critical to usability.

Over time, designers develop their own 'mental model' of a system. It is natural for them to develop their own terms to describe system concepts and become very familiar with them. This means that the designer could be the person who is least able to 'stand back' from their work and assess how a first-time user would react to it. Therefore, designers need ways of sharing design thinking. This is achieved by producing physical representations of design ideas: either computer-based prototypes or something as simple as a pen-and-paper sketch. Either way, it means that the designer can see an idea taking shape and is better able to assess it. Moreover, the design team and users can share in the process, inspecting the ideas and suggesting improvements.

Activity 6.3: Storyboard design

Based on the hierarchical task analysis (HTA) description and related plans and your statements of requirements from activity 6.1, produce a storyboard design for the online cinema ticket buying system, showing its main features and describing how your storyboard design fulfils the requirements.

6.6 Prototyping

Prototypes are ideally based on the machine rather than on paper and are therefore closer to the look and behaviour of the intended system. They consist of user interfaces that seem to look and behave like a complete system. However, it is important to remember that they only need to go this far and need not actually function like the real system. For example, if we are prototyping a system involving database searching we do not need to have an actual database behind the interface. All we need is an appropriate response to user input. So if a user tests a system by putting data in, the system can output what appears to be the result of a database search but is actually a pre-prepared response. The important thing is that the prototype appears to behave as the intended system would behave. Prototypes elicit information about functionality, the operation of individual features, sequences of operations, and the general 'look and feel'.

Different types of prototype

We briefly introduced some different types of prototype in Chapter 4; these included:

- **Horizontal and vertical**
- **Wizard of Oz.**

We shall look at these, and two or three others, in a little more detail in section 6.7.

Iterative design and prototyping

Prototyping is central to user-centred design. The creation of an artefact, whether it is a working prototype or a sketch on paper, serves to put a piece of design thinking into a physical form in which it can be evaluated. It is best to think of prototyping as a process rather than simply the creation of an artefact: it is the process of creating an external representation of some design thinking. You can then inspect and discuss the representation with other designers and users. The critical elements of the process are:

- **To turn an abstract design idea into a physical form:** this helps the designer to see if their idea can actually translate to screen designs and dialogue design in a workable way. It is not realistic for any designer to visualise a working interface in all its detail in his or her head. Making a prototype serves to alert the designer to potential practical difficulties that may be associated with an idea

- **To communicate your ideas:** consultation and teamwork are an important part of evolutionary design. Prototypes are accompanied by clear explanations of the design idea that they express. This includes the overall rationale for the approach, descriptions of how requirements are satisfied, and why the interaction style may be suitable for the intended user group

Users themselves may benefit enormously and become better able to play their role in design. A prototype is much better than a verbal or textual description of a design. Also, showing users a prototype may prompt them to suggest extra functional requirements, or describe some aspect of themselves or their work that was missed during initial requirements gathering

- **To iterate and improve:** although many design ideas may be rejected at the prototyping stage, many are selected for further development. The overall idea may be accepted (e.g. we want supermarket metaphor with product selection via pointing and clicking), but aspects of the design may need further work, or an aspect of a different prototype may be incorporated (an approach to supporting frequent users). Prototypes help to nurture, develop and document the development of the prototype.

Types of prototype

- **Throwaway:** sometimes the prototype as a physical program is not intended to develop into the final software program – but the design ideas that emerge from its evaluation are carried forward to influence the final requirements statement and design. Typically, the prototype will consist of a front-end that is partially functional, but may simply mimic the behaviour of a system. For example, the user can test a database front-end to a database that is not yet built. The prototype designer simply designs the search input and results output to behave as the finished system would behave. This means usability considerations relevant to the design of those databases can be discovered prior to their final design and build
- **Evolutionary:** this has a similar developmental role to 'throwaway' in that it helps to refine understanding and validate aspects of design, but the software program is retained and developed. The prototype has functionality added incrementally as more design aspects are added, tested and refined
- **Incremental:** in this example the system is built as separate components. The final product is then released as a series of components, each release adding a component until the complete product is delivered.

6.7 Techniques used in prototyping

There are a few important distinctions to be noted when working with prototypes:

- **Rapid prototyping:** This is becoming increasingly popular, involving a very quick computer-based simulation of the look and feel of a system using a common application such as MS Word or MS PowerPoint. If you are familiar with LaTeX, that is particularly useful, as it tends not to change in appearance when moved from one machine to another (**www.latex-project.org/**)
- **High-fidelity versus low-fidelity:** high-fidelity prototyping refers to prototypes that have practically all the functionality that the intended system would have. Therefore, the user is able to test the range of relevant usability aspects. It also has the advantage that users do not need to be directed in which features they try to use, as they do in prototypes where only a small percentage of the functions are active. However, high-fidelity prototypes are expensive and time-consuming to develop; they are often unnecessary, as more low-fidelity prototypes can be introduced at different stages as the specification of design develops. Low-fidelity prototypes are only partially functional, are much cheaper to develop, and can provide feedback into the design process
- **Horizontal and vertical prototypes:** when designing prototypes, we must carefully consider what elements of functionality should be included or omitted. One particular issue is whether we need to emphasise depth or breadth. Horizontal prototyping provides a wide range of

functions, but in a relatively superficial way with the user. This may be suitable for testing the user's ability to recognise a large range of features from their labels. The other approach is vertical prototyping. In vertical prototyping only a small subset of the system's functionality is active, but that functionality has greater depth of detail. This is useful in a system that supports a large number of similar actions

- **Wizard of Oz:** the 'Wizard of Oz' technique tests prototypes by connecting one machine (on which the prototype is shown to the user) to another (that is controlled by a design team member). This makes it seem to the user that it is fully functional when, in fact, the team member is controlling system output and responses. The user interacts with the interface, for example sending queries to a database or help system. The designer, unseen by the user, then produces a response that looks to the user like a response from the system.

  The overall objective of making the experience authentic and seem real for the users may allow further techniques. For example, imagine we want to test the design of an auditory menu for a phone-based system.

  Our test users would simply try to interact by telephone to what they will take to be a long-distance recipient. However, the role of the 'auditory menu' is not played by an electronic voice synthesiser, but by a design-team member, speaking responses from the next room. The same effect is achieved, but it is so much easier and cheaper

- **Limited functionality simulation:** as we mentioned earlier, it is not necessary for prototypes to be fully functional. The important thing is that the users who test it get the experience that they would get if this were the real design. So it is enough for them to think they are interrogating a database (which is not there) simply because you have produced a page that seems to bear search results in advance, and it appears at the point in the interaction when the user would expect it. Also, your credit card payment mechanism may not exist, but your user can still put card details into a payment form and submit, and the system can respond. So the user tells you if your form is complicated, if the feedback is adequate after the submit action, or if the interface made them feel confident that the transaction was secure.

6.8 Summary

In this chapter we have looked at the requirements gathering, design and prototyping stages of the user-centred design process.

We then looked at how to design a system by storyboard which is a hand-drawn mock up of the system to be designed. This is an important design stage which presents an argument that the system that has been mocked up fulfils the requirements listed in the statement of requirements.

Lastly, we have looked at how prototypes could be generated from the storyboards, and briefly looked at tools for rapid prototyping.

References and further reading

Carroll, JM, (2000), *Making Use: Scenario based design for Human Computer Interaction*, Cambridge, MA: MIT Press

Gould, JD, Lewis, CH, (1985), Designing for usability: key principles and what designers think, *Communications of the ACM*, 28(3). 300-311

LaTeX: **www.latex-project.org**

Nielsen J, (1994), *Usability Engineering*, London: Academic Press

6.9 Review questions

Question 6.1   What comes first, the ideas or the solutions in interactive system design?

Question 6.2   Is the best prototype a high-fidelity prototype?

Question 6.3   What applications would you use to produce rapid prototypes and why?

6.10 Answers to review questions

Answer to question 6.1   Designing an interactive system design is an iterative process. It is not too important, as long as you work through all the stages and are aware of possible biases and sources of error. UCD typically starts with task analysis when dealing with a new need or solution. However, something had to happen before that to spark off the idea that something needed to be done.

Answer to question 6.2   High fidelity captures most, if not all, important details of a proposed system. It is not always the best approach. Rapid prototyping, with lower-fidelity prototypes can allow you to respond more quickly and cheaply to proposed changes in design. The best type of prototype will best reflect both your objects and your logistical constraints.

Answer to question 6.3   You should select any applications with which you are very familiar. You should not be using a prototyping exercise as an opportunity to learn a new application. Most desktop applications have sufficient functionality to support a usefully designed prototype.

6.11 Feedback on activities

Feedback on activity 6.1: Functional requirements specification

Requirements

Functional requirement 1: *List cinemas*
- Description:
  The system should provide the user with a listing of available cinemas
- Justification:
  The user needs to know which cinemas are available before they can choose one. HTA 1

Functional requirement 2: *List films*
- Description:
  The system should provide the user with a listing of available films
- Justification:
  The user needs to know which films are available before they can choose one. HTA 3.1

Functional requirement 3: *List film show times*
- Description:
  The system should provide the user with a listing of the times of all the available film showings

- Justification:
  The user needs to know when each film is being shown in order to be able to choose one. HTA 3.2

Functional requirement 4: *Secure payments*
- Description:
  The system should have a secure method of taking payments for the tickets sold
- Justification:
  In order for an online ticket selling system to sell tickets, the system needs to be able to take payments. HTA 5.2.2

Functional requirement 5: *Ticket collection*
- Description:
  The system should have a method of the purchased tickets being physically collected / delivered
- Justification:
  Since unlike the physical task modelled in the HTA above the purchase was made online, the tickets cannot be given at the same time. There needs to be a way of collecting these tickets – otherwise there is no point in buying them. Extrapolated from HTA 5.2.3

Functional requirement 6: *Show availability*
- Description:
  The system should inform the user if a particular show has become full and hence cannot sell any tickets for it
- Justification:
  If a show is already full, there are no more tickets to sell. Extrapolated from HTA 4

Functional requirement 7: *Purchase tickets*
- Description:
  The user should be able to purchase tickets by credit card
- Justification:
  HTA 5. (Note that credit card payment is the only sensible way of paying online, and therefore the other methods outlined in the HTA will not be implemented.)

Data requirement
- Description:
  The system should output: cinemas catered for (functional requirement 1), available films (functional requirement 2), times (functional requirement 3) and availability (functional requirement 6)
  The system should take as input: users' requests for which cinema/film they wish to see (functional requirement 7) and credit card details (functional requirements 7 and 4)
- Justification:
  All these data are needed by the functional requirements.

Environment requirement
- Description:
  The system should be accessible via the Internet using an HTTP protocol
- Justification:
  An online system by definition needs to be online.

User requirements

The intended users are a very broad sample of the population who would not expect to have to be 'trained' in using the site. Therefore the system should be 'walk up and use', requiring very little explicit training. The broad nature of the user population means that care must also be taken to ensure that (for example) cultural differences do not exclude certain parts of the population.

Feedback on activity 6.2: Usability requirements specification

Requirements

Usability requirement 1: *Provide instructions*
- Description:
  The system should help the user learn how to use it, including how to recover from any errors
- Justification:
  The novice users would find a set of instructions on how to use the system especially helpful. But even the intermediate user and occasionally the expert user would find an online Help or Frequently Asked Questions (FAQ) area useful, to look for some new information or to check on something about which they are no longer sure.
  Providing instructions is supported by Jakob Nielsen's (1994) heuristic principle of 'Help and documentation' and it fits in perfectly within the principle of 'Learnability'. The users of our online cinema ticket booking system should be provided every possible facility to learn how to use the system so that by using it, they generate the business that validates the existence of our system
- Metric:
  If 5% of the test subjects cannot find out how to do their tasks, then the system has not provided adequate instructions and needs to be modified.

Usability requirement 2: *Responsiveness*
- Description:
  The system's responses to the user's actions should be fast, and any lengthy procedure must use temporal cues. The time limits described in Nielsen's article 'Response Times: The Three Important Limits' will serve as our guide. The system should respond to any user action that the user would expect to be instantaneous (i.e. within 0.1 seconds). Any actions that need a longer time to be processed and either do not or cannot give feedback to the user about their progress should not take longer than one second. No other action should take longer than 10 seconds without the user having an opportunity to interact with the process (e.g. cancel)
- Justification:
  A slow response by the system will lead to the attention of the user wandering. The user will either give up on the task altogether or go to a different, more responsive, website. The users of the online cinema ticket booking system are there to buy tickets and if they have to wait too long for a page to be displayed they will take their business elsewhere
- Metric:
  If more than 5% of the operations of the system break these time constraints, then this requirement has not been met. Also if the test subjects' attention wanders while waiting for a task to complete, or they complain about the speed of the system, then this requirement has not be fulfilled.

Usability requirement 3: *Recoverability*
- Description:
  The system should allow the user to recover from any error conditions that arise
- Justification:
  All users encounter errors eventually, even though on average the expert user will cause fewer errors than the intermediate user who in turn will cause fewer errors than the novice user. But when they do encounter an error, all users need to be able to recover from it without having to always restart the process from the start and hence lose all that they had achieved up to that point.
  In an online cinema ticket booking system where the users are there to spend money, errors can be very costly, possibly even beyond the immediate lost sales. So being able to recover from any errors that do occur would not only make the site more usable for the users but also prevent extra costs to the business.
  This requirement draws directly from Nielsen's principle of 'Help users recognise, diagnose, and recover from errors' as well as 'Recoverability' .

- Metric:
  When any errors do occur, 95% of the test subjects can navigate their way to a state that has removed the error condition without having to resort to restarting the entire process.

Usability requirement 4: *Observability*
- Description:
  The system's interface should let the user know what is happening inside the system via timely and relevant feedback.
- Justification:
  A user who has to guess what is happening in the system, or what options are available at any given point in time, will not navigate the system along an optimum path and is far more likely to make mistakes and then be unable to recognise that errors have occurred. The interface of an observable system would let the user know what the relevant internal states of the system are at that moment, as well as what options / operations are available to them at that time, hence easing the user along the correct path, possibly without the user even noticing.
  In an online cinema ticket booking system, a lack of feedback would potentially lead to the user buying the wrong tickets for the wrong films; whereas an observable system would help the user succeed in the desired task without errors, increasing the likelihood of a successful transaction.
  This requirement draws directly from Nielsen's principle of 'Visibility of system status' as well as 'Observability'.
- Metric:
  Not more than 1% of the test subjects should find themselves in a dead end where they think they have no options to proceed. Also not more than 5% of the test subjects should find themselves lost in the system, not knowing where they are and what they have achieved so far.

Usability requirement 5: *Predictability*
- Description:
  The system's design and implementation should be such that it should maximise the user's ability to correctly predict the outcome of actions with a minimum of experience with the system and/or simply based on the currently presented interface.

- Justification:
  Every user of this system will start as a novice. Even though some (due to the principle of familiarity, or other factors) will progress from a novice user to an intermediate user, to an expert user of this system faster than others, they will all have that initial learning curve. A predictable system will help the user by using interface elements and design principles that the user will find easy to predict the result of their use. This is part of the learning curve, and partly the affordance of the interface elements used.
  In an online cinema ticket booking system a predictable system will be learned faster by the users, which in turn will lead to a higher number of successful transactions.
  The design principle of 'Predictability' is one the sub-parts of the 'Learnability' design principle that overlaps with Nielsen's principle of 'Recognition rather than recall'.
- Metric:
  The successful implementation of this requirement is a hard one to measure. If more than 5% of the novice users, or more than 2% of the intermediate users, or any of the expert users have to ask basic questions relating to the functionality of an interface element, then this requirement has not been satisfied.

Design decisions

During the design stage, many decisions were made on how to design both the functional and the usability requirements into the system. Some of these would also serve other requirements not listed above.

Some of the design decisions apply across the entire website – whereas others affect only part of one page. Those that are global in scope are discussed here so as to avoid cluttering each page with the same repeated information. Some of them will still be occasionally pointed out on the actual pages to provide an in situ visual sample.

Consistency

- All menus are to be on the left-hand side, arranged vertically in the same part of the screen
- A simple colour scheme is to be used common to all pages
- The HTML links should be a different colour than the text so that they stand out
- Attention-grabbing, simplicity and minimalist design (clarity) should be aimed for
- The pages are to be very simple in layout and content so there should not be many things on the screen vying for the attention of the user
- Where possible there should not be more than seven grouping of things that the user is needed to keep track of on the same page
- This principle of 'chunking' – breaking into small elements – should also be extended into the main area of the page
- The pages should be designed to be completely visible on a 640 by 480 resolution screen, since that is the smallest resolution common to most desktop systems. Hand-held devices and other 'small' devices would have a smaller resolution still, but they are not within the expected normal range of devices that will be used to view our system, a sort of 'user-device population'.

Responsiveness

- The size of the pages should be kept to a minimum so as to speed up the download of the pages. No graphic files of any kind are to be used for the same reason. This decision does not have a specific visual object to be indicated. (In fact the simplicity of all the pages which follow is the visual proof of this decision.)

- Observability: audio or visual cues are to be used to keep the user informed as a means of feedback
- Predictability: all the pages should obey the design principle of 'operation visibility' by having all the possible operations from that point in the system visible, if nowhere else then as a link in the menu bar on the left.

Feedback on activity 6.3: Storyboard design

In all the screen representations which follow, the different elements on screen should be clearly separated from the rest, either by using white spaces or lines etc. How this segregation is achieved is an implementation issue.

The texts delimited by the [ ] are descriptions of the text (potentially more than one line) that needs to be replaced with text appropriate to the actual implementation.

Some of the decisions that affect several pages only appear listed once, spread across the pages (not necessarily the first page) so as to avoid cluttering up the initial pages.

The functional requirement, 'Available online', does not have a major impact on the design other than to cause the pages to be designed and implemented with HTML. Its main impact will be in the installation stages.

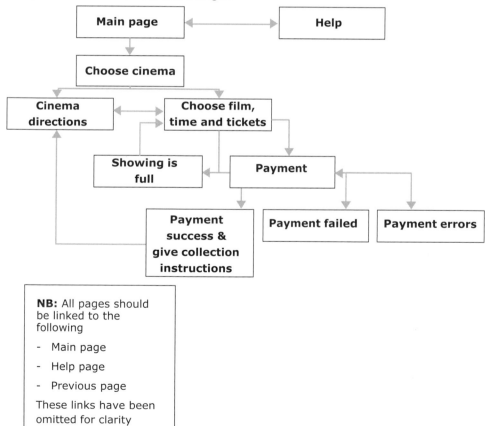

'Main/start-up' page

This first page should set the general look and layout of the website, which all other pages on the website will consistently use.

Although it will not serve a functional requirement, it will act as a portal into the system as well as a spatial landmark within the system's flow of events. Such a landmark should help the users, especially the novice users, in navigating around the system and being able to recover from errors.

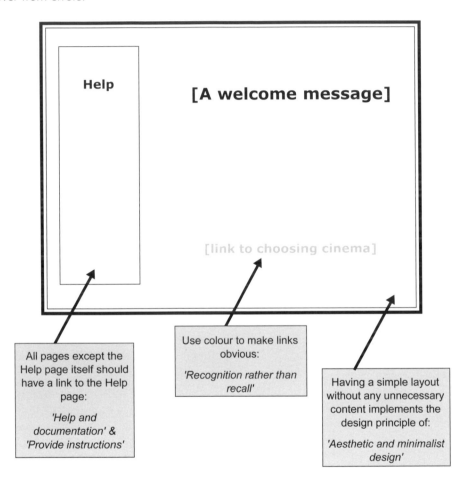

'Help' page

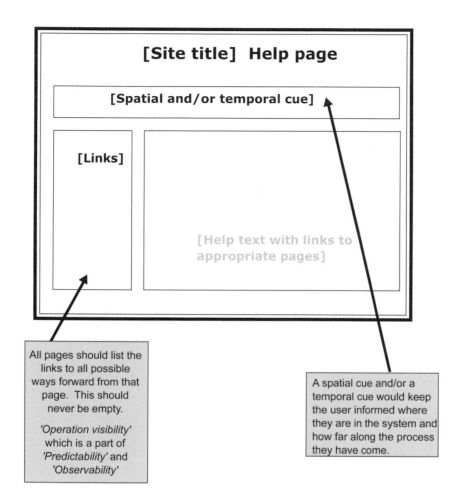

[Site title] Help page

[Spatial and/or temporal cue]

[Links]

[Help text with links to appropriate pages]

All pages should list the links to all possible ways forward from that page. This should never be empty.

'Operation visibility' which is a part of *'Predictability'* and *'Observability'*

A spatial cue and/or a temporal cue would keep the user informed where they are in the system and how far along the process they have come.

This page is the embodiment of the **usability requirement 1: 'Provide instruction'**.

It will not serve a functional requirement.

Any text within the [Help text] that refers to a page to which one can navigate should be, or contain, a link to that page.

Any text within the [Help text] that refers to some text or an object on another page should be highlighted using different colour and/or font settings so as to stand out.

'Choose cinema' page

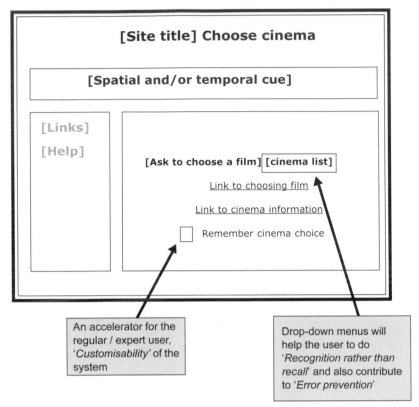

This page will fulfil **functional requirement 1: 'List cinemas'**.

The 'Remember cinema choice' checkbox should trigger a process that will cause the user's choice to be remembered the next time they come here so that the system will then automatically bypass this page and carry on to the choose film. This is an accelerator designed for the regular/expert user. Implementations of it will vary.

Colour section

This section, in association with the website, provides a range of additional imagery to support various chapters in the book.

Input devices - Chapter 10

The shape of a variety of pieces of equipment has evolved significantly. Whereas the needs of, say, left-handed users was easily and readily accommodated with a conventional symmetrical computer mouse, newer designs are unlikely to be available in left and right-hand versions.

Schools and doctors are increasingly aware of the problems of repetitive strain injury (RSI) arising out of texting and prolonged use of gaming controllers; the

mobile phone operator O2 has a website page on this, which can be found at **www.02.com/cr/repetitive_strain_injury.asp**.

Virgin Mobile reports that 3.8 million case of RSI occur annually and it takes the problem so seriously that it has a website devoted to the problem. Visit **www.practisesafetext.com**

'Gamer's thumb' and 'Blackberry thumb' are informal terms starting to rival 'tennis elbow' and 'housemaid's knee', to describe specific manifestations of RSI.

A new UK charity, Body Action Campaign, has been set up to help children become aware of the potential dangers of RSI from incorrect or prolonged use of computers, mobile phones and games machines: **www.bac.easynet.co.uk.**

On the previous page are examples of keyboards as found on some modern devices.

Images courtesy of Logitech: **www.logitech.com**

Input devices have become increasingly complex over the past few years, with an element of conflict between games and software *designers* who want – and, increasingly, *need* – to deliver greater functionality; and *ergonomists*, who need to blend this increased functionality with practical requirements. At its simplest, if there are too many controls, most users are simply unable to remember what they are for. The two keyboards above provide a wealth of direct and programmable input facilities – but are we able to cope with the assault on our senses? Vodafone has recently brought out a new, simple, mobile phone in the UK – initially intended for the older generation, but in fact a great success at all levels. According to Vodafone's research, over a third of all users believe that advances in modern technology have made life more complicated in general; this rises to over half, amongst the over 55s responding.

Tim Yates, chief marketing officer of Vodafone UK: "We've undertaken extensive research across a number of countries and a large number of our customers have told us that they want a simple handset that does the basic functions well..." Nokia, the phone manufacturer, has similarly found that 33% of users find complex instructions prevent effective use of a wide range of facilities.   And this overlaps into the field of computer software, where typically only a tiny proportion of all functionality available is ever used; Microsoft's Word program has in excess of 700 individual and specific menu bar icons: but the average user is probably aware of the function of no more than 50.

Touchscreens and interactive kiosks may be found in a wide variety of public places, such as airports, shopping malls, university campuses, museums and tourist locations; they are able to offer services, in a range of languages as seen immediately above, ranging from payment for, and printing of, airline tickets or receipts; locating shop and detailed product information; local authority services; educational course information and course bookings; detailed information on tourist attractions. The ability to 'drill down', to obtain as much information as the user wants, is a significant benefit in empowering users - and saving time or cost on staffing.

Freestanding units, so far as is practical and reasonable, need to consider and be compliant with the provisions of the Disability Discrimination Act (DDA) in terms of **access** (height, etc); **visibility** (especially in differing lighting conditions) and **usage** (touch or spoken input).

These images courtesy of DataSonic: **www.datasonic.co.uk**

Good and poor design - Chapter 11

Top image - **grill control**: to use a single grill element, you must point the knob to the *left* (to the single overhead grill indicator) - but the overhead grill that is activated is the one on the *right*.   How often is the toast put in on the wrong side of the grill?

Above left - **tumble drier:** how do you open the door? By applying firm pressure, roughly in the green highlighted area. Unfortunately, there is no marking on the door, so even for regular users there is an element of trial and error in finding the 'sweet spot' which guarantees opening! Many other appliances, including car petrol filers, have these hidden 'switches' - clean and uncluttered design – but not so good for casual users.

Above right - **computer connections**: a perfect example of good and effective colour coordination (from Dell Computers). Each socket is coloured differently - and has a matching plug.

Optical illusions - Chapter 8

This page

Top image: are the horizontal lines parallel - or do they bend in and out?

Bottom image: does the purple 'square' have parallel sides - or do they bend in at the centres?

Next page

Top row, left to right.

- Can you see the two white triangles?
- Are the thick white and black lines parallel?
- Is the circle regular or dented?

Centre: if you stare at the red arrows, do they appear to move up or down?

Bottom row, left to right.

- Can you see circles or a spiral?
- How many shades of red can you see?

The main point being illustrated here, from a design perspective, is that unforeseen effects can easily arise; what may have been clearly intended by the designer is not what always appears in the final production, so rigorous checking, considering the needs of all user groups, is essential.

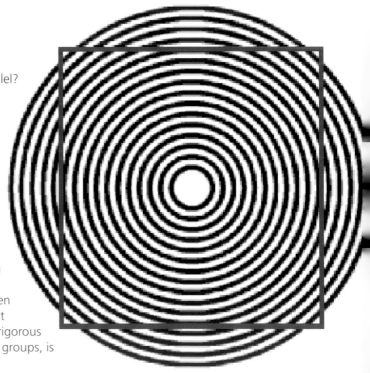

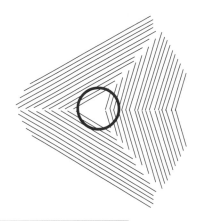

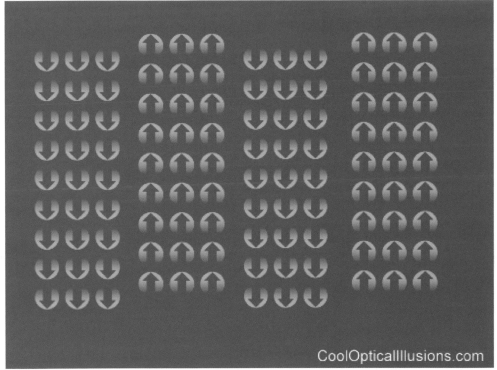

CoolOpticalIllusions.com

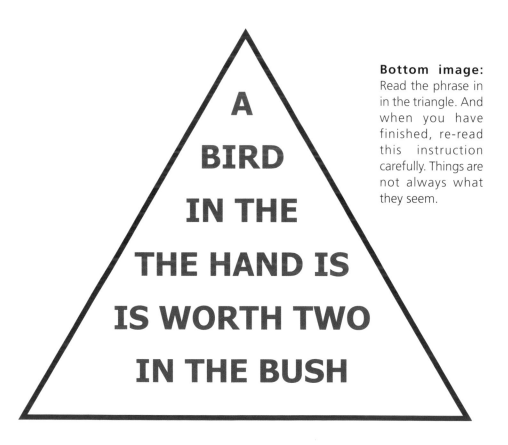

RED BLUE BLUE BLACK
ORANGE RED GREEN
BLUE RED RED BLUE
GREEN ORANGE BLUE
RED RED BLUE

Top image: Read the words aloud. How difficult is it not to say the *colour* rather than the *word*? Now repeat the exercise, saying the colour rather than the word. Experiments have shown that even simple changes in what is expected can cause significant difficulties in interpretation.

A
BIRD
IN THE
THE HAND IS
IS WORTH TWO
IN THE BUSH

Bottom image: Read the phrase in in the triangle. And when you have finished, re-read this instruction carefully. Things are not always what they seem.

'Cinema information' page

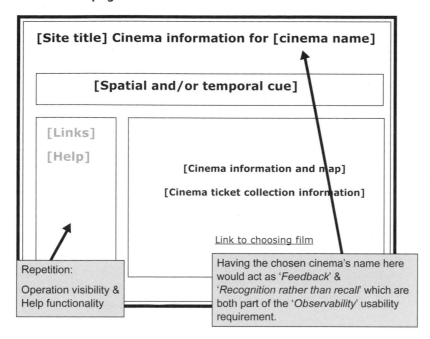

This page will fulfil **functional requirement 5: 'Ticket collection'**.

'Choose film and tickets' page

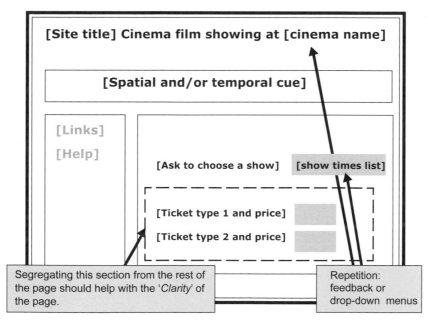

This page will fulfil **functional requirement 2: 'List films'** and **functional requirement 3: 'List film show times'**. This will be achieved by listing the films and their showing times in one drop-down menu, so each film might appear multiple times but the combination with the showing time will be unique within the list. Films on different days will be listed in the same drop-down menu.

'Show full' page

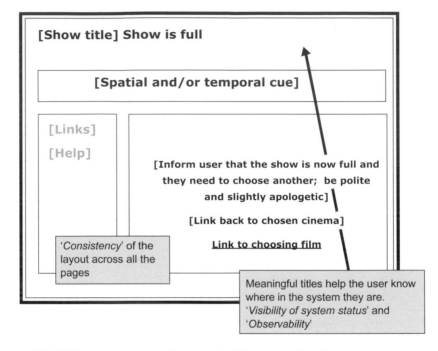

This page will fulfil **functional requirement 6: 'Show availability'**.

This page will also fulfil the usability requirement 3: 'Recoverability' by allowing the user to perform a backward error recovery and go back to the same cinema they were choosing from.

On a general note, keeping the layout of the pages consistent will conform to the usability requirement 1: 'Consistency' as well as help the usability in other ways. It will help the user learn where the main areas that need attention are. The bottom right box above is where in all of the pages the main purpose of that page is addressed and was deliberately placed as centrally as possible to help gather and keep the user's attention. Other parts of the page are designed to be at the peripheries of that area – not just physically, but functionally.

'Payment' page

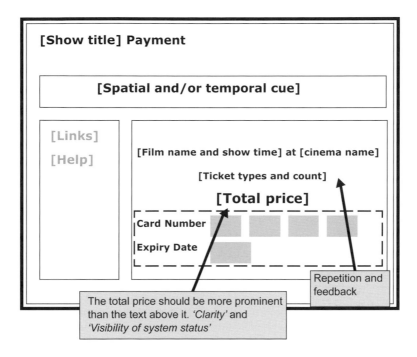

This page will fulfil **functional requirement 4: 'Secure payments'**.

This page will have to use some sort of secure connection.

Chunking (usability requirement 1: 'Clarity') of information like this will help the user in many ways. It will encourage them, by the display of the 4 boxes, (Provide instructions) to read and then type the information in small groups, which will be easier for them to remember (Error prevention). Each input box should also be set to accept a maximum of four digits, preventing the user from making mistakes (Error prevention).

The total price of the tickets being displayed on this page is important (Feedback, observability) since this is the page where users will tender payment. The user will want to know how much they are about to be charged. If that information is not on this page, they will have to either remember it (Recognition rather than recall) if they had already been informed or remain uninformed (bad observability). Also, having it on the page that invites the user to pay, mimics the real-life experiences of the user (Match between system and the real world).

'Payment error' page

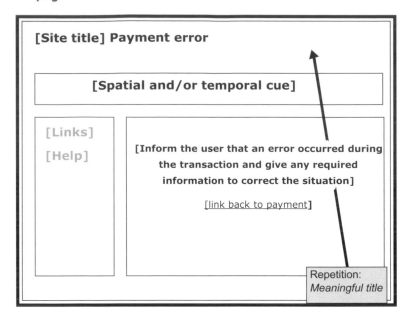

Keeping the user informed of what has happened in the system serves both the 'Visibility of system status' and 'Help users recognise, diagnose, and recover from errors'.

This will fulfil usability **requirement 1: 'Provide instructions'**; **usability requirement 3: 'Recoverability'**; and **usability requirement 4: 'Observability'**.

'Payment failed' page

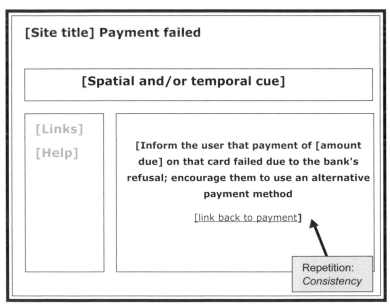

Keeping the user informed of what has happened in the system serves both the 'Visibility of system status' and 'Help users recognise, diagnose, and recover from errors'.

This will fulfil the **usability requirement 1: 'Provide instructions**; **usability requirement 3: 'Recoverability'**; and **usability requirement 4: 'Observability'**.

'Payment succeeded' page

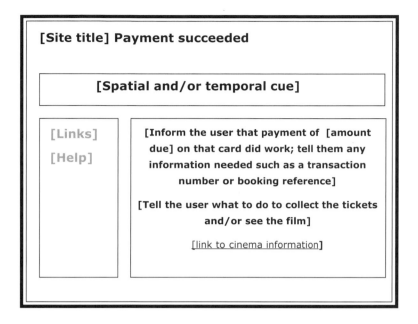

This page will help fulfil **functional requirement 5: 'Ticket collection'**.

By having the link to the cinema information on this page as well the other one, we provide the user with an alternative path to the same information (Reachability and flexibility).

CHAPTER 7

Psychology: memory

OVERVIEW

An understanding of human memory is critical to an appreciation of how users will store and use relevant information when using an application, system or website. If you want people to like and use your systems, applications or websites, then you need to know their needs and preferences, what makes them tick and how to research these issues. To quote Ben Shneiderman (2002): 'The old computing was about what computers could do; the new computing is about what users can do.'

Learning outcomes	At the end of this chapter, you should be able to:

- Describe the principles of human memory

- Identify how memory issues relate to the user-centred system design (UCSD) process

- Identify system design weaknesses that relate to human memory

- Conduct an analysis of actual or proposed designs with regard to human memory.

7.1 Introduction

In this chapter, we concentrate on understanding the psychology of human memory as a basis for developing a truly user-centred approach to interactive designs. It's about how we develop good ideas and insights into what users want. This chapter is more theoretical and less pragmatic than others in this book, but the payoff for you is that you will only need to get the basics of some important concepts. You will not need to memorise detailed procedures and methods, but the point is that if you want to develop effective, interactive systems, then you need a fundamental understanding of your users' psychology.

Building a useful theory of the human user of information and communication technology (ICT) is not easy. There have been a number of attempts to do so which, by themselves, have not proved sufficient for the task. Here, we introduce you to some relevant developments in psychology: cognitive psychology will take centre stage as the (currently) most advanced and relevant branch of psychology, but we will also briefly examine other relevant approaches.

The key feature of early research in cognitive psychology was the concept of the human mind as a processor of information. This view, though simple, unlocked the door to ways of tackling questions of how people perceive, retain and use information to perform mental or cognitive tasks.

Applied cognitive psychology also investigated practical implications of human information processing. One theory that is particularly relevant to ICT is that of the Model Human Processor (MHP). The MHP (Card, Moran, and Newell 1983) theory seeks to specify the information-processing demands on and of users – and hence the information-processing parameters of supporting systems.

The aim is to:

- Design systems that are compatible with their users
- Evaluate existing systems and their variants
- Make quantitative predictions about their use.

7.2 Psychology – memory

We shall be looking at users and at some basic psychological theory that will help you make sense of how humans behave, particularly when using interactive systems.

The idea of a psychological theory is that it explains and predicts human behaviour. A model is simply a way of presenting such a theory so that we can make useful predictions about human behaviour and thinking. Given a model of how a computer system behaves, the required tasks and how the system's users behave, we should be able to predict the behaviour of the whole interactive system. In other words, a psychological theory should allow us to design an interactive system to be more usable without having to (expensively) test it directly on large numbers of users.

We will look at an influential early model of human behaviour: the MHP, which models people as information processors with particular characteristics and abilities. MHP was never intended as a full and detailed theory of psychology, although it is sometimes criticised as if it were. Instead, it was intended as a simplistic theory to guide and illuminate good practice in ICT.

Formally, we have defined a simplistic theory as one that is intended both to guide best practice application and be able to act as a full theory – so the MHP does not quite meet that definition. However, we will explore how it is used in practice and how it can be complemented by other more recent theories. With hindsight, MHP was a trail-blazing pioneer in this field.

The use of psychological theory in HCI is, however, not always simple and we will look at some of the issues and attempts to deal with them.

7.3 Background psychology

Freud and psychoanalysis

Psychology is popularly associated with Sigmund Freud and with psychoanalysis. By today's standards, however, Freud would not be considered scientific in either his methods or his theories. This is not to belittle his genius and innovations: he was working at a time when alternative explanations were not available for consideration. To this day, leading psychotherapists look back on his work and ideas with profound respect. In fact, his former house in North London is now a museum in his honour. If today we do not use his methods and theories in cognitive psychology, he at least established the complexity of the human mind. He reminds us that the human mind needs to be considered in terms of emotions and motivations as well as cognition and rational thinking.

Behaviourism

IP Pavlov (1849–1936) and BF Skinner (1904–1990) showed how association or reward could condition human and animal behaviour. Pavlov's work showed the links between input (stimulus) and output (responses). He used objective measurements of stimuli and responses to develop a scientific theory. Skinner and his students showed how rewards could dramatically shape behaviour in a number of species, including humans.

In the behaviourist view, measuring behaviour is more objective than asking someone to describe what they are doing. The latter is more subjective and open to problems of bias and lack of insight.

Behaviourism has left a legacy of scientific rigour and objectivity, although today internal factors are given more attention. The behaviourist's view was that we should tell the outside story first, leaving complex and subjective issues about what goes on in the human mind until later. There is still some truth in this: for example, your friends may tell you that your new application is great, but what if they don't actually use it in practice? Behaviour speaks louder than words!

Neuropsychology

Physically, the brain is made up of a network of 10 billion interconnected brain cells (called neurones or neurons) – which means that there are over 100 billion billion possible interconnections. Human behaviour is an emergent property derived from the complexity of the interconnections. This approach implies that the complexity of human behaviour can be derived, in part, from the application of a set of simple rules. When combined, such rules can explain complex behaviour. The research question we face is how to discover at least some of these rules.

Activity 7.1

Evaluating an existing system

This task requires computer access; you will use a computer application – such as a word processor or a spreadsheet – and assess how easily you can perform certain tasks.

Activity 7.1

URLs and memory

This task requires computer and internet access; you will need to find a dozen website addresses of sites with which you are familiar, and consider how easy they are to remember.

Activity 7.2

7.4 Cognitive psychology

Cognitive psychology builds upon the strengths of each of these approaches:

- Following Freud, it accepts the complexity of human cognition and the need to consider a combination of cognition, emotions and motivation
- Like behaviourism, it looks at stimulus (input) and response (output), emphasising an objective and impartial scientific approach. It also seeks to explore the internal mechanisms that give rise to behaviour
- An additional theme is that of artificial intelligence, which is based upon early computer simulation work, seeking to understand human cognition by building computer programs that appear to respond like people
- Finally, phenomenology emphasises people's subjective experiences and seeks to relate existing behaviour and experience.

Thus, modern cognitive psychology has a wealth of research methods, types of theory and objectives.

Combined with computing science and neuroscience, this overall approach to understanding human performance and related issues is now called cognitive science. What we call 'applied cognitive science' (or cognitive technology) is directed to the solution of real-world problems such as the design of interactive systems and websites. That is why it is of vital interest to the field of human–computer interaction (HCI).

7.5 The Model Human Processor

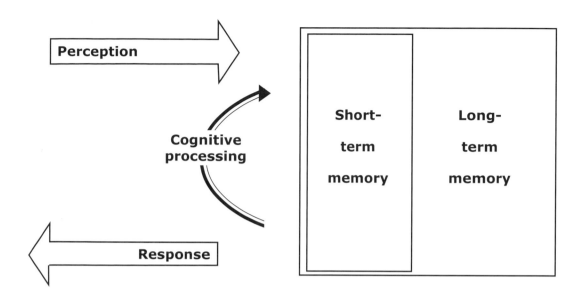

Figure 7.1: The Model Human Processor

The MHP, introduced earlier in this chapter, is the first simplistic theory of human cognition. It aims to combine current research knowledge with a simple approach that can readily be applied to the solution of applied problems such as system design.

Working memory limits

MHP postulates a short-term memory with the following properties to model and predict human performance:

- Short-term memory has a decay time of 10–20 seconds
- Memory is maintained and increased with rehearsal
- It can hold a small number of items, typically 7 ± 2. (Informally, an 'item' is a chunk of information: a word, a letter of the alphabet, a meaningful sentence etc)
- The size of chunks appears to have only a small influence on memory, if at all.

Note that the original concept of short-term memory has now been replaced by the more advanced notion of working memory, with a greater emphasis upon holding information in mind when carrying out cognitive tasks.

Long-term memory

Long-term memory (LTM) contrasts with short-term or working memory, having strikingly different properties and thus implying two distinct modules within the one system.

Long-term memory is organised as a network of connected 'chunks' of knowledge. It includes facts, definitions, meanings and procedures. Recall from long-term memory is by means of the two processes of recollection and association, and by matching with the available information.

Such processes generate practical rules for systems design, including:

- Support recognition rather than recall
- Reduce working memory load
- Support the production of chunks of items to facilitate memory
- Frequent activities become 'automatic' and so don't require conscious attention
- For highly practised responses, requiring confirmation of responses will not necessarily reduce errors.

MHP, Broadbent's Maltese Cross and Simplex

MHP has led to a number of more advanced, simplistic theories such as Simplex that provide an even better account of current research.

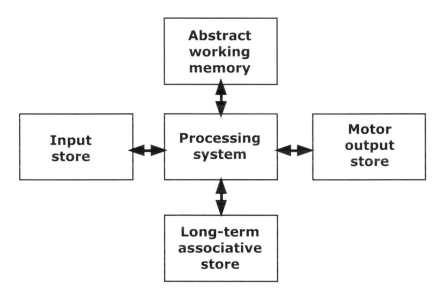

Figure 7.2: Simplex One

Simplex One is typical of current views of the architecture of human cognition. It was developed from pioneering Cambridge psychologist Donald Broadbent's 'Maltese Cross' model by Adams and Langdon (2003).

While new information enters via the input store from the senses, the above type of structure allows information to flow both back and forth and not simply in one direction as expected by linear theories such as MHP. Simplex One postulates that there are five components of human cognition:

- **Input store:** this takes information from the environment or system. It holds and maintains information
- **Abstract working memory:** accepts the information required to be active while conducting a cognitive task
- **Long-term associative store or long-term memory:** holds information on a long-term basis and thus supports performance
- **Motor output store:** responses or sequences of responses are held here pending action
- **Executive functions or processing system:** this has the role of exchanging information between the four main stores, according to demands of the task and upon prior experience.

This approach supports the design of interactive systems, as follows:

- An interactive system must provide suitably designed input to the user (input store)
- A well-designed system must support the user's responses and allow them to be made easily (motor output store)
- A system should not require an excessive amount of information to be stored in working memory
- A system should provide the user with appropriate information for long-term associative store or long-term memory use, in the correct form at the right time and so that learning may be optimised
- Finally, the system should support the executive or processing system by ensuring that the tasks required by the system are not too complex to be mastered and maintained.

7.6 Alternative theories

Cognitive psychology provides a rich variety of architectures for working models:

- Simplistic architectures, such as Broadbent's Maltese Cross, capture an overview of cognition, but do not attempt to be complete
- MHP attempts to be a cut-down, but still accurate, theory that both captures current knowledge and guides current best practice
- Theories such as SOAR (Newell 1990) and ICS (Interacting Cognitive Subsystems) (Barnard 1985) take a parallel processing approach that attempt to address the complexity of human cognition (see Chapter 3 for references)
- In addition, there are neural networks, which aim to mimic the human brain and provide a computer instantiation
- Production systems such as Anderson's ACT (1983) reflect both cognitive psychology and computer simulations of cognitive processes.

Whereas any of these could be used to model the assessment of cognitive skills, we have adopted a simplistic approach based on Broadbent's Maltese Cross model.

7.7 Advancing simplistic theories

The formal definition of a simplistic theory of human cognition is one that captures leading-edge research findings, but can equally guide good practice in the solution of applied problems such as system design.

MHP was the first such theory. Simplex One builds upon the strengths of Broadbent's Maltese Cross model (1984), but is much more modular, has a formal definition of its simplistic status and is applied to systems design. The aim is to develop a simplistic framework that provides a first approximation for a model of cognition. It should be possible to show that the model of cognition can be unpacked to act as a framework for highly detailed sub-models such as a model of memory processes.

Simplex Two, shown in Figure 7.3, aims to be a simplistic theory, capturing both current knowledge and practice, but has been expanded to include those factors that are important to interactive system designers. Reviewing the literature, as well as studying designers and designs, we have added four more factors:

- Emotions and drives
- Feedback management
- Output programs (for complex, skilled responses)
- Cognitive modelling.

Each of the nine aspects or zones in the Simplex Two model indicates an area where the designer needs to consider user needs. They can also be used as a basis for developing situationally specific design principles, known as heuristics. Simplex Two is shown in Figure 7.3; the four additional zones are shown with dotted lines.

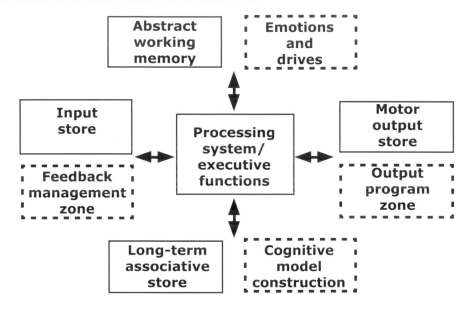

Figure 7.3: Simplex Two

Understanding human memory

For practically any task you undertake, you will need to use your memory to hold information. That information guides and supports your mental activities, and human memory is thus both important and complex. How do we cope with the evident complexity of human memory and why should we try to understand it?

- **Why should we try to understand it?** Here we are concerned not only with understanding human abilities, but also with understanding the implications of such abilities for the creation of systems which are useful, usable and accessible. If we need to create interactive systems that people will use and enjoy using, then we must ensure that they do not create unacceptable pressures and problems for users. In particular, we need to ensure that we do not overload the memory capabilities of the people who use our systems

- **How are we to develop a sufficient understanding of the memory skills of these people who use our systems?** How do we cope with the evident complexity of human memory?   For almost any task, some memory resources are required.

We could attempt to understand the memory demands of any task. However, that seems to be an overly complicated and difficult endeavour. Also, many interactive system designers do not have a sufficiently strong background in psychology, so they would find a complicated model of human memory to be virtually unusable. Our solution is to use a simplistic theory (like Simplex Two) to set out the basic ground rules of human memory that both research psychologists and interactive system designers can use.

Simplex Two is not the only relevant theory available, but it does provide an overall model of human memory that we can apply to system design.

Simplex Two portrays human cognition in terms of nine semi-autonomous factors or zones – including an executive functions zone (or processing system) that mediates and manages the others. Each zone, including the executive functions zone, has both processing capabilities and memory capacity.

We will consider each zone in turn, drawing out its contribution to overall human memory; the description of each zone is accompanied by a reduced size image of the Simplex 2 model, as a reminder of the zone under discussion.

This cannot be a complete picture, but it does provide designers with a simple, useful, structured list against which to evaluate their designs.

Memory to support perception

We are all owners of a remarkable perceptual system, which is sensitive to faint stimulus events yet also able to make sense of complex perceptual events. Perception is associated with sensory memory, which holds incoming inputs while the system makes sense of them.

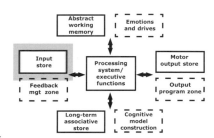

For perception to work smoothly, we need a form of supportive memory to hold the information as we process it. Here we are dealing with incoming information via or from the senses.

Information comes in via the senses and is held in brief buffer stores while it is processed. Information is fed back by the executive from the other modules. (An example of the latter would be recalling a visual image of a well-known face in response to a spoken name.) Sensory memories can form the basis for more durable memories if the system design allows the information that is to be remembered to be processed appropriately. A good system designer will enable the users of a system to perceive, process and retain the information they need to achieve their objectives.

Memory to support feedback (feedback management zone)

Simplex Two distinguishes between sensory input / perception and feedback. Designers have told us that this is an important distinction for interactive system design. We are adept at taking in new information – and we need to be good at observing the consequences of our actions. Hence, the management of feedback is of central importance both for human learning and for effective system design:

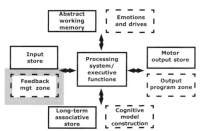

- A person without any feedback memory would be unable to keep track of where they are and what progress they had made in a task

- Remembering feedback will help a person to learn a task

- Feedback provides a basis for new learning.

The memories derived from feedback can form the basis for more durable memories if the system design allows the information that needs to be remembered to be processed appropriately. A good system designer will enable the users of a system to perceive, process and retain the information they need to achieve their objectives.

Working memory (abstract working zone)

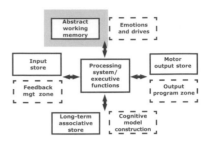

The information required to perform a task comes from a number of sources, including long-term memory and the external world. Working memory consists of those memories that support the achievement of a task. We all know the experience of holding information in the front of our mind while carrying out a task. That is working memory.

Working memory is a potential bottleneck, and good designers will ensure that their designs do not overload it. In contrast to long-term memory, working memory is limited in both capacity and duration. It is vital that a system design does not make unrealistic demands on the user for the information required to use a system effectively. If we have to hold too much information in mind when we use a system, we will make mistakes, work slowly and find the system unpleasant to use.

Emotions and drives

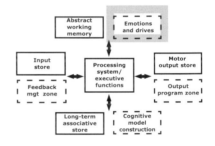

There is growing evidence that our moods influence our ability to learn and retain information. It is also evident that the emotional status (pleasant, unpleasant or neutral) of items may influence their memorability. A poor design may be unpleasant to use or ignore the nature of the items involved.

Some tasks are emotionally unpleasant or stressful by their nature. For example, consider online banking when it is necessary to check the balance in an account or to query a transaction. Features intended to enhance security, such as pin numbers, passwords or security questions, may make the process unnecessarily stressful – in an emergency situation, users of mobile phones may even have difficulty remembering their phone number. A good design will avoid unnecessary stress and should be pleasant to use.

Long-term data warehouse (long-term memory or associative store)

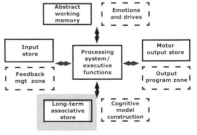

Any interactive system design assumes that users will have access to a lot of information, either in long-term memory or in the environment. Clearly, a good design will not require users to hold too much information in long-term memory.

An experienced designer would ensure that the system provides the necessary information when and where it is required. We know that familiar items are easier to deal with than unfamiliar items. A good designer will not make unwarranted assumptions about what is familiar to users. There is always a danger that designers will underestimate the difficulty of a new design. Although they will be familiar with it, it may be new and unfamiliar to users.

Cognitive model construction

There is considerable evidence that people construct mental models when using a complex system or attempting a difficult task. For example, most people who live in London have either a paper map of the London underground train system or have developed a mental model of it over time and through repeated use.

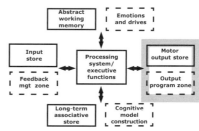

This applies equally to websites, applications or eLearning systems. A good system design will enable the development of such mental models by new users.

Output responses (output zone and output program zone)

Simplex Two distinguishes between simple responses and complex response sequences.

Interactive systems require responses from the people who use them. People need to remember the responses they have already made as well as those they intend to make next. This applies both to simple responses and the more complex sequences of responses that experienced users learn when using applications. A good design supports users and enables them to respond appropriately.

A dangerous example of a complex response occurs when a user selects an option by going through a number of menus. As a safety feature, a system will often ask for confirmation of an action if a user selects an apparently risky option such as deleting a file. However, there is a danger that an experienced user will have learned a response sequence including the automatic confirmation of an action, even when it might be wrong.

Executive functions

Although the above components of memory are all important to user performance, they will be of little impact if they are not organised and integrated. These are executive functions, which transfer information between other zones and provide the overall task organisation and management.

Memory is important for the executive function in at least two ways. It must:

- Retain long-term information about task requirements
- Hold short-term information about its progress in the task.

A good designer will ensure that a system design does not produce so much complexity that the executive cannot cope with it.

Perception and information

This task requires computer and Internet access. You wil need to revisit one of the URLs you previously identified.

Activity 7.4

Applying different theories

Imagine that you have developed a system to enable you to recall your business appointments. Represent it by a simple diagram. Now explain how you would evaluate your design using MHP, Simplex One or Simplex Two.

7.8 Summary

In this chapter, we have looked at some simple theories of cognition and memory. Human memory can be difficult to understand, particularly by non-psychologists. Simplistic theories such as Simplex can, however, be used to guide designers and other practitioners who are involved in the design and evaluation of new systems.

You should now be able to explain relevant aspects of the cognitive psychology of memory, why it is particularly suited to understanding HCI issues, and how psychological models of memory can be used in the design of interactive systems.

References and further reading

Adams, R and Langdon, P (2003, SIMPLEX: a simple user check-model for Inclusive Design. In *Universal Access in HCI: Inclusive Design in the Information Society*, Stephanidis, C. (Ed.). 4, 13-17. Mahwah, NJ: Lawrence Erlbaum Associates.

Anderson, J. (1983), *The Architecture of Cognition.* Cambridge, MA: Harvard University Press.

Barnard, PJ (1985), *Interacting Cognitive Subsystems: A psycholinguistic approach to short term memory.* In A Ellis (Ed.), *Progress in the Psychology of Language*, Vol. 2, London: Lawrence Erlbaum Associates, 197-258.

Broadbent, DE (1984), The Maltese Cross: A new simplistic model for memory, *Behavioral and Brain Sciences*, 7, 55-68.

Card SK, Moran, TP, and Newell A. (1983), *The Psychology of Human-Computer Interaction*, Hillsdale, NJ: Lawrence Erlbaum

Preece J, Rogers, Y and Sharp, H. (2002), *Interaction User: Beyond Human Computer Interaction*. Chichester: Wiley.

Shneiderman, B. (2002), *Leonardo's Laptop: Human Needs and the New Computing Technologies,* Cambridge MA: MIT Press.

7.9 Review questions

Question 7.1 What factors from MHP or Simplex One would you use to evaluate a system design? Explain how you would do this.

Question 7.2 How do MHP and Simplex One differ? Describe and evaluate the two approaches.

Question 7.3 How do Simplex One and Simplex Two differ? Describe and evaluate the two approaches.

7.10 Answers to review questions

Answer to question 7.1   Input, output, short-term memory and long-term memory.

Answer to question 7.2   Simplex One gives more focus to executive functions. Can the user understand and cope with the complexity of the tasks that they must do with your system?

Simplex One takes a modular approach, covering input, working memory, long-term memory output, and executive functions (which reflect the complexity and feasibility of the tasks which users carry out).

Answer to question 7.3   Simplex One covers input, working memory, long-term memory, output and executive functions. Simplex Two adds four more factors of importance to designers, that is, emotions and drives, feedback management, output programs (for complex, skilled responses) and cognitive modelling.

7.11 Feedback on activities

Feedback on activity 7.1: Evaluating an existing system   The typical applications designer must rely on the users having *reasonable* powers of memory. They cannot be always explaining where to find functions; there would be no room on the screen. However, some functions are so well buried that they cannot be found even with the 'help' of the help function. We have tried to suggest functions that you might have not used before, but ideally try to identify functions that you use rarely at all. Make a note of them (but not how to use them) and, several days from now, try to remember how to use them. All applications of any size present memory challenges to users.

Feedback on activity 7.2: URLs and memory   This activity demonstrates the fallibility of human memory. You may have been able to remember only a few URLs. Don't worry: that is the normal result. Initially, individuals who browse the web mainly use search engines. As people become more familiar with what they want, they make less use of search engines. Instead, they go directly to the site they want.

The importance of easy-to-remember websites and web addresses is increasing. Make sure that users find it easy to remember where to find you. Addresses should be as short and as meaningful as possible. Avoid unusual features unless they are memorable.

Feedback on activity 7.3: Perception and information   Did you have problems remembering how to find the website? The longer you leave it, the more intervening tasks you do, the more difficult it becomes. This is a common experience, so try to make it easier for your users!

Unless you found a particularly simple website or have a photographic memory, you will have overlooked many features on the website. This may because they were either unimportant to you or because they were not obvious or salient. Human perception is highly selective, often in quite complex ways, so remember to direct your users in your designs.

Feedback on activity 7.4: Applying different theories   MHP looks at the incoming stimuli that users perceive, the responses that they make and the memory requirements (short and long) that the system places on users.

Simplex One takes a modular approach, covering input (storage and dedicated information processing), working memory (storage and dedicated information processing), long-term memory (storage and dedicated information processing), output (storage and dedicated information processing) and executive functions (which reflect the complexity and feasibility of the tasks which users carry out).

Simplex Two shares the above factors with Simplex One, but adds four more factors of importance to designers; that is, emotions and drives, feedback management, output programs (for complex, skilled responses) and cognitive modelling.

CHAPTER 8

Cognitive psychology: perception

OVERVIEW

In a previous chapter, we introduced the Model Human Processor (MHP) theory. Now, we look in depth at the key concepts of attention and perception. First, we consider human attention, its nature and limits. Next, we consider perception, primarily visual and auditory perception. The section on perception introduces several important theoretical analyses and discusses their relevance to interface design.

Learning outcomes	At the end of this chapter, you should be able to:

- Describe the different ways of studying human perception

- Explain the direct or structuralist approach to perception

- Explain the Gestalt approach to perception

- Explain the constructivist approach to perception

- Discuss the implications for interactive system design of the different approaches to perception

- Discuss how cultural and social factors impact the design of interactive systems.

8.1 Introduction

An understanding of human perception is vital to the creation of usable and accessible interactive systems. In this chapter, we look at how users perceive objects, symbols and events, concentrating on visual and, to a lesser extent, auditory perception. The question we ask is: how can we design systems to make the most of users' perceptual skills and preferences?

Elsewhere in this book you have been introduced to a number of guidelines and tools for human–computer interaction (HCI). Many of them were designed for the non-specialist, intentionally hiding the cognitive psychology on which they are based; however, it is not always possible to use such knowledge effectively: Jakob Nielsen's heuristics, for example (introduced in Chapter 3.4) are the basis of a popular evaluation method in industry. They consist of ten quite general design principles which can be used as a reminder of the sorts of issues to look for when evaluating an interface design.

One of them is *'Ease the user's memory load'*. This seems like a sound principle but, by itself, may be difficult to interpret. To take a second example, the meaning of the design principle *'Support recognition rather than recall'* needs to be explained in terms of psychological theory if it is to be useful – even if it is possible to guess its meaning.

Moreover, following any one principle may well cut across others: interpretation and judgement are always necessary.

This chapter is designed to help you gain a deeper understanding of the underlying cognitive psychology of perception so that you are better able to interpret and apply such guidelines.

8.2 Attention

The word *attention* is used in at least three senses:

- **Attention is about how we make the choice between different stimuli.** Our attention is selective. We process some information, but reject other inputs, either at an early stage or after significant amounts of processing before we decide it is not important
- **Attention refers to our capacity to process information.** Clearly, we are limited in the amount of information we can deal with overall. Our attention is limited
- **Our attention often declines over the time that we spend on a task.** We talk of changes in our concentration or vigilance.

Practical implications for design

Each of these aspects of attention has implications for design:

- Since our **attention is selective,** we need to understand how to design interfaces such that users' attention is drawn to the important features or information on the screen. An item on a screen should be sufficiently striking in size, location, colour or style to attract attention. It should also be in an expected location. A 'click here to continue' button which appears on the screen at different points – even just at different heights – can prove very frustrating
- Since our **capacity for attention** is limited, if your website or application bombards people with lots and lots of information, they will make mistakes or even give up
- Our **ability to *maintain* attention** is limited. Over time our concentration will tend to decrease, particularly if we are tired. If the task is uninteresting, the decline will be even more marked – so make your applications as interesting and attractive as possible. Either that or supply free coffee!

8.3 Theories of human perception

Human perception is complex

Human perception is a complex and difficult achievement that we usually take for granted. How, for example, do we recognise familiar objects, symbols or people? Visual perception is not like pointing a camera at a scene. Look across the room or out of the window. What do you see?

Now look again. What things did you overlook previously? Look carefully, now with an artist's eye. Notice colour, shades, shapes, relative proportions.

What we are interested in here is how the brain *processes* the information that the eye manages to *capture*. If we are to create usable interfaces, then we need to examine how the brain processes the information presented to it. We *look* – but do not always *see*.

Introspection

Early psychologists attempted to study perception by introspection alone. Yet many processes seem to be unavailable to introspection: how do we perceive the passage of time, or why is one person attractive to us and another not? Introspection may be necessary to answer such questions, but it is clearly not sufficient.

Direct or structuralist approaches

The simplest modern view of perception is structuralism, which corresponds to our everyday, common-sense view of the world.

This structuralist, common-sense view suggests that perceived objects are made up of elementary features. When we encounter an object or event, our senses subject it to a sequence of increasingly complex analyses of its features. These analyses lead to perception. The emphasis is on bottom-up, data-driven processes based on the stimulus inputs. A visual event is defined by, for example, location, movement, wavelength, intensity, shape and size.

What this common-sense view does not explain, however, is how:

- The input to our senses varies continually (to take a simple example, when we move our heads) yet we perceive a relatively unchanging world
- We make use of incomplete information
- We are selective in the information to which we attend and respond.

Nor does it explain the existence of visual or other illusions.

Why does grass always look green?   How does the phenomenon of colour constancy work? How is it that we perceive grass to look green, whether in deep shade or in full sunlight? At least three types of explanation have been produced:

- You are looking at grass; therefore the reasonable *inference* is that grass is green. Hence, you see it as green in all lighting conditions. This theory, however, does not make clear whether such inferences start as conscious processes, or if they are innate or learned
- A second approach supposes that *other sensory events* (e.g. pupil dilation) *provide the necessary information* to maintain colour constancy. However, this is generally seen as an inadequate explanation
- A third explanation is to suppose that *memory is involved in perception*. In this view, the information in memory guides the conversion of sensory input into perception.

Currently, it is not clear if any of these three explanations suffice. There is a growing consensus that top-down processes must also be included in any adequate account of human perception.

Gestalt

One of the first substantial approaches to human perception was developed by the Gestalt psychologists, Christian von Ehrenfels (1859–1932), Max Wertheimer (1880–1943), Wolfgang Köhler (1887–1967) and Kurt Koffka (1886–1941).

In formulating their approach, the Gestalt psychologists were strongly influenced by the philosopher Immanuel Kant (1724–1804) and the physicist Hermann von Helmholtz (1821–1894). Kant put forward the distinction between the external world (objects and events) and the internal world of subjective phenomena. The human mind, he argued, applied rules to produce subjective phenomena from stimuli; the external world as such is unknowable. Helmholtz was one of first scientists to show that neuropsychological issues could be researched experimentally. He distinguished between sensations (raw sensory experience) and perception (the meaningful interpretation of sensory experience). He concluded that unconscious inferences link sensations to perceptions, that they become unconscious through experience, but can be altered by learning.

The Gestalt psychologists believed that the production of perceived objects from the many features of sensory experience was carried out automatically by the human nervous system. They thought that our minds create 'wholes' from a collection of attributes, and identified a number of important phenomena of human perception, some of which are illustrated below.

Contextual information

Consider Figure 8.1 below and the look at letter 'A'. What do you see? Is the next symbol the letter 'B' or the number '13'? It really depends whether we are reading across or down. The context in which we see a symbol has a huge influence over how we 'see' it.

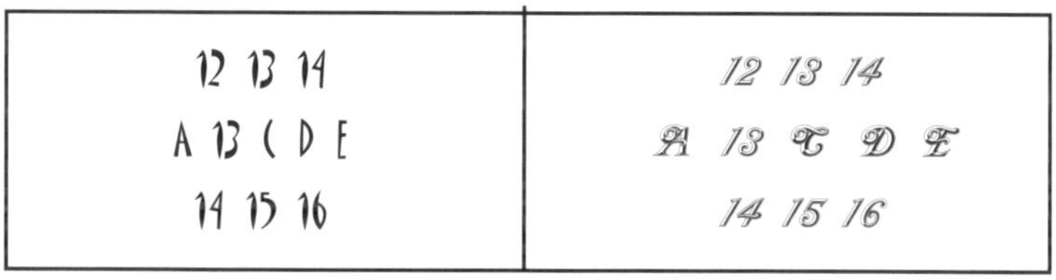

Figure 8.1: 13 or B?

In Figure 8.2 below, the symbols in the middle of the words 'THE' and 'CAT' are identical, yet we are able to 'see' it differently in each context.

THE DOG AND THE CAT

Figure 8.2: H or A?

Our brain is able to use information about the context in which a symbol appears. It can use the contextual information to disambiguate the symbol, so that we 'see' complete and meaningful words.

Contextual perception has obvious applications for interface design. For instance, an icon design that means one thing in one part of the interface might mean something completely different in another place. A good example of this is the checkbox in Figure 8.3:

Figure 8.3: Checkbox

Usually this symbol shows whether an item is selected or not. However, it is also the symbol for 'Close' when located in the top right corner of a window in Microsoft Windows. We 'see' different buttons in the different contexts, even though the representation is identical.

World knowledge

From childhood, we accumulate a vast range of knowledge about the objects in our everyday world. Our perceptual systems exploit this knowledge, allowing us to recognise objects even when they are partially obscured. In Figure 8.4 below, we can readily identify the middle wine glass, even though roughly half the original information is obscured. The final glass is much harder to identify, however. Much more information is missing, including crucial contour details of the glass.

Figure 8.4: Using world knowledge to recognise partial shapes

Much research has been conducted into the types of information our perceptual systems need to identify objects. Edge information and contour information is vital; other information, colour for instance, is largely redundant. (Even an object that is heavily reliant on colour to identify it, such as a banana, can be as quickly recognised in black and white). Hence, where screen resolution is limited, we may show an object in silhouette or only those edges that most clearly define the object.

Figure and ground

'Figure' and 'ground' refer to the way we identify an object by distinguishing it from its background. Look at Figure 8.5; what do you see? Do you see a triangle with a circle on top of it? Or do you see a triangle with a circular hole, through which you can see the square beneath? In other words, is the circle part of the 'figure' or is it part of the 'ground'?

Figure 8.5: What is *figure* and what is *ground*?

Distinguishing clearly between figure and ground is essential if we are to produce pictures and icons which are unambiguous. Consider the symbols for 'Exit' in Figure 8.6:

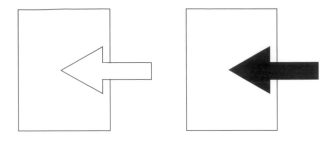

Figure 8.6: Designing symbols

By using a contrast boundary, the black arrow stands out more than the outlined arrow. One rule that we can infer therefore is that in marking boundaries it is better to use a solid shape than an outline.

Activity 8.1

Icon design

Look at the laundry labels below. Each represents a separate class of operation you can perform on your laundry: for instance, wash, dry, iron or bleach. Can you guess which operation each (large) symbol represents – and what the smaller symbols mean? Do you think that the symbols exploit world knowledge sufficiently well to depict each action? If not, suggest some alternatives.

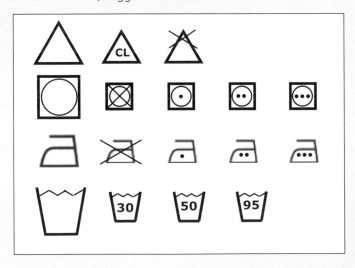

Constructivist approaches

Constructivist approaches emphasise the active, constructive nature of perception. They could be described as top-down, in contrast to the bottom-up structuralist or Gestalt approaches. For example, Richard Gregory, an expert of perception and illusion, proposes that human perception involves a much greater level of hypothesis testing than is usually understood.

Gregory describes perception as a 'building up' of layers of meaning around a perceived object, a process that is strongly influenced by experience and long-term memory. When designing icons and visual elements, therefore, the designer needs a good understanding of users' prior knowledge. A poor design will mislead users in this process of hypothesising.

One of the consequences of this approach is an explanation of visual illusions in terms of a process of hypothesis testing that goes wrong.

Some examples are shown collectively as Figure 8.7

- Ambiguous figures: where several hypotheses are feasible. Do you see a young woman – or an old lady?

- Unstable figures: where the picture appears to change in front of your eyes. Are the black diamonds the ends of lozenges pointing towards you – or the top face of lozenges pointing downwards?

- Illusory figures: where we 'see' a figure that does not exist. Is there a white square in the centre of the image?

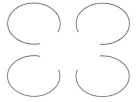

- Impossible figures: where we 'see' a figure that could not possibly exist

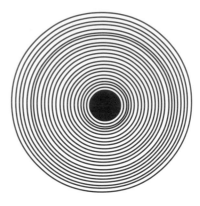

- Apparent movement: where no real movement exists

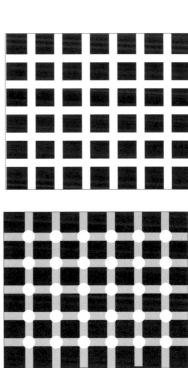

- Non-existent shapes: illusory shapes caused by after-images. Can you see small grey squares at the intersection of each set of four black squares or, in the lower figure, black dots at the centre of the circles, as you move your eye across the squares?

Figure 8.7: Visual illusions as hypothesis testing

Practical implications for design

As you can see, there are several different approaches to understanding human perception. Each provides insights that are relevant to the design of interactive systems. Some guidelines that we can extrapolate are:

- As top-down processes (expectations, context, ideas, preferences and biases) are important in perception, your system design should match the expectations and preferences of your users
- To take bottom-up processes into account, the objects and events presented by your application should be designed carefully to attract, retain and boost the attention of your users and be sufficiently clear that their use can be easily understood
- Automatic processes (or perceptual habits) and deliberate processes should be allowed for. In other words, will your screen designs be compatible with users' habits and automatic responses? The design should also make it clear how users should deploy deliberate actions
- Do your screen designs enable users to identify key objects and events?
- Do your designs enable users to develop a stable perception of the system and develop an adequate mental model of it?
- Users are accustomed to automatically filling in the gaps of incomplete information. Will users be able to fill in the gaps in the right way, given your system design?
- Will users be able to select the right information and respond appropriately?

The concept of 'affordance'

The Gestalt psychologists believed that perception is a direct process. When we encounter stimuli, the human brain automatically turns collections of features into perceptions of objects or events. James Gibson developed this as the concept of 'affordance', based on the meaning 'to afford or make available, give forth or provide naturally or inevitably' – as in, for example, 'The sun affords warmth to the earth' or 'The roof afforded a fine view'.

Using the concept of affordance, Gibson suggested that we directly perceive the attributes and functions of an object. In this sense, affordance means giving an indication of what an object can be used for. In terms of the relationship between the user and the system, affordance is an 'invitation to act'. The user not only recognises the purpose of an interface feature, but also immediately recognises how it can be used and which actions are needed to operate it.

One psychologist who recognised the importance of affordances in designing interfaces was Donald Norman (1998). Norman distinguishes between real and perceived affordances. In real life, an object has real affordances. Perceived affordances, on the other hand, are those of the icons, symbols or objects of interactive systems. They are supported by custom and experience, but are not intrinsic. After all, we can easily design objects with different or contrary qualities. For example, most menus have a stable structure, but it is possible to create menus in which the items change with frequency of use, as in the Microsoft XP operating system.

Norman showed that interface elements could be designed to afford how the user should interact with them. Consider the button below, part of the original Apple Macintosh interface:

SUBMIT

Figure 8.8a: Button

How do we know that this is in fact a button? How does it afford pushing? A better version of the button would be:

SUBMIT

Figure 8.8b: Button

In this case, we can see that the button is 'raised' off the page, so it could perhaps be pushed 'level' with the page.

Norman used a wide variety of examples, ranging from computer interfaces to door handles, showing how badly designed objects could afford one style of interaction, but actually use another. Door handles are a common example of this. Handles of the type found in figure 8.9a afford pushing, while those in figure 8.9b afford pulling. In figure 8.9c, what appears to be a 'push' plate is in fact a 'pull handle'. It's confusing. This is why people often push 'pull' doors (or indeed pull 'push' doors) as the handle affords the wrong type of interaction.

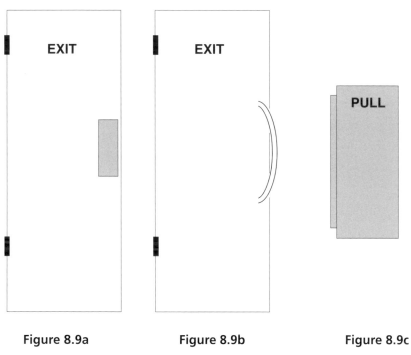

Figure 8.9a   **Figure 8.9b**   **Figure 8.9c**

Figure 8.9: Affordance

Can we afford affordance?

Is the concept of affordance useful – or is it merely jargon? There is some indication that Norman now feels that the word is often abused. He comments: 'I shudder at the misuse of the concept, however well intentioned.'   We occasionally read that 'a handle affords pulling or lifting', or that 'a button affords pushing' – worse, that someone has 'added an affordance' to an icon. Perhaps the word 'affordance' affords misuse?

Grouping

The perceptual regularities that the Gestalt psychologists demonstrated have been well established, particularly with regard to perceptual organisation and grouping.

They include:

- **Proximity**: we organise the objects we see on the basis of what is near to what:

  In Figure 8.10a, the 25 dots could be organised in rows or columns.

  In Figure 8.10b, the 25 dots arrange themselves in columns.

  Conversely, the 25 dots in Figure 8.10c appear in rows.

  Proximity need not only apply to organised items; the tendency to group by proximity can be seen in random allocations such as in Figure 8.10d. (These are the stars forming the Plough – Ursa Major.)

Figure 8.10, a-d: Proximity grouping rules

- **Similarity**: we perceive objects of similar shape or colour to be grouped together, as in Figure 8.11a

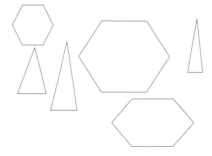

- **Continuity**: we organise the objects we see by finding continuous sequences. By using continuity in perception, we tend to see two distinct trails of dots in Figure 8.11b, not a single dot shape

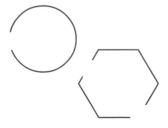

- **Closure**: the application of closure to perception means that we see a circle and hexagon in Figure 8.11c, rather than three separate lines

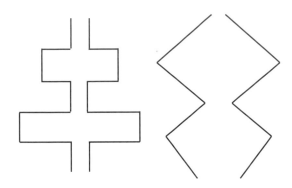

- **Symmetry**: areas that are surrounded by symmetrical lines, as in Figure 8.11d, tend to be recognised as shapes, rather than the lines being perceived as shapes in their own right.

Figure 8.11, a-d: Additional grouping rules

These five grouping rules provide designers with hints about how to arrange interface objects so that they will be perceived to belong together in some way.

Activity 8.2

Grouping rules

For four different computing applications that you use frequently, consider how grouping rules have been used to create the dialogue boxes and toolbars that are used within each.

8.4 Beyond visual perception: other perceptual channels

We have focused mainly on visual perception so far. Vision, of course, is not the only way we are able to perceive the world around us. We now turn to the properties of some of our other senses, especially hearing, and the implications these properties have for user interface design.

Sound

It is often said that most of the information we receive about the world comes to us through our visual sense. Although this is true, it is also the case that sound plays a central role in communicating with others (through speech), receiving information and entertainment (through radio broadcasts or musical performances) and enabling us to be aware of events outside our visual field (for example, police sirens or ringing telephones). Sounds that are apparently in the background often give us vital clues about the status of ongoing processes: for instance, the varying sound of a car engine as we are driving along or the noise made by machinery in a factory.

Sound has a very different set of properties to vision. Consequently, a designer can use auditory stimuli in different ways to visual stimuli. For example, a user cannot see around a corner, but they can hear what is around a corner. This means a user could get auditory stimuli from a computer without being in direct contact with it.

Sight and sound – important differences

- **User control:** visual interaction consists of a number of features (information tokens), each of which may remain constant or vary over time. In most systems, the user is able to manipulate and control the visual display for much of the time. On the other hand, a sound is a single information token, and is not under the control of the listener

- **Access time**: the visual channel also has a much faster access time. For example, a large amount of information may be made simultaneously available on a visual display – whereas presenting the same information in the audio channel will take longer because it can only be presented sequentially. Moreover, while listening to part of a message, users must remember what has gone before. With a visual display, the parts previously read usually remain visible

- **Non-directionality:** another relevant property of the audio medium is that, unlike vision, hearing is non-directional. Admittedly, we do possess some ability to detect the direction of a sound source, but we cannot decide to listen in a particular direction. Similarly, while we can easily control our visual sense (for example, by looking in a particular direction) it is much harder to be selective about what we listen to.

A further property of sound and hearing that designers need to be aware of is that we are relatively poor at separating out a single sound or sequence of sounds from a background of similar sounds. Imagine trying to hold a conversation in a noisy environment where many other people are talking – or trying to follow two conversations at once. It follows that using auditory signals only is likely to be ineffective in noisy environments such as financial dealing rooms.

Moreover, it is well known that people are skilled at noticing changes in sound levels. For example, you may not be aware of the low humming sound of your PC's fan or of an air conditioner in the room, but you will certainly notice it if it suddenly stops. If a background sound remains relatively constant, however, we tend to become less aware of it, and eventually cease to notice it at all.

Practical implications for design

Sound is currently used in many computer interfaces and other interactive devices: sometimes as an important source of information, and sometimes simply as a means of making the interface seem more impressive. Sound can be used for both input and output; and the kinds of sounds that are used include abstract tones and bleeps, naturally occurring sounds, music, and, of course, speech.

Audio alerts

Almost all computer systems 'bleep' when an error of some sort occurs. What is the purpose of such a bleep, and what can the user infer from it?

Clearly, the sound indicates that something has happened, but it is typically left to the user to find out:

- **The nature of the event:** an erroneous input, or a system-generated warning or simply the arrival of e-mail?
- **Its source:** one of several applications, the operating system, or networking software?
- **What should be done about it.**

In 1979, at the Three Mile Island nuclear power station in the US, where one of the most serious nuclear accidents in history took place, control room operators were faced with an array of instruments and displays giving information about the state of the power station. As the situation worsened, auditory alarms sounded as well; a reported 100 alarms of one form or another were operating within minutes.

Partly because of the confusing alarms, the operators failed to diagnose one of the serious problems with the reactor for two hours, during which time extensive damage and leakage of radioactive material occurred.

The world of power stations and control rooms may seem far removed from everyday design, but the same issues are relevant in the interfaces of desktop systems and the design of web pages. The point is that although alarms and alerts can be successful for indicating that some event has occurred, they often carry little useful information about the nature or location of the event or what should be done in response. More significantly, if several such events occur together, then providing an auditory indication of each is going to confuse users. Used with care, however, sound can enhance an interface and provide users with an important source of information.

Providing extra information

An idea that researchers have experimented with is to add sounds to many of the familiar features of some visual interfaces. Sounds chosen match the interface objects with which they are associated, so, for example, folders on a desktop may have the sound of paper crumpling (presumably because, in the real world, we put paper into folders); dropping an item in the wastebasket might produce a sound of breaking (things sometimes break when we throw them in the bin).

Voice input

Voice input is a useful way of interacting in particular circumstances. It may be, for example, that the user has difficulty with typing because of a medical condition.

Several products exist that enable designers of interactive telephone-based services to incorporate voice recognition technology. This allows users to provide information, commands and so on. For example, the Vocalis Group markets a range of products and has made demonstrations available over the telephone.

Speech output

Speech synthesis has been possible for some time, but it is only relatively recently that using synthetic speech has become a reality in everyday interfaces.

- **Voice as an alert:** recent versions of the Apple Mac operating system include a speech synthesiser 'speaking' pop-up alert windows. If a pop-up window appears with a text message, this will be accompanied by a voice speaking the text.   Although this will undoubtedly be a valuable feature for some users, others simply find it unnecessary, and turn it off (as we have already discussed, it can take rather longer to listen to the verbalisation than it does to read the corresponding text).

In Apple Mac's implementation of this feature, there is a delay between the pop-up box appearing and the start of the speech: if the pop-up is actioned, closed or cancelled during this delay, then the speech is never started. Users are quite surprised when, the first time they are slow to close the dialogue box, the computer starts speaking to them!

- **Voice as information:** synthesised speech output can reduce demands on the visual sense; on modern aircraft flight decks, synthesised speech is used for many applications. For example, in the final stages of an approach to landing, the aircraft's height above the ground is critical. On some aircraft, the computer system monitors the height and provides a verbal read-back of the height in intervals of 10 feet as the aircraft approaches the ground.

This is one instance where speech has the potential to add real value to an interface. On approach to landing, a pilot's visual sense is usually in high demand – looking out of the window at the runway below and monitoring instruments. If the critical height information were available only on a visual display, then the pilot's vision would be stretched even further by the requirement to look at yet another display, and by the need to continually refocus on different things. On the other hand, if some of the information can be offloaded and presented acoustically instead of visually, then the demand on the pilot is lessened, reducing the potential for error.

Touch

In everyday life, our sense of touch gives us information and feedback about objects and events with which we are interacting directly: for example, their temperature, texture, pressure, position or orientation.

A simple, but effective way of combining input and output for user interfaces is to use a pointing device such as a mouse or joystick that provides physical feedback.

The dataglove, an input/output device that has been developed for use with virtual reality systems, senses the position, orientation, and movement of the user's hand, allowing gestures to be used as inputs and objects to be grasped. Some datagloves add force, pressure or vibration, enabling the user to 'feel' the virtual objects they touch or grasp.

Perception and culture

Our perceptual systems are shaped by the culture in which we grow up. In the western world, for instance, rooms tend to be rectangular, with right-angled corners. Consequently, our assumptions about distance or depth depend upon our processing of the perspective of rectangular objects or spaces.

If you are creating an interface for a different culture than your own, it is well worth investigating cultural differences between you and the target user group.

Activity 8.3

Culture

Although not strictly a perception problem, there are strong cultural reasons why the most-used computer menu (usually the 'File' menu) is in the top left corner of the screen.

- Why is this and how would you change the interface for a user who is from a distant continent?

- Produce a paper prototype of your design.

8.5 Summary

In this chapter we have looked at how we perceive objects, symbols and events. We have focused mainly on visual perception, but have also discussed auditory and other perceptual channels.

Our guiding concern has been what practical implications for system design can we infer. How can we design systems that make the most of users' perceptual skills and preferences – while not conflicting with those perceptual skills and preferences?

Elsewhere in this book we have introduced you to a range of guidelines and heuristics for interface design. Underlying the design of most successful interfaces, however, is a sound understanding of human cognitive limits such as limits to attentional focus, and how we perceive and understand the world.

References and further reading

Gibson, JJ (1979), *The Ecological Approach to Visual Perception*, Hillsdale, New Jersey: Lawrence Erlbaum Associates.

Norman, DA, (1988), *The Design of Everyday Things*, New York: Doubleday.

Norman, DA, (1999), Affordances, Conventions, and Design, In *Interactions*, 6 (3) p. 38-41, Hillsdale NJ: Lawrence Erlbaum Associates

Norman, DA, (1999), *Invisible Computer: Why Good Products Can Fail, the Personal Computer Is So Complex and Information Appliances Are the Solution*, London: MIT Press.

Norman, D, (1998), *The Invisible Computer*, Cambridge MA: MIT Press.

McGrenere, J and Ho, W, (2000), Affordances: Clarifying and Evolving a Concept, *Proceedings of Graphics Interface*, Montreal: Quebec.
www.graphicsinterface.org/proceedings/2000/

Richard Gregory: **www.richardgregory.org/**

James Gibson: **www.huwi.org/gibson/index.php**

Donald Norman: **www.jnd.org/bio-sketch.html**

8.6 Review questions

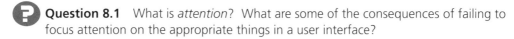 **Question 8.1** What is *attention*? What are some of the consequences of failing to focus attention on the appropriate things in a user interface?

Question 8.2 What user interface design features affect users' attention focusing? In what situations might the use of each be appropriate for a user interface?

Question 8.3 Why is context important when designing an interface?

8.7 Answers to review questions

Answer to question 8.1   *Attention* is the selection of one of a number of possible perceptual and mental activities to focus on. The idea is that we have limited cognitive capabilities, and therefore have to be selective in what we perceive or think about.

Lack of attention can result in failing to carry out tasks (forgetting them – a 'lapse') or carrying out a similar, more familiar, task in place of the desired one (a 'capture error'). Focusing attention of the wrong elements of a user interface can lead to distractions, making the user's task harder, and to the user missing important stimuli (such as notification of an emergency).

Answer to question 8.2

- Visual and audio alerts: to draw the user's attention to specific and important events and conditions (e.g., emergencies, or system-generated warnings)

- Motion, blinking, annoyance etc: can be a distraction and an annoyance. Use only occasionally and with care!

- Colour, intensity, size etc: to make specific pieces of information stand out from the background

- Spatial and temporal cues: to help the user to focus on where they are currently working in a large space (e.g., a form) or what stage they are at in a process with several stages (e.g., online purchasing)

- Structure and layout: structuring can help users decide what to focus attention on when a large amount of information is presented, and to stay focused.

Answer to question 8.3   Context gives meaning to a symbol. Without context, symbols such as the box with a cross in it can be ambiguous, and confuse users about its meaning. This makes it both hard for the user to match the feature with what is being searched for, and increases the chances of an error.

8.8 Feedback on activities

Feedback on activity 8.1: Icon design

- The triangles represent bleach. The crossed-out triangle (obviously?) means no bleach.

- The squares represent tumble dryers, and the dots in the centre of the squares represent the heat at which the garment may be dried – three dots being (obviously?) the hottest.

- The third row of symbols represents ironing. Again, the dots represent the heat of the iron.

- Finally, the last row represents how the garment should be washed. Numbers denote temperature in degrees Celsius; a hand in the 'bucket' would indicate hand wash only.

These symbols would be more effective if laundry equipment (e.g. irons and washing machines) used the same symbols so that the user need not even understand the meaning of the symbol. This is the best solution, as you will discover if you try to design alternatives. If you sell garments worldwide, symbols will inevitably be misinterpreted.

Feedback on activity 8.2: Grouping rules In the many dialogue boxes, light grey lines are used to enforce grouping. Proximity is used to group functions which have a similar task, or work on the same object (file, clipboard etc). Shape similarity is also used for drawing tools. Word allows the insertion of a Word table or a table from the Excel spreadsheet package. The icons are identical, except the Excel table has the Excel logo placed on it.

Feedback on activity 8.3: Culture The menu is here as people in a western culture start reading from the top left-hand corner and proceed across the top until moving on to the next line. Someone from China, on the other hand, reads in columns, so it might be more sensible to put the menu down the left edge of the screen.

CHAPTER 9

Evaluation

OVERVIEW

So far, we have looked at component activities in the user-centred design system (UCSD) along with the underlying cognitive psychology theory. In particular, we have looked at how heuristics can be used to evaluate systems and how models of the human mind can be used to measure performance.

In this chapter, we look at the role of evaluation in the UCSD process. We will look at more of the key techniques and their contribution to the evolutionary development of systems. As we have seen, the Waterfall model is criticised because we cannot revisit and revise aspects of the design process once they are completed. In the user-centred design approach, this is very much encouraged. It is evaluation that is the central activity in this process. The product of evaluation is knowledge. This could be knowledge about a design, knowledge about the user or knowledge about the task.

Learning outcomes   At the end of this chapter you should be able to:

- Explain where evaluation sits in a user-centred design process

- Discuss the key evaluation techniques and be able to compare and contrast them

- Explain how to design a user observation

- Describe how to interpret evaluation data.

9.1 Introduction

In this chapter, we will look at the final stages of the design process. The ultimate usability test for a system is to be used by real users who give opinions on why or why not they find it usable. We will also look at observational techniques.

We will also look at observational techniques in which users are given a prototype system and are recorded attempting several broad, but representative, tasks (usually drawn from the task analysis). The observer can then analyse the recordings to see if the users are performing as expected with the system. In particular, the observer needs to put together a convincing argument that the usability requirements of the system are met.

Based on the outcome of the observation, decisions then need to be made about what to do with the system prototype; whether it is good enough to be fully implemented or whether modifications need to be made. If modifications are required, then a detailed description of those modifications should be presented along with a rationale for them.

We will also look at ways of recording user behaviour, ways of measuring how successful a system is, and ways in which the act of observing users can interfere with what the users are actually doing and how to reduce the impact of this.

9.2 Evaluation as part of user-centred design

User-centred design is based on the belief that usable systems are created gradually rather than being produced in one go. This means that a good system can only evolve through a process of generating, representing, testing and refining ideas.

There is an important distinction between formative and summative evaluation (Hewitt 1986).

- Summative evaluation takes a finished system and assesses it for aspects of usability. This can tell companies what off-the-shelf packages they should or should not buy, or compare two alternative designs

- Formative evaluation (which we are more concerned with here) is evaluation within the design process. Usable interfaces are never produced spontaneously by a designer. The process produces good usability through evolution. Formative evaluation provides ways of learning about design options, the user group, and the task-space by deep analysis of prototypes. The data from formative evaluation will point to problems and strengths of proposed designs. This information feeds back into new prototypes which are themselves evaluated. This process continues until a final design gradually emerges. Therefore, your prototype may have many usability errors when evaluated. Your response would be to look at each problem in turn, and reason about how the design can be changed to remove the problem. It also means that there is no embarrassment for the designer when evaluations find problems with a design. This is a natural and normal part of the design process.

It is reasonable to say that evaluation is the pivotal activity of user-centred design. The other phases of design help add content and generate possible solutions, but formative evaluation takes those ideas, looks at how they might work in practice and assesses what they contribute to the overall solution. In the early stages of a project, the design team may generate quick paper sketches (mock-ups) of possible screens or early attempts at a specification. They may be very simple and quick, but they are a representation of an idea that a design team member has in his/her head and are very valuable. Because the idea is given this physical form, the team can discuss the idea in a way that could not be done when it was only an abstract concept. The designer can provide rationales for their ideas and describe them to other team members.

The design process will move on from producing paper mock-ups to electronic prototypes that can be interacted with, as well as inspected. However, the same principle applies at this stage as applies to the paper-prototyping activities. A design idea is not easy to imagine as a complete reality. Although the designer will have ideas about things such as the look of the pages, the way that users will interact, the use of icons and text and so on, even quite a simple system will have a number of interrelated usability aspects that can only be brought out by building a representation of the design idea.

Is evaluation necessary?

Evaluation is essentially the process of testing and refining design ideas. Within this broad purpose there are specific issues that it addresses, depending on the particular circumstances. It may be that we want to compare two or more designs to see which is the better design; we may want to check a design to see if it conforms to the requirements that we specified, or to a set of standards.

A particularly important reason for doing evaluation is to find unforeseen problems. It is very difficult for designers to spot potential problems without evaluation. Furthermore, it may be that the evaluators want to understand how the system will work in the real world.

When do we need it?

The simplest answer is to say 'all the time'. As soon as an idea is generated, it can be tested. All we need is a rough representation of the idea, even on a piece of paper. Evaluation exercises are useful at all stages of a project. For example, if we are designing a system that supports similar tasks to ones that already exist (e.g. shopping websites) you can look at existing systems. They can give us hints about good and bad ways of supporting the tasks that we want the system to support. Early paper prototypes allow us to check various ideas for design without having to make any programming effort. This allows us to compare ideas and refine our ideas about usability. These are limited in that the designer and design team can inspect them, and they can be shown to users, but the user cannot interact with them.

The ability to interact with a prototype makes usability testing (or 'think-aloud protocols') possible. This is very important, as it is the closest that we can get to the reality of using the system. As we have seen, prototypes can be made to look like a complete system when in fact they only look like they work. For example, imagine that we want to test alternative interfaces on a project to build a database querying system. We can ask users to test the interface design by giving them the task of formulating the query to a database that does not yet exist. If we instruct them to find a flight from London to New Delhi on a particular day, all we need to do is to produce an output that looks like the database has been searched. In fact it may simply be a pre-designed page that fully represents the final item. Thus with minimal programming effort, we can get interesting and useful data from users before we make a significant investment in design. This makes it cheap and simple to make comparisons between design ideas.

Quantitative and qualitative data

- Quantitative data simply means statistical results from evaluation. As we will see, a questionnaire may tell you that 80% of users who were asked, said they liked the system. Alternatively, it may tell you that skilled users take 12.5 seconds to complete a task using one package and 16 seconds to complete the same task on another system. This can be very useful in some circumstances

- Qualitative data provides evidence about why a system performs well or badly. As we will see, observations of users can easily give us counts of, for example, how many times they failed to complete a task, or stopped, or went to the help system (quantitative measures). To diagnose why they are having problems and what may usefully be changed, however, we also need qualitative data such as descriptions of their reasoning while performing the task.

9.3 Observational evaluation

A critical feature of UCSD is the choice between user observation and user experimentation. The former places more emphasis on natural tasks and environments, whereas the latter stresses rigour and replicability of results. There is a trade-off between the benefits and problems of these approaches. In an ideal world, you would wish to use a range of different methods in order to be reasonably sure that your results and consequent conclusions are reliable. The common features of many such approaches include user observation, testing a system with real users. The aim is to see if the defined requirements are met. There are a range of observational techniques, so you must get to grips with the basics of how to design a user observation which will produce a useful evaluation.

Observational-based design is an important activity in HCI. It is critical that problems are identified by users rather than by the observer. Observation provides a more natural setting than an experiment. It overcomes many disadvantages of experiments, but it is not without its own problems. With natural observation, it may be difficult to replicate findings and it enjoys less scientific rigour. The data itself may be more difficult to analyse, though there are emerging methods which promise to overcome such difficulties.

Subjectivity and observations

To increase the quality of research, we must avoid the following effects during the observational study:

- **Hawthorne effect:** users increase performance to please the observer or simply because they are being observed
- **Observer bias:** an observer only sees and records what they want to see (e.g. positive aspects of the interface)
- **Halo effect:** the observer's judgement is influenced by another, separate, positive judgement. For example, 'My friend who made this is good, so this must be good too.'

9.4 Protocol analysis

Verbal protocols

The simplest approach is to observe people using the user interface, making notes on what they are doing and videotaping them for later analysis. This is useful in some circumstances, but can only show us what people do, not why. In order to discover deeper information about the design, we need to know the user's reasoning. The best way of doing this is to ask the user to talk about what they are doing as they go. This method is referred to as protocol analysis.

There are at least two components to a verbal protocol:

- **Talk aloud:** verbalise your silent decisions: what you would say to yourself while solving this problem, or doing this task
- **Think aloud:** verbalise whatever thoughts occur doing this task.

Protocol analysis involves users 'thinking aloud' while carrying out a task. The users describe their reasoning and their interpretation of the system as they use it. What they say is recorded and analysed for explanations of what they are trying to do (and any plans or predetermined ideas they may have); how they interpret items on the screen; and explanations of any difficulties that they may have.

Designing observations

When designing observational work, there are some key issues to consider, most of which are discussed in more depth on subsequent pages:

- Select:
  - **tasks:** identify a representative set of tasks that help users evaluate most of the system (e.g. from the task analysis)
  - **users:** your users should be a representative sample of the user population or populations (e.g. background, age, sex, abilities, experience, disabilities, and environments)
  - **environment:** use a realistic setting for your observational evaluation that allows users to feel natural and comfortable
  - **one or two significant functional requirements:** and test them to see if requirements are fulfilled. (However, don't test all requirements)
- Observe (at least three users)
- Give users their set of tasks to complete
- Describe the decisions you made about how the observation(s) should be carried out
- Explain to the user how to conduct a think-aloud study (e.g. 'Say out loud whatever thoughts occur to you while doing this task, or if you encounter any problems')
- Conduct a think-aloud study
- Keep protocols (transcripts for each user)
- Record at which point in the task/system these responses occurred
- Record the users' comments, facial expressions, body language (e.g. user frowns, user hits computer)
- Analyse usability requirements as part of observation
- Analyse the protocols
- Are the functional requirements fulfilled?
- What can you say about the usability requirements?
- Build prototype to test (only) those requirements.

Writing a verbal protocol

A verbal protocol (i.e. record) should have the following:

- Description of the environment
- List of tasks completed by the user

- Users' background and demographic details (e.g. age, sex, computer experience)
- Record (tape, shorthand) and write up users' comments, body language, facial expressions
- The aspects of the interface that these responses relate to should also be detailed.

How to conduct a session

- **Choose the tasks:** it is important that you select tasks that are representative of how the system will be used. You will give these to your users on an instruction sheet. This will describe what they should do, but without giving them any hints about how they will do it. For example, if you were testing a drawing tool you could simply show a diagram and ask them to reproduce it using the tool

- **Select users:** it is equally important to choose a representative set of users. It is important that you find out the level of experience that they have with computers generally, the type of system that is being tested and their experience of the task. Other details such as their age may also important and are worth knowing. If you get the wrong users for testing, it may give misleading information – and you could fail to find serious problems that will affect real users. For example, if all your test users have years of experience using Windows, you will not find out if the package being tested causes problems to those who do not have that experience

- **Explain the purpose to the users:** it is important that the user understands the purpose of the test. For example, make clear the user interface is being evaluated, not the users. They may feel that they are on trial, particularly as you are analysing errors and problems. Also, if they know that the system being tested is your (or your team's) design they may believe that you want them to say only positive things about it

- **Conduct the evaluation:** sometimes the user may find it difficult to both concentrate and provide verbal commentary. One way of helping is simply to remind them to say something. One variation of protocol analysis, called 'cooperative evaluation', recommends that you ask a limited set of questions at key points such as when the user appears to be stuck, or has encountered a problem. These are typically:
  - *'What are you trying to do here?'*
  - *'What are you looking at now?'*
  - *'What just happened?'*
  - *'What are you going to do next? Why?'*
  - *'What do you think this means?'*
  - *'Had you thought of doing this?'*

  It is important to bear in mind that this approach is an attempt to simulate a real-use situation and can never do this perfectly. In a sense, your user is like an actor playing a role. You are telling them to imagine they are motivated to do the task, and to imagine the circumstances and environment in which the task is situated. You must always be aware of factors that threaten to corrupt the data that you are collecting. The fact that you are observing, or a video-camera is recording, may affect their behaviour. If you choose to ask questions as they are performing the task, you must be aware that questioning can be disturbing and affect their concentration. You need to find the balance between getting information from them and ensuring the session is as 'natural' as it can reasonably be.

Analysing a protocol/transcript

The data that you will have at the end of a session is known as the transcript, which details the physical actions and verbal commentary that the user has made.

The commentary will include information about the user's interpretation of what they see and what they expect to happen and their response to what actually happened.

We can therefore trace the causes of problems that they may have had and isolate any parts of the system that they found difficult. Transcripts tend to contain critical incidents that often involve the user having difficulties or doing something unexpected.

When analysing a transcript of an evaluation session, the aim is to categorise the comments according to:

- **Frequency:** identify groups of issues that frequently arise around a specific event encountered, such as interface element or user problem
- **Fundamentality:** identify issues that although don't frequently arise are deemed by you to be fundamentally important.

In the example that follows, we look at a transcript from a test of a tool for drawing diagrams. The user subject has been asked to reproduce a dataflow diagram. In this first example the user is looking for cut-and-paste facilities that are typical of Windows or Macintosh packages.

The transcript references are:

Mental action = **M**   Physical action = **P**   System action = **S**

M	"I want to move this block of text"
P	Drags down the 'edit menu' and runs the cursor over each option
M	"So where is move?"
P	Drags down the 'edit' menu again and a third time
M	"It doesn't look like I can do it. I could drag it but I don't really want to."

We know from this fragment that the user has failed to match the term 'move' in their mental model of the task with 'cut' and 'paste'. Therefore, there is a mismatch between the user's model of this sub-task and the system's representation of it. A further check of the user's background reveals that their experience of this task is from an older package that used a menu option called 'move' and a different procedure for this action. Therefore, we are able to explain this problem as a gulf between what the user is accustomed to doing to complete this sub-task and the different way that is offered in this package. We also know from it that the subject is not confident about dragging and dropping objects.

It may be that you need to look further than the critical incident itself to reason about the data. As we saw in the example above, the evidence from the transcript was usefully cross-referenced with the user profile.

In the second example, the same user is trying to connect two boxes with an arrow:

M	"I want to connect these two boxes"
P	Selects a line option, plots the first coordinate, drags mouse to end coordinate
S	*Line appears*
P	Releases mouse button
S	*Arrowhead appears on the line*
M	"I didn't want an arrow. Why has it given me one?"
S	*Deletes the line*
M	"Ok, let's try again"
P	Repeats line-drawing action
S	*Arrowhead appears on line*
M	"And again! Why on earth has it done that?"

What we know from this communication is that the system is not doing what the user wants, and that the user cannot explain it. To diagnose the problem, we need to go back to an earlier point in interaction.

Earlier the user had drawn another line that did require an arrowhead. There are two ways of doing this:

1. Select line option; draw line; go to arrows menu; select arrowhead

or

2. Select line option; go to arrows menu; select arrowhead; draw line.

The system allows the user to do it either way – and this user did it the second way. To the user, it appears that they are identical in their effect and that it does not really matter about the order. However, if it is done the second way the system also sets the arrowhead as default. In other words, the user (unwittingly in this case) tells the system to put an arrowhead on every line that is drawn. It is only several minutes later that this shows itself as a problem.

Therefore, we need to have the whole transcript in order to trace the problem to its original cause. It is clear that the user cannot explain the behaviour of the system because the action had effects that the user was not informed about.

9.5 Experiments

Experiments usually define a hypothesis (or a question) and adopt a clear experimental method (a way of answering the question). The experiment itself has two distinct stages: implementing the experiment and analysing the results. The latter often involves some type of statistical analysis to indicate if the observed results are just random variations or are statistically significant. The data and analyses then enable you to ask if the hypothesis holds. You can then go on to draw some conclusions – usually, that more work is required!

Experiments have some advantages. A good experiment tends to be systematic, with a repeatable approach to testing based on scientific rigour. Disadvantages often include a reduced consideration of specific variables, questions which are hard to relate to real-world holistic problems and an artificial setting which may lack real-world validity. In some cases, an experimental design can be overly restrictive, with the question or questions defined beforehand: no real exploration is possible. Perhaps it would be a good idea to combine experimental and observational methods, starting with an exploratory approach first and moving into more experimental methods with increasing precision and rigour. Caution is advisable, however, as current research shows that we have a tendency to be satisfied with evidence sufficient to support or views and preferences, but not to explore further.

In designing user testing, we usually strive for realism. We want the users to be representative of the population, we want the task they try to be typical and the prototype to be as intended. Of course, if they are sitting in our test laboratory or our office they are not in the situation where the intended system will actually be used. One way of overcoming this problem is to take the evaluation study to the user's location. Then we can see how the system would integrate with the user's own environment. This may be the user's workplace or home or even (where we are testing a mobile system) during travel. It would also be easier to get our user to relax and concentrate on the task, which makes it more likely that the data will be useful.

Another technique involves creating an environment that resembles the actual circumstances of use. A good example of this is a flight simulator, where pilots can test new software in realistic conditions. This has the advantage of informing us of how the safety-critical software will integrate with the pilot's work. It also has the advantage of allowing testing to take place without putting the pilot in danger. We could not test prototypes on a real flight.

Similarly, user experience laboratories are a way of making evaluation studies more realistic. These 'laboratories' are very different in appearance to conventional experimental laboratories. They are designed to look like a familiar environment for the user, typically a room in the user's home. This has been used, for example, to test interactive television applications.

9.6 Cognitive walkthrough

A cognitive walkthrough is an approach to formative evaluation without users. Members of the design team perform it. The user is 'represented' by a set of relevant questions that are applied to each action in the system. So the team goes through each action just as the user would need to perform such a task on the system. For each action, the design is scrutinised and reviewed, with problematic features noted so that alternative designs can be explored. This technique is particularly aimed at usability for first-time users of systems that are walk-up-and-use. These are systems which we would expect to be immediately usable and for users not to need any training.

The cognitive walkthrough is based on the assumption that users explore the interface to learn. This learning is example-based where users look to learn how the system in general works by trying some of its features and learning general principles. This is referred to as exploratory learning. Good systems allow the user to learn by exploring some of its features and using that experience to reason about how the system works and explore further. As we will see, the method prompts participants to simulate a first-time user learning by exploration. This is a team exercise in which a particular design idea is put under the scrutiny of other team members. They examine each action that the user will have to perform and predict potential usability problems. The fact that they are imagining this from the perspective of the first-time user also helps them to suggest possible fixes for the problems that they identify.

Preparing a cognitive walkthrough

You need to make a reasonable estimate of the knowledge, skills, and experience that your user will have. The team of evaluators will specify this before the walkthrough begins. You then need to identify a set of representative tasks. These are likely to be the most typical tasks encountered by a new user. If these are not designed well, the user is likely to struggle with the system as a whole. After you choose the tasks, you will need to specify each component action that the user requires in order to complete them successfully.

Conducting the walkthrough

The team looks at each action and considers the relevant questions; stock walkthrough questions at each step of the task include:

- Will the user be trying to achieve the right effect?
- Will the user know the correct action is available?
- Will the user realise it is the correct action?
- If the correct action is taken, will the user understand the feedback and recognise that progress is being made towards the goal?

The team will assess each action according to these criteria.

Experiments in support of design

Sometimes we want to test something very specific about some aspect of our systems. An experiment involves two sets of users whose situation differs in only one respect – that which is being tested. For example, in an experiment to determine whether a trackpad is quicker to use than a mouse for selecting objects on the screen, the two sets of subjects would be treated identically except that one set would use a trackpad and the other a mouse. In this example experiment, the hypothesis might be that 'using a mouse is quicker than using a trackpad for selecting objects on the screen'.

This simple example highlights many aspects of experimental design.

- Initially, the hypothesis is some prediction we wish to test (here that a mouse will be quicker to use than a trackpad) – this has itself probably been derived from some previous research or observation

- Secondly, we need to be explicit about what kind of difference we expect to see – this is the thing we are going to measure in the experiment and is referred to as the dependent variable. In this case it is the time to complete tasks with the computer (the prediction was that using a mouse would be quicker than using a trackpad)

- Thirdly, we need to state what we are going to change between the different sets of subjects – the thing that we change is referred to as the independent variable. In this case it is the kind of input device used – either a mouse or a trackpad. Usually in experiments to do with user interfaces we keep the task the same across all subjects so that we can determine the difference between user interfaces for the same task – therefore it is important to select tasks which can be performed using the different user interfaces

- Finally, it is important in experiments to avoid confounding variables. These are things, which are beyond your control and might effect the result of the experiment and should therefore be avoided. In this case, the fact that most users of computers currently use mice rather than trackpads could be a confounding variable as the subjects would be more experienced with the mouse and so probably quicker by default. In order to remove this confounding variable we could select only novice computer users for the experiment (i.e. those without any experience of using computers and, we might assume, without experience of using a mouse).

Dependent variables

Dependent variables are those things that we are trying to measure to support or disprove our hypothesis. Therefore, they need to be things that are easily observed and measured, for example:

- The time it takes to complete a task
- The number of errors made during the experiment
- The time taken to recover from an error
- Number of times help is used
- Length of time help is used
- Time spent before responses formulated.

These dependent variables produce quantitative data – that is, with numerical results. We might also use qualitative data such as subjects' preferences – how much they liked the system, or the quality of product produced at the end of the experiment. Qualitative data such as user preference can be gathered using interviews or questionnaires, as discussed previously.

Independent variables

As already mentioned, independent variables are the factors that we change between sets of subjects. Previously we considered the type of input as an independent variable – either mouse or trackpad: these are levels of the independent variable. In this example, there are two levels of the independent variable. More complex experiments may involve more than two levels of independent variable, and may also involve more than one independent variable. Each unique combination of independent variable levels is referred to as a condition. So, for our simple example there are two conditions in the experiment – one where subjects use a trackpad, and another where they use a mouse. If we were to build on the design of this simple experiment by including another independent variable we would increase the number of conditions in the experiment. For example, we may want to change the hypothesis to be that 'using a mouse is quicker than using a trackpad, and providing online help makes them easier to learn to use'. In this case we would have an extra independent variable – the kind of help provided. We might wish to have three levels of this independent variable – no help, simple textual help, and interactive help.

The following table illustrates how these two independent variables and their levels combine to produce six conditions in the experiment.

| | | Type of input device | |
		Mouse	**Trackpad**
Type	**None**	**Condition 1:** No help, mouse input	**Condition 2:** No help, trackpad input
of	**Simple text**	**Condition 3:** Simple help, mouse input	**Condition 4:** Simple help, trackpad input
help	**Interactive**	**Condition 5:** Interactive help, mouse input	**Condition 6:** Interactive help, trackpad input

Table 9.1: Table of conditions

Assigning subjects

Recruiting enough subjects is one of the hardest parts of conducting an experiment. Typically, at least ten subjects are needed per condition to provide statistically significant results – results that we are pretty sure could not have happened by chance. For the more complex experiment just proposed, this would require sixty subjects (ten per condition). Attracting so many potential subjects usually requires some incentives, such as cash or unit credits for students.

The use of each subject in only one condition is referred to as between-groups design. We can reduce the number of subjects needed by reusing subjects in different conditions – referred to as within-groups design. However, subjects may then carry over experience from one condition to another and so introduce a confounding variable into the experiment.

Suppose we were setting up the simple experiment just described, which attempts to show that using a mouse is quicker than using a trackpad. The independent variable in this case is the type of input, with two levels – mouse or trackpad. There are therefore two conditions: mouse or trackpad. If we found ten subjects for the experiment (Ann, Bert, Carol, Derek, Eric, Fred, Gary, Harry, Iris and Joan), then we could assign the subjects as follows:

Between-groups design					
Mouse input:	Ann	Bert	Carol	Derek	Eric
Trackpad input:	Fred	Gary	Harry	Iris	Joan
Within-groups design					
Mouse input:	Ann	Bert	Carol	Derek	Eric
Trackpad input:	Ann	Bert	Carol	Derek	Eric

Table 9.2: Assigning subjects

Statistics

We use statistics to determine whether an independent variable (such as the kind of input device) has an effect (positive or negative) on a dependent variable (such as the time to complete a task), and that this has not come about by chance.

We are looking for results that are statistically significant: that is, we believe that they did not occur purely by chance. A detailed coverage of statistical analysis is, however, beyond the scope of this book.

Summary of user experimentation

To sum up, performing an experiment involves the following stages:

- Formulate hypothesis – some statement that you wish to test in the experiment
- Identify the variables – independent, dependent, and confounding
- Decide on the levels for the variables
- Select subjects – decide who would make suitable subjects
- Decide on the experimental design – within-groups or between-groups
- Decide what tasks are to be performed
- Perform the experiment
- Analyse the results.

9.7 Other evaluation methods

The first thing to say about the two techniques which follow, interviews and questionnaires, is that they must be seen as supplementary to the techniques already described, and have a limited usage for design. They tend to be used to find out information about the users' backgrounds, their views and their opinions about the system. These methods help us understand the user population. For example, if we want to select a representative sample of users, observational evaluation questionnaires will help us find those people. We can also use them to gauge levels of satisfaction with a system.

Although these techniques yield qualitative data, they are not seen as having the same power in diagnosing usability problems as the other techniques discussed. This may seem odd, given that they seem at first to be very simple direct ways of probing users, but it is important to remember that they are limited in what they can tell you.

- If your user uses the system while you watch and listen to their verbal accounts, you can get a clear as-it-happens response to your design
- If you interview them, even a few minutes after using it, you are likely to get 'reconstructed' accounts of their reasoning. So it is better so see interviews and questionnaires as something that can be used as a supplement to the main techniques.

Interviews

Interviews can be structured or unstructured:

- **Structured interviews** provide a *strict sequence of questions*, useful for comparing the responses of several interviewees. However, they are limited because they do not allow the evaluator to ask follow-up questions – even when more information would be useful
- **Unstructured interviews** allow the interviewer to choose the order and nature of the questions. One critical advantage is that it allows the interviewer to follow up interesting issues and topics. This approach is useful in situations where we are not sure about the scope and nature of the answers that we will get. For example, we may want to ask a user about aspects of their lifestyle. This would need to start with quite an open question, such as 'What tends to interest you in your leisure time?'. The response from the user may include something in particular that you want to explore further. So the next question will ask for further information about it. The absence of a strict structure makes this possible. The interview can therefore develop in a natural way.

  It can, however, be difficult to collate and analyse data provided by an unstructured interview.

Questionnaires

Unlike interviews, questionnaires (usually) involve subjects filling in responses to questions themselves rather than responding to an interviewer. Therefore, questionnaires can involve a larger set of people as there is no need for the interviewer to ask each subject for their answers. Extensive use of questionnaires is usually referred to as a **survey**.

Questionnaires can generate a lot of data, because you can distribute them to many people. However, it is often hard to get people to respond to them.

A potential problem with questionnaires revolves around questions that may be confusing or need clarification, as you are not there to clarify it for them: it is critical to pilot your questionnaire, in order to remove any such confusion or ambiguity. Try the questions on a few people to see if the questions – or the answering structure – that you have designed are clear for users. If you survey thirty people, your data would be useless if they interpret the questions in thirty different ways.

Another problem is that people may not want to devote time to answering long lists of questions. So questionnaires should be kept within two sides of A4 paper.

There are two main types of question to be found in questionnaires:

- **Open questions:** the subject is free to write their answers in any way they see fit. Of course, this means that analysis time must be devoted to trying to understand what subjects meant by their answers and, moreover, subjects may not provide appropriate answers at all
- **Closed questions:** the subject selects an answer from a set of presented possibilities. This provides less ambiguous results than open questions and can even be used to provide some numerical results such as 'Nine out of ten cat owners, who expressed a preference, said that their cat preferred Super-Sweet cat food'.

Closed question questionnaire design involves not only choosing the questions, but also choosing the form in which the user is able to respond. This is important as an inappropriate choice or poor design can corrupt your data. Preece et al (2002) identify several kinds of scale from which subjects can choose their response including:

- **Simple checklist:** simple responses such as 'yes', 'no', or 'don't know' are provided
- **Ranked order:** this approach requires the user to specify their preference for items in a list. For example, a user may be asked to rank (using, for example, the numbers one to four, with one being 'most useful') their perception of the usefulness of four different commands
- **Multi-point rating scale:** a number of points on a scale are provided which give a range of responses (e.g. ranging from 'strongly agree' to 'strongly disagree', as shown in Figure 9.1).

strongly
agree

strongly
disagree

Figure 9.1: Basic scale

A variation of this is the Likert scale (illustrated in Figure 9.2) which indicates the meaning of each point (e.g. instead of simply putting 'strongly agree' at one end of the scale and 'strongly disagree' at the other, the intermediate points of 'agree', 'slightly agree', 'neutral', 'slightly disagree', and 'disagree' are included).

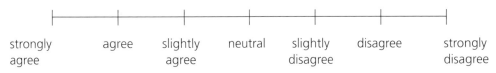

strongly
agree

agree

slightly
agree

neutral

slightly
disagree

disagree

strongly
disagree

Figure 9.2: Likert scale

Activity 9.1

Design a user evaluation survey

Design a user-based evaluation of a prototype for a new website selling clothing to teenagers. Detail your preparation for the study. How it would be carried out, and how you would analyse the data?

Activity 9.2

Comparing user evaluation techniques

Compare the use of experimental studies to user-based observation. Discuss the differences between the approaches and the different kinds of information that can be acquired from them. Also, consider the different situations in which they are appropriate.

Activity 9.3

Activity 9.3: Designing a user experiment

In an experiment to determine which user interface (command-line, desktop metaphor, or virtual environment) allows users to perform their task quickest, what might the following be?

- The independent variables and their levels

- The dependent variables

- The conditions

- The confounding variables.

9.8 Summary

An important choice for evaluators is to select the appropriate method to use. This will depend on what it is being tested, who the users are and the context of use for the intended system. For example, the main purpose of a supermarket checkout computer is to support many transactions by trained staff. So we may want to do comparative experiments to study the time taken per interaction.

We are less likely to want to use a cognitive walkthrough, because the staff would be trained and learnability for first-time users would not be the most important issue. In evaluating a commercial website, we would want to know how easy it is to use for first-time users. However, we also know that they want customers to keep coming back, so the site has to be pleasant to use to encourage customers to return. So testing would include subjective measures of satisfaction. We would want to do user testing, but satisfaction questionnaires and interviews may also be helpful.

In this chapter, we have looked further at the theory and practice of usability evaluation. We have considered three important distinctions. One is the contrast between formative and summative evaluation. Formative evaluation is a direct contributor to the continued design, and the techniques described are mainly targeted at this. We have made the distinction between qualitative and quantitative usability data.

Quantitative data gives us statistics but qualitative data is what we require to help us diagnose and reason about problems in the design. We have also drawn the distinction between methods that use users, such as think-aloud protocols, observation, interviews and questionnaires. Each of these methods has something to offer and is often used in combination. A key part of the skill that you are developing is the ability to make judgements about the appropriate use of evaluation techniques, when they are used and why.

References and further reading

Dix A, Finlay JE, Abowd GA, and Beale R, et al. (2004), *Human Computer Interaction* (3rd edition). Harlow: FT Prentice Hall International.

Hewitt T, (1986), *Iterative evaluation*. In Harrison M D and Monk A F (Eds), *People and Computers: Designing for usability*, Proceedings of the second conference of the BCS HCI Specialist Group.

Nielsen J, and Mack RL, (1994), *Usability inspection methods*, New York: John Wiley & Sons.

Nielsen J, (2000), *Designing Web Usability*, Berkley, CA: New Riders.

Preece J, Rogers Y, and Sharp H, (2002), *Interaction Design: Beyond Human–Computer Interaction*, Chichester: John Wiley & Sons.

9.9 Review questions

Question 9.1   What are the differences between concurrent and retrospective protocols involved in user observation? What effect do these differences have on user observation?

Question 9.2   We have discussed four different purposes of evaluation. Complete the table below to indicate which techniques are appropriate or not for the purposes given (mark a tick or cross).

Technique	Find usability problems	Compare designs	Understand real world	Check conformance to standard
User observation				
User interviews/questionnaires				
User experimentation				
Cognitive walkthrough				
Heuristic evaluation				

9.10 Answers to review questions

Answer to question 9.1   Concurrent protocols involve the subjects of the observation verbalising what they are doing and why while they perform the task that is the subject of the observation. Retrospective protocol is used after the observation – subjects recount what they did and why.

Concurrent protocols may distract the subject while they are attempting to perform their task. On the other hand, retrospective protocols rely on the subject remembering what they did and why, and involve the subject in extra time as part of the evaluation.

Answer to question 9.2

Technique	Find usability problems	Compare designs	Understand real world	Check conformance to standard
User observation	✓	✓	✓	✓
User interviews/questionnaires	✗	✓	✓	✗
User experimentation	✗	✗	✓	✗
Cognitive walkthrough	✓	✓	✗	✗
Heuristic evaluation	✓	✓	✗	✗

9.11 Feedback on activities

Feedback on activity 9.1: Design a user evaluation study   The first job is to select teenagers to act as subjects. You need to check each subject's age, gender, computer experience and web experience, then prepare a task-sheet. This should contain a simple set of instructions, telling them to attempt to select some items for purchase but not hinting about how they will do it. Set up the computer that they will use in a comfortable, quiet room where you will not be disturbed. When the users arrive, be careful to put them at ease, and clearly explain the purpose of the evaluation and the nature of their role. Ask them to comment on themselves as they go. Make notes on their thoughts and actions (record on video if you are able) as they use the system. Prompt them to speak if they go quiet. At the end of the session make a note of the most important incidents that occurred in the session and isolate apparent problems with the design.

Feedback on activity 9.2: Comparing user evaluation techniques   Experimentation typically requires a large number of subjects who are given quite restricted tasks to perform. User observation, on the other hand, requires a smaller number of subjects who may carry out larger and more realistic tasks. Moreover, whereas experimentation typically requires quite specific physical surroundings such as a usability lab, user observation is more flexible and can even be employed in the workplace. Results from the two approaches also differ – experiments provide quantitative data, whereas user studies typically give qualitative data.

Feedback on activity 9.3: Designing a user experiment   There is only one *independent variable*, which is the type of user interfaces. It has three levels: 1) command-line, 2) desktop metaphor, and 3) virtual environment.

There is one *dependent variable* – the time it takes to complete the task using a given interface. As there is only one independent variable and it has three levels, there are three *conditions* – the three levels of the independent variable.

Confounding variables might include: subjects' experience of any of the interfaces, and typing experience (for command-line interface).

CHAPTER 10

UCSD and advanced technology

OVERVIEW

This chapter takes a step back from the business of designing interactive systems and looks at how technologies develop in the long term. Things like radios were complicated and difficult to use one hundred years ago and only determined enthusiasts bought them. Nowadays radios are ubiquitous, simple to use and owned by anyone who can afford them.

In this chapter, we will also look at the different types of technology (hardware and software) that are emerging in today's information society. We will discuss how these different technologies can be designed so they are useful, usable and accessible.

Learning outcomes   At the end of this chapter you should be able to:

- Describe the differences between emerging human–computer interface technologies

- Describe how people typically respond to new technologies

- Explain what is meant by the phrase 'the invisible computer'

- Evaluate and give examples of Donald Norman's concept of an 'information appliance'.

10.1 Introduction

Typically, when we think of IT, we consider current systems or applications running on desktops or laptops. However, there is much more to information technology than that. For example, the human–computer interface of a website might need to be very different from that of an ATM or a ticket machine – and the range of design issues we consider may be different too.

In this chapter, we look at the different types of technology (hardware and software) that are emerging in today's information society. How will these different technologies be designed so they are useful, usable and accessible?

10.2 Emerging human–computer interface technologies

Desktops and laptops are still the most common forms of individual user systems, but there is an increasing interest in newer forms of hardware. These include:

- **Tablet PCs,** where a digital pen is used to write onto the screen
- **Handheld computers** or **personal digital assistants** (PDAs)
- **Smart phones** that provide a range of powerful new functions, including video messaging and Internet access.

Each form of hardware has different properties and functions. They may all need different interface designs to be usable and accessible. For example, the tablet PC design calls for the effective use of a digital pen. The screen display must support the use of such a pen. Specifically, the contents of the screen cannot be obscured by the use of the pen. Selection of objects by the pen must be designed to be both intuitive and easy.

The personal digital assistant (PDA), while providing a wide range of useful functions, must do so using a relatively small screen. Since the PDA is intended to be portable, the system needs to be designed to be functional without depending on too many peripherals, such as a stylus or digital pen, mini-keyboard, external disk drive or digital camera.

Figure 10.1: Pictures of small screen devices

Issues relating to a small screen and portability apply even more to the smart phone, which usually has a very small screen and is used almost exclusively on a portable basis.

Another type of system that has enjoyed some popularity is the public information kiosk, offering a dedicated information service to members of the public or to specialists. The system often presents difficult design problems, since it is used by people with a wide variety of objectives and levels of skill, experience and ability. Here, the system cannot readily be customised or adapted to the requirements of an individual person, but must be designed in such a way as to be usable and accessible to the greatest number of people.

Figure 10.2: Information kiosks and touch screens
(images courtesy of www.datasonic.co.uk)

All of these systems attempt to provide a large number of useful functions to the maximum of number of people. They are often called 'multipurpose information systems'. Donald Norman, in his book *The Invisible Computer* (1998), argues strongly against this approach. He suggests that such general-purpose information systems (such as the desktop, the laptop and PDA) carry out a large number of useful functions badly. He argues that they are difficult to use because of the inherent complexity of the task of supporting a wide range of functions.

If this complexity is intrinsic to the design of the PC, then simply redesigning the system will not be an effective solution. Instead, Norman predicts, we will move into the age of the 'invisible computer' in which information technology is embedded within appliances that we do not view as computers at all. The standard phone, the washing machine, the vacuum cleaner and the e-mail machine are all examples of single- function appliances, which contain very powerful silicon chips and can carry out complex sequences of actions when required to do so.

Research in this area is known as **pervasive computing** or **ubiquitous computing**, from a phrase first coined by Mark Weiser (1988) who envisioned future computers to be embedded in everyday objects. This research field covers a wide range of topics including distributed computing, mobile computing, sensor networks, human-computer interaction, and artificial intelligence. Around the world there are number of leading research labs and technological organisations with an interest in this area:

- Ubiquitous Computing Research Group at Georgia Institute of Technology
  http://home.cc.gatech.edu/ubicomp
- MIT Media Lab
  http://www.media.mit.edu

- Interactive Workspaces project at Stanford University
  http://iwork.stanford.edu
- The Distributed Systems Group at the ETH Zurich
  http://www.vs.inf.ethz.ch/
- e-World Lab at University of South Australia
  http://e-world.unisa.edu.au/
- Grid and Pervasive Computing Group at University of Southampton
  http://www.gpc.ecs.soton.ac.uk/
- Mobile & Pervasive Computing Lab at University of Florida, Gainesville
  http://www.harris.cise.ufl.edu/

IBM's project *Planet Blue* is largely focused on finding ways to integrate existing technologies with a wireless infrastructure. Carnegie Mellon University's Human Computer Interaction Institute (HCII) is working on similar research called *Project Aura*; their goal is to provide each user with an invisible halo of computing and information services that persists regardless of location. The Massachusetts Institute of Technology (MIT) has a project called *Oxygen,* so-named as MIT envision a future of ubiquitous computing devices as freely available and as easily accessible as oxygen is today.

In practice, however, the world of information technology is not yet dominated by 'invisible' information technology. Although many single-function appliances are now available with advanced information processing, we still see that multi-function systems are still very visible indeed. Will Norman's prediction come true in the future? You may find it useful to take a moment to pause and think about this issue, before you move on.

10.3 The invisible computer

Donald Norman is a leading light in HCI. He edited *User-Centred System Design: New Perspectives on Human–Computer Interaction* (1985), which is still seen as one of the most important books on HCI, even two decades after its publication. Norman has written several other important popularising books about HCI.

In his book *The Invisible Computer*, he presents an argument based on a study of how technology has developed in the past, and therefore predicts how information technology will develop in the future.

- **Good products sometimes fail:** often companies put an awful lot of effort into developing extremely advanced technology or into sophisticated marketing, but their products still fail in the marketplace. No one buys them. Why is this?

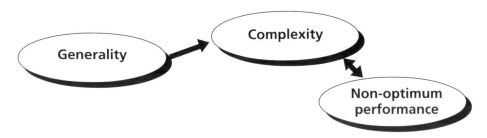

Figure 10.3: Why some products fail: built-in mediocrity

What makes a good product?

If you have invented something new, how can you ensure that it sells? Is it important to get the underlying technology to be as good as possible? Or should you put a lot of effort into a marketing campaign? Or do you need to ensure the usability of your product?

Norman argues that, on their own, none of these factors is sufficient to ensure the success of a product.

Figure 10.4: Why some products succeed

- **Good technology:** In the late 1970s two technologies emerged for recording video data on magnetic tape: Betamax and VHS. Betamax was the first format available, and it is often argued that Betamax was technically superior to VHS. Yet today, VHS is the only format available: Betamax has disappeared from the consumer market.

  So why did VHS win out? The argument usually revolves around Betamax having a clearer picture, higher resolution and better colour. What this does not tell us, however, is how much better Betamax was. In reality, the technical superiority of Betamax could only be detected in the laboratory.

  VHS scored over Betamax in many non-technical ways. VHS tapes provided up to two hours recording time whereas Betamax tapes were only an hour long, which meant that users could record a feature-length film with VHS, but not with Betamax. Furthermore, there were many more pre-recorded films available on VHS than on Betamax, which meant that users were more likely to be able to rent the film they wanted to see if they had a VHS player. So, although the technology of Betamax was superior, users could do what they wanted (record films, see the films they wanted to) more easily with VHS.

- **Good marketing:** Maybe products fail because not enough attention is paid to marketing the product. However, one of the most famous failures of the 'dot com boom' the clothes retailer Boo.com went out of business despite having spent an enormous $30 million on advertising. They created a 'Boo' brand and tried to position themselves in the market as the most trendy and cool place to buy clothes.

  Despite this, users were either simply not interested in buying clothes online, or if they were they were put off by Boo.com's famously over-complicated and slow to download website. A typical user comment was 'The website was very good looking but very slow. The average visit to a site is five minutes, but to get into Boo and reach the chance to buy something took 20-30 minutes.

So we can see that advertising only works if the product being advertised is something that users actually want or can use.

- **Good usability:** In the above two examples we seem to have suggested that what is missing in the case of Betamax and Boo.com was that they were not useful and usable, and therefore failed because of that. So is it the case that good usability guarantees a product's success?

  Unfortunately, good usability is not necessarily a strong selling point. If we consider Microsoft Office, it is the leading product in the market, but it contains many usability problems; simply applying Nielsen's heuristics to an Office application demonstrates this.

  Therefore if Microsoft Office is market leader then usability is not the determining factor in the success of a product.

Norman argues that any one of the above factors (technology, marketing and usability) will not guarantee the success of a product, but that a successful product needs all three. The above diagram should be thought of as a three-legged stool: if a product has good technology, marketing and usability, then it will 'stand up', if it only has two legs (i.e. the technology is bad, but the marketing and usability are good) then it might stand up, but it will be very wobbly. If it has only one leg it is guaranteed to fall down. This three-legged stool has to stand on a solid business case – the product has to be actually needed by its customers, and the customers must be willing to pay the producer more money for it than the producer spends on making it.

Complexity of computers

PCs are general-purpose information technology devices. They try to do everything, but this makes them inherently complicated and difficult to use.

In previous chapters, we have looked at ways of improving usability by understanding users' abilities (cognitive psychology) and what they want to do (task analysis). However, for the PC the task is 'everything' and the users are 'everybody', which makes it almost impossible to make sensible design decisions.

Norman argues that in order to accommodate all these possibilities, we have to design PCs to be far too complex. We typically interact with all these applications through the same physical interfaces of keyboard, mouse and screen, and that can be very restricting. Reading e-mail and modelling the airflow over a wing are two very different tasks. Would you expect to use the same tools for both?

Assume that someone invented a general-purpose piece of clothing – something that could be stretched and pulled and thus used either as a skirt, top, hat, shoes, gloves or trousers. That could be a useful garment: all we would have to do is buy one rather than all those other different garments. The problem is that this general-purpose piece of clothing might not be very comfortable, elegant or easy to slip into.

Norman argues that, because PCs are general purpose, they force us to do things in uncomfortable, inelegant and difficult ways.

A lot of this book has been about ways we can get designers to understand the capabilities and needs of users. The HCI maxim is 'Know your user; understand what they want to do'. But when it comes to designing PCs, who are the users? Everyone! And what do they want to do? Everything! So the HCI maxim becomes impossible to implement: you cannot design a system that does everything for everyone in the most efficient, easy-to-use way.

For example, synthesisers are general-purpose machines for producing sounds; they produce lots of different sounds and do so well. Pianos are single purpose: they produce one type of sound, but they do it excellently.

The early computers were not very powerful – you could only get a few applications to work on them (typically a word processor, spreadsheet and a drawing program). However, those applications could sometimes be easy to use, because they did not try to do everything – they could do very few things but did them well, despite using (by today's standards) slow, inefficient technology.

There is a relationship between generality, complexity and non-optimum performance. Because PCs are general purpose they have to be complex to cope with all the different things we expect them to be able to do – yet this complexity means that they are inherently difficult to use, and therefore will be used inefficiently in a non-optimum way. In general, the less the product offers, the easier it is to use, as shown in figure 10.5.

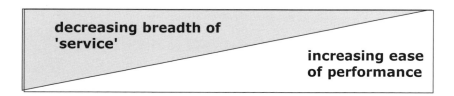

decreasing breadth of 'service'

increasing ease of performance

Figure 10.5: Continuum of complexity

However, it is all very well to criticise computers – but the fact remains that millions of them are sold, therefore they must be fulfilling some needs.

Information appliances are the solution

Norman defines an 'information appliance' as something that does the job of a computer (i.e. processes information) but invisibly and in a much more focused way.

Activity 10.1

Comparing different technologies

A good way of looking at the complexity of technology is to compare what you want to do with how you have to do it.

Let's assume you want to listen to a radio station:

- Write down what you have to do to listen to that radio station on a radio

- Write down what you have to do to listen to a streaming audio version on a PC.

Assume neither your PC nor your radio are switched on when you start.

Compare the two lists of instructions. Which is less complicated and why?

10.4 The technology adoption/innovation diffusion cycle

Whenever a new technology is invented and becomes available, the first people to buy it are, generally, technophiles or early adopters. These sorts of consumers like complexity and the challenge of working out how to use some new technology. By definition, however, technophiles or early adopters are not the mass market. Most people do not like complexity at all and have better things to do than work out how to use technology – they want things to be simple and easy to use. Yet the transition from marketing your product to early adopters, to marketing your product to everyone else, is risky. For example, imagine that the year is 1920 and you have designed a radio that is simple and easy to use. All the technology is hidden.

The current users of radios, who are all early adopters and love their radios with the technology hanging out of the box, will most likely hate your radio. What they want is more and more overt technology. Your radio, however, is going to have to break into a new market of people who want to listen to the radio without fiddling around with rheostats and such like, and leave the old early adopter market behind. This is a brave and big step to take, and if you do not get all three of technology, marketing and usability right, your new radio is likely to fail.

PCs are in much the same situation nowadays. They are still targeted at technophiles and are sold according to how good the technology is: 512MB of memory is better than 256MB, a 2.4GHz processor is better than a 1.2GHz processor. From a user's perspective, however, is this really an improvement? What can you do with a 2.4 GHz machine that you cannot with a 1.2 GHz machine? It sounds as if it's twice as fast – but does it really mean that? Can you do twice as many things with it, twice as fast? In reality, both do the same things – except that one does them marginally faster than the other.

Advertisements for PCs are full of technical specifications – which rarely translate those into things that people can actually do.

Imagine that you are a radical software designer, and you decide to produce simple, easy-to-use word-processing software to compete with Microsoft's Word. Instead of having 1,000 functions, you conduct a user study to determine which word-processing functions users actually need and use. You implement those few functions well. You follow Nielsen's 'aesthetic and minimalist' design heuristic and present those functions through a simple, elegant interface. Who is going to buy your word processing software? Certainly not all the computer experts who love having extra menus and tool palettes with lots of icons and tools. The computer trade magazines will hate it: they will call it trivial, simplistic and a word processing package for idiots.

You have to prove all these people wrong in order to market your software. It is, perhaps, much safer to keep making increasingly complex software for technophiles.

10.5 Information appliances

If PCs are immature information technology, then Norman speculates what a mature information technology will look like. He calls mature information technology 'information appliances' and suggests that they have the following properties:

- **Single purpose:** an information appliance should do only one thing and be specifically designed to just do that one thing well.

  Information appliances should overcome the problems with PCs that we have discussed in this chapter. Because an information appliance is single purpose, it can be designed to do one task, and do that task excellently. We argued that PCs are more complex than they need to be because they are multipurpose. A single-purpose device need only be as complex as the task the user is trying to do

- **Hidden technology:** the underlying technology should be hidden from the user. The user only needs to know what the appliance does, not how it does it.

  If the technology is hidden, users do not need to understand how it works. They can concentrate on what the system does. Most people do not understand how a television works, but this does not stop millions watching them. In a similar way, users should not need to know how an information appliance works, how much memory it has or how fast is its processor

- **Enable free interchange of information:** information technology is all about processing and moving information. Information appliances should make moving information seamless: one information appliance should transfer and accept information from other appliances without the user needing to worry about whether the formats are compatible.

If information appliances allow free interchange of information, it means that data produced by one appliance can be easily transferred to another appliance. The user should not need to worry whether a spreadsheet program can use the output produced by a word-processing program: the computer should be able to work that out and do the translation automatically.

Furthermore, data formats should not be proprietorial. All companies should use the same or interchangeable formats. This means that if you take a photo using a Canon digital camera, you do not need to buy a Canon printer to print out the photo. You can buy any printer and your camera should be able to freely exchange information with the printer

- **Serendipitous flexibility:** free exchange of information also allows users 'serendipitous flexibility'. This means that the users (not the designers) can choose how to put several information appliances together to make a 'new' system.

For example, assume that someone designs a shopping list information appliance. The user keeps the appliance in the kitchen, and every time something is used up in the kitchen they note this down on the gadget. At the end of each week, the gadget prints out a shopping list so that the user can do the shopping and not forget the things they need to buy.

Now assume that supermarkets issue pricing information appliances, which users also keep in their kitchens. These gadgets tell users what is available in the local supermarket, the price of the goods and allow users to order food.

If these two gadgets allow free interchange of information, then it is possible for users to put the two together and build a new gadget that automatically reorders anything that they run out of from the supermarket. The designers of the two gadgets may not have intended users to use them in this way, but this is not the point: the users, not the designers, determine how the gadgets are used.

Early adopters versus late adopters

Write definitions in your own words of the following terms:

- Early adopter
- Late adopter.

Are you a late adopter or an early adopter? Explain why.

Are most people late or early adopters? Explain why.

10.6 Different types of input device

There is a wide range of input device which can be used to enhance the performance of most of the systems previously discussed, from desktop to smart phone. As mentioned, the more portable the device, the fewer the number of additional input devices it can conveniently support. Information can be input from a range of external disk drives or memory storage devices, but the system must be able to both represent the presence of such devices and depict any information input from them in such a way as to make that information useful, usable and accessible.

Keyboards

The traditional keyboard is being offered in many guises, and also supplemented by alternatives such as the mini-keyboard (convenient but difficult to use?), the ergonomic keyboard (shaped to be easier to use) and the on-screen keyboard for people who have limited hand movement (through disability or limitations in their working environment). Such on-screen keyboards can be controlled by a pointing device such as a mouse or by voice-activated commands.

The mouse

The mouse is a familiar example of the range of pointing devices now available. The optical mouse is increasingly replacing the mechanical mouse; it has no moving parts and uses sensors to detect movement. It tends to be more sensitive and may be easier to use. Of course, the mouse cord is often a nuisance, so there is increasing use of a cordless mouse, where the signal to the host machine is by radio waves or by infrared ligh However, if you use a cordless mouse, be careful not to lose it!

If you are among the ten percent of the population who are left-handed you can adjust your mouse settings to suit. Although a mouse seems to be an innocent-enough device, there is some evidence that prolonged use can result in repetitive strain injury (RSI).

Trackballs, touchpads and pointing sticks

The trackball is increasingly popular, particularly with users with limited manual dexterity. A trackball is rather like an upside-down mouse, where the ball is in contact with the palm of your hand. The touchpad is another alternative to the mouse. As a flat, rectangular shape inset into the keyboard, particularly on laptops, it is sensitive to touch and movement. It may also imitate mouse click actions.

Figure 10.6a: Computer devices (not to scale)
(Images courtesy of Logitech **www.logitech.com**)

The pointing stick is a small, stick-like item usually set in the middle of a keyboard. It responds to pressure to move the cursor and is used in combination with the additional buttons on the keyboard. Perhaps difficult to use at first, it dispenses with the mouse and can be more convenient in experienced hands.

Joysticks and wheels

Computer game players ('gamers') will be familiar with the joystick and wheel, or the game controls of devices such as the PlayStation. They are much more suited to rapid response tasks (such as action games, driving or fight sequences) than the keyboard or mouse. Even a trackball or touchpad would not be suitable. Imagine trying to drive a real car with a trackball or touchpad rather than a steering wheel.

Light pen

A light pen is used to select items on a screen by pressing the end of the pen to the screen (some pens may require a special monitor, some not). It is particularly useful when the systems in use are predominantly menu- or icon-based, where desk space is limited, where health professionals do not want to get contamination onto their hands or where staff work with chemicals which could damage a computer.

Digital pen and graphics tablet

A digital pen is often used with a graphics tablet – a flat, rectangular electronic board. Architects and graphic artists use them to produce designs or drawings. Such input devices are often intuitively acceptable but are, of course, no substitute for artistic ability.

Figure 10.6b: Computer devices (not to scale)
(Images courtesy of Logitech **www.logitech.com**)

Touch screen

A touch screen is an option often found in information kiosks in public places (such as airports, libraries, museums, universities and shopping malls) as seen in Figure 10.2. The advantage is that they do not require the individual to be familiar with specific input devices. People simply touch the screen as necessary. Conversely, they do require a lot of hand and arm movement. This can be a disadvantage for tasks that require a large amount of data input or where people have limited psychomotor abilities. Positioning height is a consideration, to ensure that they are accessible to users in wheelchairs or young people.

Voice input, audio input

Voice input is an important alternative to keyboard input – though in appropriate circumstances only. We have all experienced the individual with a mobile phone and very loud voice on trains or buses. The thought of someone sitting on a train talking to their laptop is simply too awful to contemplate!

Other settings and tasks, however, may be much more suitable for voice input. Individuals working on phone-based activities may benefit from voice input. It may also be beneficial if someone has psychomotor disabilities, or severe dyslexia, thereby making the use of a keyboard problematic.

Where voice recognition software is used, a good-quality microphone is essential. The software possesses a pre-set of existing words, but for additional words it will still need to be trained to accept your voice. Most software of this kind now accepts continuous speech – so you no longer need to separate each word with a pause. Even so, word recognition software is only 90-95% accurate. Although this sounds good, on a typical page such as this, with around 280 words, there would be 14 errors – assuming a 95% accuracy rate. On the same basis, in the complete chapter (which contains around 6,000 words) there would be 300 words containing an error.

Clearly, voice recognition software has both disadvantages and benefits. Careful system design is vital to get the best balance. It is apparent, however, that voice input/voice recognition is the way of the future for the personal use of information technology.

Voice input is a subset of audio input. This is also a growth area for effective system design. Systems with suitable sound cards can take high-quality auditory input from microphones, tape players, CD / DVD players, radio or television.

Other input devices

A number of methods have been developed to overcome the challenges of using handheld computers or PDAs. In addition to the stylus (the main input device for PDAs) and portable keyboards, voice input is increasingly popular. The virtual keyboard can be a usable approach for certain users and tasks. This produces an infrared image projected onto any flat service. As the person 'types' on the keyboard, the resulting data is transferred to the PDA by a receiver. This is a powerful method for mobile users.

If you want to look in more depth at input devices, you should also consider digital cameras, webcams, video-conferencing, scanners, optical character recognition (OCR), barcode scanners, terminals and specialist data collection input systems.

Finally, for security and other reasons, there is considerable interest in biometric data input. Mainly seen at airports and major businesses, such inputs can now include fingerprint scanners, face recognition, voice verification, signature verification and smart cards that store biometric information.

10.7 Output devices

We are accustomed to dealing with output in terms of the information on a PC screen or printed on paper, but there are now so many more ways to provide output from a system.

- **Screens:** cathode ray tube (CRT) monitors have been subject to a considerable amount of research to determine the most user-friendly ways of working in terms of posture and perception. Flat FST and plasma screens are becoming more popular and are now considered both space-saving and less taxing on the eyes

- **eBooks:** these (as seen on Star Trek) are another mobile device that can download a text from the Web and present it on a small but conveniently sized screen
- **Electronic paper:** a fascinating new type of output device is 'electronic paper' currently being developed at the Palo Alto Research Center
- **Interactive television:** the television is a familiar fixture in most homes these days, with many people owning multiple sets. Interactive television is perhaps an example of Donald Norman's idea of the 'invisible computer'. There is both local and remote information processing capacity in most such systems, but we are not strongly aware of it: to us it is just a TV.

  Interactive TV is very different from the conventional PC. First, people sit at a distance, not up close. Screen designs need to reflect this fact. Second, since television viewing is usually a social event, it cannot be treated in the same way as a solitary person sitting in front of a PC. Third, TV is seen as entertainment rather than work. For these reasons, interactive television needs to be treated differently. Screens cannot be packed with information, different metaphors need to be used and more appropriate ways of interacting with the system selected

- **Self-monitoring systems:** although we think of systems as being under our control at all times, there are circumstances where we would want a system in a hostile environment to be able to detect when it has been damaged and be able to take steps to repair itself. Think, for example, of a moon rover craft exploring the surface of the moon. What happens if it is damaged? Ideally, it would be capable of repairing itself.

  Similarly with ICT systems. For example, when an operating system is attacked by a new computer virus, it probably needs a very rapid response if it is not to sustain damage. The question here is: 'What are the HCI design implications and how can we make these systems usable?'. At first sight, it looks as if we are taking the human out of the loop, although in practice the people are simply being involved in a different way.

  Modern networked computer systems frequently have protection systems, which hold a reserve of power together with software to allow a system to be elegantly closed down in the event of a power failure, and RAID (redundant array of inexpensive disks) devices which allow for duplication of data and an automated switchover in the event of any hardware failure.

  Perhaps the key question is: 'How can such systems be designed to be self-monitoring and self-repairing without making them impossible to use or dangerous to deploy?'

10.8 Summary

Clearly, there is a vast proliferation of input and output devices, which not only create new options for designers, but also create new challenges for system and interface design. These devices now differ so significantly from each other that they may often need different design solutions if they are to be sufficiently useful, usable and accessible.

References

Dourish P, (2004), What We Talk About When We Talk About Context, *Personal and Ubiquitous Computing*, 8(1), 19-30.

Norman, DA & Draper, SW, (Ed.), (1986), *User-centered system design*, Hillsdale, NJ: Lawrence Erlbaum Associates.

Norman D, (1999), *The invisible computer*, Cambridge, MA: MIT Press

Weiser M, (1991), The Computer for the 21st Century, *Scientific American*, Vol. 265, No. 3, September, 94-104

10.9 Review questions

Question 10.1   Fill in the blanks:

_____1 argues that for a product to be successful, primarily it must have a sound _____2. This means that people must actually want to buy the product and are willing to pay more for it than it costs to _____3 and distribute. However Norman also argues that _____4 other properties must be fulfilled in order to ensure success of a product, they are: good_____5, good _____6 and good _____7.

Norman illustrates his argument by showing that some products, despite having good _____8 , were not successful in the marketplace, because they failed in their marketing or usability. Norman argues that having all three properties _____9 success, but that a product with _____10 out of three of the properties may succeed, but this is not guaranteed.

Question 10.2   Fill in the blanks:

Norman's definition of an '_____1' is a gadget for which:

- the technology is _____2

- there is a _____ _____3

- the _____ _____4 of information is possible.

The first two properties of an information appliance mean that they overcome most of the problems with _____5. If the technology is hidden, users do not have to understand _____6 a system works in order to understand _____7 it does. If the gadget is single purpose, it can be designed to do its single task _____8. The third property means that several information appliances can be used in concert together to effectively create _____ _____9. How this is done is up to the user, not dictated by the designer. Norman describes this property as '_____10'.

10.8 Answers to review questions

Answer to question 10.1

1 Norman	2 business case	3 make	
4 three	5 technology	6 marketing	
7 usability	8 technology	9 ensures	10 two

Answer to question 10.2

1 information appliance	2 hidden	3 single purpose
4 free interchange	5 PCs	6 how
7 what	8 excellently	9 new appliances
10 serendipitous flexibility		

10.10 Feedback on activities

Feedback on activity 10.1: Comparing different technologies Your answer will be dependent on your particular hardware and software, but here is one example.

Listening to a radio station on a radio:

1. Switch on radio.

2. Press button corresponding to station you want to listen to *or* adjuster tuning dial controller until you find the station you wish to listen to

3. Listen.

(Note also that most people only listen to their one favourite radio station and leave their radio tuned to that station. So in most cases step 2 can be omitted.)

Listening to streaming audio radio on your PC:

1. Switch on PC.

2. Wait while PC boots up (1 – 3 minutes).

3. Press the 'Start' button, then select a web browser.

4. Wait for browser program to start.

5. Select web page of your radio station from Favourites menu.

6. Wait for page to download and display.

7. Click on 'Listen live' link.

8. Wait for plug-in to load up.

9. Wait for station to be buffered.

10. Listen.

(Note that we have omitted any reference to downloading the appropriate plug-in and setting it up for your Internet connection speed ...)

Clearly using the radio is quicker and less fuss. In fact, it is so little fuss that we do not even think about doing it. In this case, how we do something ('switch on radio, listen') is as simple as what we want to do ('listen to a radio station').

In the case of the PC, how we listen to the radio is much more complicated than what we want to do. The reason for this is simple: the radio only does one thing and therefore makes the doing of that one thing very simple and straightforward. The PC does hundreds of things and therefore has to be more complicated.

In this chapter we will continue making this argument: that PCs make things more complicated than they need to be and that some future ideal will be to simplify things according to the required task.

Think about some other tasks you might want to do on your PC and compare what you want to do with how you have to do it. Maybe you've found an interesting picture on the Internet and you want to put a copy of it (properly credited, of course) in your lab exercises.

What you want to do is simple; it can be described in one or two lines of text. Can you find anything on your PC where how you do something is as simple as what you want to do?

Feedback on activity 10.2: Early adopters vs late adopters (Remember we asked for these in your own words. Just copying a glossary or dictionary definition does not show you understand the definition, only that you can copy it.)

- Early adopter: someone who buys technology for the sake of having the latest technology. Whether the technology is actually useful or reasonably priced is irrelevant to them. The important thing is having the latest technology

- Late adopter: someone who does not care about technology, but only buys a product if it actually does something useful for them and it is reasonably priced. How good the technology is in a product is not important to them. What is important is whether it is easy to use and looks good.

Whether you are an early adopter is entirely up to you. Most computing students are early adopters, because they would not be doing a computing course if they were not interested in technology.

Most people are late adopters. Most people do not care about technology and only buy a technology if it is clearly useful to them.

CHAPTER 11

Universal access and 'design for all'

OVERVIEW

All products exclude some users, often unnecessarily. In this chapter, we look at different approaches, methods and practices for the design of interactive systems that can be used by anyone, anytime, anywhere.

The different approaches have much in common, even if they are known by different names in the US and Europe. Universal access, for example, refers to system designs that can be used by anyone, anytime, anywhere. In Europe, the term 'design for all' has a similar meaning. It indicates a system design that can be used by all users, regardless of their strengths and weaknesses, their level of expertise, disabilities and environments.

Learning outcomes   At the end of this chapter you should be able to:

- Describe and distinguish between accessibility and usability

- Describe common accessibility and usability issues in website design

- Evaluate the accessibility and usability of a website or other interactive product.

11.1 Introduction

In this chapter we look at different approaches, methods and practices for the design of interactive systems that can be used by anyone, anytime, anywhere.

The different approaches have much in common, even if they are known by different names in different parts of the world. In America, for instance, the term **universal access** refers to system designs that can be used by anyone, anytime, anywhere.

Universal design, which we consider below, is defined as:

> ... the design of products and environments to be usable by all people, to the greatest extent possible, without the need for adaptation or specialised design.

In Europe, the term **design for all** has a similar meaning. It indicates a system design that can be used by all users, regardless of their strengths and weaknesses, their level of expertise, disabilities and environments.

Overall, the different approaches share a common purpose of simplifying life for everyone by making products, communications and the built environment more usable by as many people as possible.

11.2 Universal design ('design for all')

Universal design (or 'design for all') is an inclusive and hands-on approach which aims to accommodate diversity in the users, applications and services. The requirement for universal design stems from the impact of emerging technologies and the different dimensions of diversity intrinsic to the information society – as well the cultural diversity between and within different countries.

The following 'Principles of Universal Design' can be found at the website of the Center for Universal Design, North Carolina State University: **www.design.ncsu.edu/cud**

The authors are a working group of architects, product designers, engineers and environmental design researchers who collaborated to establish these principles to guide a wide range of design disciplines, including environmental, product and communication design. These seven principles can be applied to evaluate existing designs, guide the design process and educate both designers and consumers about the characteristics of more usable products and environments.

---

1 EQUITABLE USE

The design is useful and marketable to people with diverse abilities

Guidelines:

- Provide the same means of use for all users; identical whenever possible; equivalent when not
- Avoid segregating or stigmatising any users
- Make provisions for privacy, security and safety equally available to all users
- Make the design appealing to all users.

---

2 FLEXIBILITY IN USE

The design accommodates a wide range of individual preferences and abilities

Guidelines:

- Provide choice in methods of use
- Accommodate right- or left-handed access and use
- Facilitate the user's accuracy and precision
- Provide adaptability to the user's pace.

3 SIMPLE AND INTUITIVE USE

Use of the design is easy to understand, regardless of the user's experience, knowledge, language skills or current concentration level

Guidelines:

- Eliminate unnecessary complexity
- Be consistent with user expectations and intuition
- Accommodate a wide range of literacy and language skills
- Provide effective prompts and feedback during and after task completion.

4 PERCEPTIBLE INFORMATION

The design communicates necessary information effectively to the user, regardless of ambient conditions or the user's sensory abilities

Guidelines:

- Use different modes (pictorial, verbal, tactile) for redundant presentation of essential information
- Maximise 'legibility' of essential information
- Differentiate elements in ways that can be described (i.e. make it easy to give instructions or directions)
- Provide compatibility with a variety of techniques or devices used by people with sensory limitations.

5 TOLERANCE FOR ERROR

The design minimises hazards and the adverse consequences of accidental or unintended actions

Guidelines:

- Arrange elements to minimise hazards and errors: most used elements, most accessible; hazardous elements eliminated, isolated, or shielded
- Provide warnings of hazards and errors
- Provide fail-safe features
- Discourage unconscious action in tasks that require vigilance.

6 LOW PHYSICAL EFFORT

The design can be used efficiently and comfortably and with a minimum of fatigue

Guidelines:

- Allow user to maintain a neutral body position
- Use reasonable operating forces
- Minimise repetitive actions
- Minimise sustained physical effort.

7 SIZE AND SPACE FOR APPROACH AND USE

Appropriate size and space is provided for approach, reach, manipulation and use, regardless of user's body size, posture or mobility

Guidelines:

- Provide a clear line of sight to important elements for any seated or standing user
- Make reach to all components comfortable for any seated or standing user
- Accommodate variations in hand and grip size
- Provide adequate space for use of assistive devices or personal assistance.

Principles © 1997 NC State University, The Center for Universal Design

---

Activity 11.1

Testing websites' accessibility

You will require computer and Internet access for this activity, which invites you to see how accessible certain websites are.

Assessing standards

There are several standards bodies that aim to provide standards for design for all – which means there are a number of different sets of standards, including different systems for Europe and the US.

There are also guidelines and toolkits for evaluating website accessibility. Check out the *Web Content Accessibility Guidelines 2.0*, available at: **www.w3.org**

One such automated toolkit is *Bobby*, available at **www.watchfire .com**

11.3 Inclusive design

All products exclude some users, often unnecessarily. Inclusive design (an umbrella term for the broad collection of approaches, methods and practices for designing inclusively) aims to highlight and reduce such exclusion. As we have seen, the Center for Universal Design at North Carolina State University defines *universal design* as the design of products and environments to be usable by all people, to the greatest extent possible, without the need for adaptation or specialised design. The main purpose of universal design is to simplify life for everyone by making products, communications and environment usable by as many people as possible at little or no extra cost. Universal design benefits people of all ages and abilities.

In Europe, the term *design for all* has a similar meaning to universal design. However, the definition of inclusive design includes the concept of 'reasonable'. It refers to the design of mainstream products and services that are accessible to, and usable by, as many people as reasonably possible on a global basis, in a wide variety of situations and to the greatest extent possible without the need for special adaptation or specialised design.

Poor inclusive design

Regrettably, examples of poor inclusive design are everywhere. Many products present unnecessary difficulties for many users and thus they are often 'disabled by design'. When you look closely at everyday products, you will quickly begin to notice where people may have difficulties using them. Many of those difficulties will be caused by design decisions made without considering the user. As such, their causes are often trivial – but, fortunately, the solution may often be trivial as well. For example, if a button is difficult to operate because it is too small, then replace it with a larger one. The following pictures are typical examples of this.

A typical household's collection of remote controllers - all looking very different!

Helpful colour coding of sockets *and* connectors

The control on the left clearly has a 'top' and a 'bottom'; not so the one on the right

Keyboard and mouse connections - colour coded, but it might have been better to have the symbols *alongside* the sockets.

Is the coffee machine 'on' when the shaded bar is out – or pressed down?

Figure 11.1: Good and bad design examples

Solutions that are more inclusive may be inherently more usable and accessible As we have just seen, products do not necessarily need major revisions to improve them. Often just a little early thought and common sense are all that is required.

Universal access refers to practically applying principles, methods and tools of universal design in order to develop information society technologies that are accessible and usable by all citizens, including the very young and the elderly as well as people with different types of disability, without the need for a posteriori adaptations or specialised design. Universal access in the information society signifies the right of all citizens to obtain equitable access to, and maintain effective interaction with, a community-wide pool of information resources and artefacts.

The requirements for universal access and quality in use for the broadest possible user population progressively merge into first-order objectives for an 'Information Society for All'.

11.4 Accessibility

Accessibility is about design for everyone. It is about making the information and services that you provide online available to users, irrespective of age and ability.

An accessible system design ensures that system functions can be accessed by users with disabilities or those working in extreme circumstances.

Web accessibility

The Royal National Institute of the Blind (RNIB) is the UK's leading charity, offering information, support and advice to over two million people with sight problems. In the RNIB's view, an accessible website design means that:

> ... the design enables all users to access, no matter whether they need to change the colour and text settings inherent with their browser, or whether they are using access technology such as magnification, screen readers or Braille display to access. An accessible website displays all parts of the website and all the functions and information as is available to sighted users. A site may be accessible but still unusable because it is not a satisfactory experience or is simply too tedious or difficult to work through.

See **www.rnib.org.uk/webaccesscentre** for further information.

Examples of poor accessibility

Many visually impaired users have a screen resolution of 640 x 480, so, if the page layout is not fluid, parts of the screen can be virtually inaccessible. This can happen, for instance, if the page is designed for a 1024 x 768 screen with table measurements in absolute pixel sizes.

On the next pages are representations of a multi-column table at a fixed width of 1,000 pixels, seen at screen resolutions of 1024 x 768, 800 x 600, and 640 x 480.

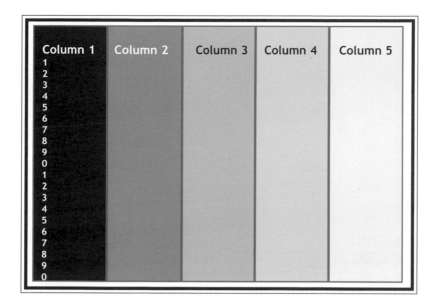

Figure 11.2 Representation of a 5-column table, 1024 x 768

Table width 1,000 pixels, screen resolution 1024 x 768. All columns are visible.

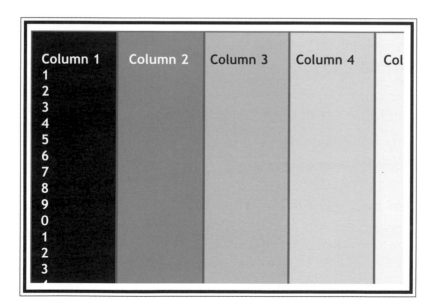

Figure 11.3: Representation of a 5-column table, 800 x 600

Table width 1,000 pixels, and commonly used screen resolution of 800 x 600. Column five is no longer visible without horizontal scrolling, and some depth has been lost, necessitating vertical scrolling.

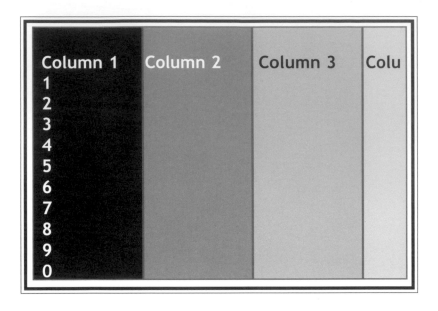

Figure 11.4: Representation of a 5-column table, 640 x 480

Table width 1,000 pixels, screen resolution 640 x 480, as used by many visually impaired people. Only three columns are now (partially) visible; horizontal and vertical scrolling is necessary.

By using percentage measurements for the table layout, a page can be made to fit whatever screen resolution is being used.

Activity 11.2

Activity 11.2: Seven principles of universal design

For this activity, select one of the following products to carry out an evaluation to see if it accommodates the seven principles of universal design satisfactorily.

- Television

- DVD player

- Mobile phone.

What design features do you like? What features do you dislike?

Make a list of:

- All the problems that you encountered

- The design features that you like or dislike.

Examples of accessibility problems

If a website has not been designed to accommodate flexibility, use of access technology such as magnification, screen readers or Braille display can cause a number of problems. Here are some problems related to accessibility outlined by RNIB:

- Some websites only fix the background colour and leave the text colour to default. If the user changes colours without setting their web browser's *Accessibility options* to *Ignore Colours*, a very poor colour combination can result – or text may even 'disappear' altogether

- Sometimes developers assume that a particular font and font size will be used, and put text in frames with no scroll bars. This is fine if all the text fits into the frame but users will be unable to use the site properly if their screen resolution is set differently or text size is increased as, without scroll bars, they won't be able to get to it

- Forgetting to include alternative text descriptions for images, graphical links or buttons so that they are accessible to visually impaired users who are using a screen reader.

11.5 Usability

In general terms, a usable system design is one which ensures that the functions are presented in such a way that they can be used by users.

Usability is defined by the International Standards Organisation (ISO) as

> ... the effectiveness, efficiency and satisfaction with which specified users achieve specified goals in particular environments.

If a user is unable to find what they want within a reasonable time, then your site needs to be re-examined. Usability is a huge subject and there are plenty of resources dedicated to this topic. Jakob Nielsen's website, for example, is very useful: **www.useit.com**

Examples of poor usability

Here are some of the most common usability errors:

- **Not using the title tag:** this tag goes inside the <head> tag and can be a full description of the page. It is also picked up by search engines, so helps all users to find your site. The title is the first thing that a screen reader 'reads' and so the user quickly finds out if they are on the right page without wasting too much time

- **Using <blockquote> to create an indent:** some screen readers read out the underlying code; this can make the page tedious to listen to.

User diversity

In user-centred design, the role of the user is central. In traditional methods like Waterfall, however, the emphasis is more upon the technology and on signing off individual stages in the design process.

The user has a role at each stage of user-centred design. Task analysis, for example, involves the user in carrying out the tasks that the new system is intended to support; and the requirements specification forms the basis for the development and evaluation of a prototype system by the users.

However, user-centred design may not always pay sufficient attention to user diversity. There is a natural tendency to look for evidence in favour of a design, perhaps with too small a sample of users.

There is also a tendency for design to be aimed at a 'typical user', which is very convenient when hoping to produce only one system design. Yet designing for a typical user is not only to risk loss of market share, but also reduced levels of user satisfaction because of a poor fit between user needs and design.

In the real world, there is considerable variance within a group of users. This variance should be taken into account: either by providing a wider range of designs ('design for all') or by providing alternative means of access to the new system (e.g. 'universal access'). These solutions can be supported by the judicious use of adaptable and adaptive systems to provide greater variance in the design solutions available. Moreover, as users become more expert in the use of a system, they will need faster methods with which to access the features of that system. Experienced users tend to prefer shortcuts such as keyboard commands, rather than working through a set of menus.

Another aspect is ageing. As people get older, they tend to accumulate minor disabilities, including:

- **Sensory problems** (vision or hearing),
- **Cognitive difficulties** (perception, concentration or memory)
- **Psychomotor skill deficiencies** (hand or arm movement or posture).

Overall, many designers assume that users form a single group, whereas it seems more likely that there will be distinct groups of users within the population. Finally, designing for groups of users may not be enough. There must also be provision for individuals with special needs.

User modelling

Capturing the diversity and variability of users in system design is at the same time a difficult and a vital task. Without diversity, initial production costs are low; with diversity in design, production costs are higher – but so may be profits. An appreciation of user diversity can be:

- **Ad hoc**
- **Systematic.**

We can respond passively to user differences or seek to understand user diversity on a systematic basis by means of a user modelling framework. Examples of user modelling frameworks that are clear and powerful include Simplex and MHP . These were discussed in Chapters 3 and 7 respectively.

11.6 Summary

In this chapter, we have looked at different approaches, methods and practices for the design of interactive systems that can be used by anyone, anytime, anywhere.

We have focused on accessibility and usability. We have reviewed specific examples of poor accessibility and usability and discussed how they might be improved.

As we have seen, the different approaches share the common purpose of making interactive systems, products, communications and the built environment accessible to and usable by everyone.

References and further reading

Bobby (automated toolkit), available at **www.watchfire .com**

Jakob Nielsen's website: **www.useit.com**

The Center for Universal Design (1997), *The Principles of Universal Design*, Version 2.0, Raleigh, NC: North Carolina State University

Royal National Institute of the Blind (RNIB): **www.rnib.org.uk**

Web Content Accessibility Guidelines 2.0, available at: **www.w3.org**

11.7 Review questions

 **Question 11.1**   The population is getting older, we are living longer, and these trends are due to continue. How do you see the future of inclusive design and its counterparts such as universal design? What is going to affect companies' design practices?

Question 11.2   Is there a gap between usability and accessibility?

11.8 Answers to review questions

Answer to question 11.1   Companies will have to change their design practices to reflect the changing nature of their consumers. Ultimately, inclusive design issues will become so ingrained in the design process that they are an automatic element of the design requirements and regarded as inherent activities.

Answer to question 11.2   Generally, usability is often regarded as a specialist activity. Current usability techniques provide methods for developing usable systems for specified users. However, they are severely limited in their suitability for design accessibility.

11.9 Feedback on activities

Feedback on activity 11.1: Testing websites' accessibility   Check first to see if your web authoring tool or the program developer's website can check for valid code and accessibility. Ensuring that HTML and any coding such as CSS is correct aids accessibility (**http://www.w3.org**) Try any or all of the following:

- Change your browser colours – for example, white font on black background, and then change Internet options (from the Tools menu), followed by checking boxes in Accessibility options (e.g. *ignore page colours, ignore font styles* and *ignore text sizes)*

- Change your screen resolution to 1024 x 786 | 800 x 600 | 640 x 480. Many partially sighted people use a 640 x 480 screen size (to be able to this go to your computer's control panel, then select *display option* and then finally select *Settings*)

- Change your computer display settings options (e.g. to *large, high contrast white* or *yellow on black)*

- Disable frames if your site uses them

- Try greyscale – or print the pages in black and white – to see if the contrast between colours is sufficient to distinguish elements

- If your browser allows it, try using your own stylesheet.

During this test you may put the following questions to yourself:

1. Does the site still make sense and does it still function as planned?

2. Is the structure consistent and therefore predictable?

3. Is the navigation intuitive?

4. Has any information been lost?

5. Is there good colour contrast?

6. Are all parts of the site accessible?

7. Do all visual elements have appropriate *alt text* and full descriptions if necessary?

Feedback on activity 11.2: Seven principles of universal design: The design of products and environments to be usable by all people, to the greatest extent possible, without the need for adaptation or specialised design.

- **Equitable use:** the design is useful and marketable to people with diverse abilities

- **Flexibility in use**: the design accommodates a wide range of individual preferences and abilities

- **Simple and intuitive use**: use of the design is easy to understand, regardless of the user's experience, knowledge, language skills, or current concentration level

- **Perceptible information:** the design communicates necessary information effectively to the user, regardless of ambient conditions or the user's sensory abilities

- **Tolerance for error:** the design minimises hazards and the adverse consequences of accidental or unintended actions

- **Low physical effort:** the design can be used efficiently and comfortably and with a minimum of fatigue

- **Size and space for approach and use:** appropriate size and space is provided for approach, reach, manipulation and use, regardless of user's body size, posture, or mobility.

CHAPTER 12

Review

OVERVIEW

HCI is a rich and broad academic field, with an attendant growth in employment opportunities. It brings together theory and practice: not only from computing science, but also from the human sciences such as psychology and sociology.

The aim of this book has been to introduce you to the fundamental and exciting area of human–computer interaction (HCI), and also to prepare you for more advanced work in HCI.

| **Learning outcomes** | At the end of this chapter you should be able to: |

- Recall and review the main issues we have addressed in this book.

12.1   Introduction

The aim of this introductory book in human–computer interaction (HCI) has been to give you an insight into this dynamic field, starting with theoretical concepts as a foundation upon which to build practical skills in analysing and designing interactive systems.

We have discussed a number of reasons, both theoretical and practical, as to why HCI is a worthwhile field of study:

- HCI provides a context in which to consider user-centred system design (UCSD) methods. We often encounter systems that are badly designed, that do not consider the needs of users or which are difficult to use without substantial training. As users become more selective in their choices of software, there is an increasing emphasis on usability

- HCI provides a basis on which to evaluate the efficiency and effectiveness of design methods. The art of system design is more than just a collection of methods: systematic ways of evaluating those methods are also required

- HCI provides a real-world environment in which to develop new theories of user psychology. It provides a test ground for existing theories, and the data for developing new theories

- HCI is one of the fastest-growing areas of employment in computing science.

In this review chapter we revisit the various chapters and bring together the various strands of HCI; we also provide a glossary of the most important terms that have been introduced. There are four activities which, at this stage, do not attract any feedback; they have been included to give you practical issues to consider in the light of your completed study of the subject.

12.2   HCI: what it is and why it is important

We have reviewed a wide range of interactive systems in the case studies and activities in this book. Together, we have explored how to:

- Look at interactive systems from a user's point of view
- Systematically analyse the usability and accessibility of existing systems
- Design and construct systems that are useful, usable and accessible
- Evaluate different design options
- Argue convincingly for the viability of constructing easier-to-use systems.

The challenge has been to encourage critical and inventive thinking about how people use interactive systems, including computers, to support what they do.

We defined an interactive system broadly as any technology-based system that requires interaction with users. So we've considered a ticket machine, a money-dispensing machine (ATM), a central heating or air conditioning control to be interactive systems – as is a calculator, a word processor or spreadsheet or a website.

We argued that interactive systems are frequently not designed with the user in mind. We discussed why this is so – and some of the consequences. For example, in Chapter 1, we proposed that the issue with the ticket machine we examined was not so much that it was poorly designed, but why.

If we could answer that question, we suggested that we have a good chance of answering the follow-on question: 'How can we ensure interactive systems are better designed?'

In fact, for many of the examples we have looked at, the fundamental questions are:

- What is wrong with this system?
- Why?
- How can we redesign it to make it more useful, usable and accessible to a diversity of potential users?

12.3 Interactive system design and natural computing

Early in this book, in Chapter 2, our inquiry led us to the emerging research field of natural computing.

Natural computing – or natural computation – is the study of how people process and store information, manipulate symbols, ascribe personal values to events, attribute cultural and emotive judgements and so on – and how we use interactive artefacts such as personal digital assistants (PDAs) or mobile phones to enhance our lives.

What insights were there to be gained – and how might they be applicable in the context of interactive system design?

The main idea of natural computing is that people are naturally capable of processing information. It is a natural process for us: it is how we have survived as a species. The relevance of natural computing is that it provides us with three perspectives:

- **The user's perspective:** natural computing provides us with a conceptual framework within which to address the issues of user modelling
- **The designer's perspective:** if we have a better understanding of human information processing, then we will be more able to develop interactive system designs that support users in their activities
- **The sustainability perspective:** as a species, we have learned to make use of tools, artefacts and systems to increase our chances of survival. The need for well-designed systems is no mere luxury: it is a necessity. Thus, the link between the user perspective and the designer perspective is motivated by the human need to create artefacts that support our strengths and weaknesses, our activities and the achievement of our objectives.

12.4 User modelling and user-centred system design

One approach that is congruent with natural computing is user-centred system design (UCSD), which places the user, their needs, goals and activities at the centre of the design process.

The question we asked in Chapter 3 was:

- How do we understand – or model – the live, flesh-and-blood people who use our systems?

We argued that what's needed is a psychologically valid way of representing those users that includes their cognitive processes, individual differences, social context, needs and preferences, internalised cultural factors and lifestyle, and task objectives.

We showed that there are several ways of constructing a user model, discussing the strengths and weaknesses of each in turn.

- One way is to take a well-established psychological theory. In cognitive science, for example, there are a number of powerful models to choose from. Examples are Broadbent's groundbreaking Maltese Cross model and Barnard's Interacting Cognitive Subsystems (ICS)

- A second way is to do a task analysis, the idea being that this will lead on to a consideration of how users will undertake those tasks. We looked at task analysis in Chapter 5
- Another way is to use a cut-down psychological theory such as the Model Human Processor (MHP).

Or we can combine these in a hybrid way, using a simplistic model. Such a model seeks to systematically combine the benefits of the three methods above. In this book, we have focused on Simplex One and Simplex Two as representative of current simplistic models, particularly in Chapters 3 and 7.

12.5 The user-centred system design process

UCSD places users, their needs, goals and activities at the centre of the design process. In so doing, we suggested, we need to rethink traditional development processes, which are often too sequential and rigid.

Traditional methods – which we characterised as the 'Waterfall' model – tend to have a technology focus. The requirements, preferences and training needs of users are overlooked and the user interface is often designed around a technical view of how systems work. Part of the problem, we argued, lies with the processes by which systems are developed.

In contrast, UCSD is informed by a three-phase cycle of requirements gathering, prototype design and evaluation in which we:

- Analyse users and their world
- Storyboard or prototype design ideas
- Evaluate to ensure the design works well for users – and iterate again.

However, while the UCSD process focuses on the user, it often stops short at groups of typical users rather than the individual. Good design practice allows – if not mandates – customisation to meet the needs and preferences of individuals, particularly those with limited sight, hearing or physical mobility.

Activity 12.1

Chocs away! Evaluating the design of a chocolate machine

On the next page is the design for a chocolate dispensing machine: the machine dispenses several different types of chocolate. The user can either select a chocolate from the panel and then feed coins into a slot; or can feed in coins first and then select a chocolate.

The user can keep on feeding in money and (assuming an endless supply of chocolate, money, electricity and teeth) continue selecting chocolates for ever. Once the user has finished, they can press a button and any unspent money will be returned.

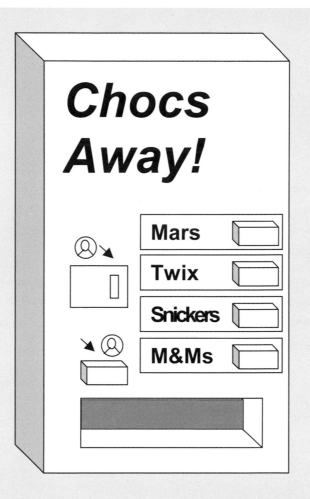

How does the chocolate machine measure up against Nielsen's usability heuristics?

For instance:

- Visibility of system status
- Match between system and real world
- Error prevention
- Flexibility and efficiency of use
- Aesthetic and minimalist design.

Can you improve on the design of the machine? If you can, why is your design better?

12.6 Task analysis

We identified hierarchical task analysis (HTA) as a method useful in many, if not all, settings. We noted, however, that there are other ways of doing task analysis and other notations that may be more appropriate in certain contexts.

The purpose of a task analysis is primarily to establish requirements: to help designers understand existing systems, job roles, tasks and necessary skills. We saw, however, that task analysis can also be useful in the design and development of new systems. For example, we can use task analysis to ask 'What if?' questions:

- Could this task be done more efficiently or effectively?
- If so, could the existing technical system still support it?
- What usability issues might be encountered?
- What errors might arise in the proposed task design?
- How can we error-proof the new design? (Think of the sequencing of sub-tasks when you use a bank's money-dispensing machine.)

12.7 Requirements gathering, storyboarding and prototyping

As we have seen, task analysis is a key aspect of requirements gathering, but we also need to know about the context within which the proposed system, device or – to use Don Norman's phrase – 'information appliance' is to be used. We need to know about the intended user group – and about any organisational, environmental, technological, legal or ethical constraints on its deployment.

How do we find out all that we need to know? Typically in UCSD, requirements emerge as the team builds up a rich picture of the intended circumstances of use. As we've discussed, it can be an untidy and iterative process of interviews with stakeholders, workplace observation, user surveys and analysis of existing or competing systems or products. In contrast with sequential Waterfall methods, in UCSD the process of requirements gathering does not – nor is it expected to – happen once and for all. New requirements can emerge at any point in the UCSD requirements gathering, prototype design and evaluation cycle.

You'll remember that we discussed design rationale and the **question-option-criteria** (QOC) technique of design space analysis in Chapter 6. Clearly, design solutions need to meet requirements. If, for example, you are designing a walk-up-and-use information kiosk then:

- One **question** might be 'How can we support ad hoc database queries?'
- Some design **options** might be *query by touch-screen category* or *selection by pointing within a pull-down list*
- **Criteria** are likely to be derived from a usability principle such as 'Speak the user's language' – or, more specifically, 'Hide the complexities of SQL database query language'.

Design space analysis is usually done collaboratively within the team and with representative users. During a QOC session, you will probably have one or more storyboards to hand as a way of visualising typical scenarios of use and their flow.

But storyboarding can also be considered as a form of 'low fidelity' prototyping. We develop our early design ideas through making quick sketches on paper – rather than going to the expense of building throwaway, incremental or evolutionary machine-based implementations. That we do later, as we converge on an agreed design.

Why do we storyboard or prototype our designs?

- **To turn an abstract design into a physical form**. From a user perspective, this answers the question 'How do I know what I want until I see what I can have?'
- **To communicate your ideas** – 'Show and tell'
- **To be iterative and improve**.

Prototyping a hand-held interactive visitor's guide for visitors to London Zoo

Imagine that you are a member of the team designing a hand-held interactive visitor's guide for London Zoo. The guide will be used by visitors to help find their way around and to learn more about the large and varied collection of animals. Here is a hierarchical task analysis (HTA) prepared by one of your colleagues outlining the 'tasks' of a visitor to the zoo.

0. Visit zoo

1. Purchase ticket
   1.1. Find ticket kiosk
   1.2. Get ticket

2. Visit animals
   2.1. Decide which animals to see
   2.2. Find where they are housed
   2.3. Go to appropriate place
   2.4. View animals

3. Visit shop
   3.1. Find out where shop is
   3.2. Go to shop
   3.3. Browse
   3.4. Buy items

4. Visit restaurant
   4.1. Find out where restaurant is
   4.2. Go to restaurant
   4.3. Buy meal

5. Visit toilets
   5.1. Find out where toilets are
   5.2. Go to toilets
   5.3. Use toilets

6. Leave zoo
   6.1. Find out where exit is
   6.2. Go to exit
   6.3. Leave

Plan 0: Do 1 first, followed by any of (2, 3, 4 and 5) in any order as many times as needed. Then do 6.
Plan 1: Do 1.1, then 1.2.
Plan 2: Do 2.1, then 2.2, then 2.3 then 2.4.
Plan 3: Do 3.1, then 3.2, then 3.3 then 3.4.
Plan 4: Do 4.1, then 4.2, then 4.3.
Plan 5: Do 5.1, then 5.2, then 5.3.
Plan 6: Do 6.1, then 6.2, then 6.3.

... *continued*

Here is a first paper-prototype of the device:

London Zoo Interactive Guide

Bears

Lions   Tigers   Birds

Press to move through the zoo

The screen presents a map of a section of the zoo. The arrow buttons enable the visitor to scroll the map left and right or up and down.

- Given your colleague's HTA, what is your evaluation of this prototype?
- How would you redesign it so that it better supports the tasks in the HTA?

12.8 Cognitive psychology: memory, attention and perception

We looked in greater depth in Chapters 7 and 8 at current cognitive models of memory, attention and perception.

Elsewhere in this book (for instance, in Chapters 3, 4 and 11) we introduced you to a range of guidelines and heuristics for human–computer interaction and interface design. Our guiding concerns have been:

- What practical implications for interactive system design can we infer?
- How can we design systems that make the most of, rather than conflict with, users' abilities, attentional focus, perceptual skills or preferences?

Underlying the design of most successful interfaces, however, is a sound understanding of human cognitive processes, their strengths and limitations.

The purpose of a psychological theory is to explain or predict human behaviour. A model is simply a way of presenting such a theory.

Remember Nielsen's *'Support recognition rather than recall'*!

12.9   Evaluation as part of the UCSD process

Perhaps the ultimate usability test of a system is that it be used by real users, enriching and becoming a natural part of their everyday lives:

> Instant messenger … is an integrated part of my life. With it, I have a sense of connection to many of my friends and colleagues around the world. Without it, I feel as though a window to part of my world is bolted shut.   Quoted in Norman (2004)

Stepping back a bit, in Chapter 9 we looked at the role of evaluation in the UCSD process. We distinguished between:

- **Formative evaluation:** this is carried out within the overall design process to deepen our understanding of requirements, learn more about user needs and test prototype designs
- **Summative evaluation:** this is external to the design process, which takes the finished product and assesses it for usability or fitness for purpose – typically as part of an organisation's procurement process.

As we have seen, UCSD is based on the belief that usable and useful systems evolve through an iterative process of generating, representing, testing and refining design ideas. What that means is that we are mainly concerned with formative evaluation here.

When do we carry out a formative evaluation? The simple answer is: 'As early and as often as possible'. Evaluation is helpful at all stages of a project, even during our earliest design ideas – whether storyboards or paper prototypes.

Which method of evaluation should we use?

- Cognitive walkthrough?
- User satisfaction questionnaires or surveys?
- A comparative experiment under controlled conditions?
- User observation with 'talk aloud' and 'think aloud' protocol analysis?
- Simulation?

The answer is that it depends on what your purpose is, what is being tested, when, who the users are and the context of use of the intended system. For instance:

- In evaluating early design ideas you might well do a task-analysis-based **cognitive walkthrough** with other members of the design team
- If you were evaluating a new supermarket checkout to be operated by trained staff, a **comparative experiment** would be the most appropriate method to measure throughput (i.e. the time taken per transaction)
- When evaluating a prototype for a commercial website, we would probably want to know not only how usable it is for first-time visitors, but also how pleasurable it is so as to encourage customers to return. Here you might use an **observational study and 'think aloud' protocol analysis** with a sample of potential customers – supplemented perhaps by a questionnaire to gauge subjective measures of satisfaction

- For safety-critical train or aeroplane cockpit automation software, a **full-blown simulation** is probably the only realistic choice.

Evaluating a prototype portable communicator for Mollusc Oil

Mollusc Oil has developed a working prototype of a portable communicator for use by divers in the North Sea who repair underwater damage to offshore oil rigs. The communicator will enable the divers to communicate with each other and with controllers on the surface. Diving is dangerous and highly skilled work. Mollusc currently employs 20 divers. The prototype now needs to be tested. The independent usability consultancy firm that has been contracted to conduct the tests has drawn up the following test plan:

- The prototype is to be tested by user observation

- 100 subjects will be chosen to test the prototype. They will be a carefully selected group who will not be biased by culture or gender. To limit costs, the subjects will be chosen from the experimenters' friends, family and work colleagues

- The subjects will be asked to use the prototype communicator in our usability lab where they will be put in a comfortable, non-threatening environment

- The experimenters (who will include some of the developers of the communicator) will help the subjects use the communicators

- At the end of the experiment, the subjects will be asked to complete a comprehensive user-experience questionnaire.

You are the manager of the diving crew. When asked to comment on or approve the plan, you have serious reservations about the real-world validity of the tests.

- Can you suggest how the user observation could be redesigned to improve its real-world validity?

12.10 Emerging human–computer interface technologies

As long ago as 1999, Donald Norman predicted that we would soon be living among 'invisible computers' or 'information appliances' that we do not regard as computers at all. Norman speculated that information appliances would have the following properties:

- **Single purpose:** an information appliance should do one thing and do it well
- **Hidden technology:** users need to know what the appliance does, not how it does it
- **Enable free interchange of information:** requesting, accepting or moving information from one appliance to another should be seamless – making possible what he refers to as 'serendipitous flexibility'.

What do you think? Has Norman's prediction come true?

Today, the long-awaited convergence of computer technology, consumer electronics and mobile, 'always-on' telephony is gaining momentum. Increasingly we live in an information-rich world that is no longer bounded by the desktop or laptop PC. Personal digital assistants (PDAs) and smart phones that provide Internet access, video messaging and more are commonplace.

Comparing different technologies

In Chapter 10, we invited you to compare the experience of tuning in to a radio station on a conventional (or digital) radio with that of streaming audio on PC.

How do they compare with tuning in to a radio station on your mobile phone – assuming that your phone has that capability?

- Which is less complicated?

- Why?

- Which do you prefer?

A related issue that we explored in Chapter 10 was the technology adoption / innovation diffusion cycle – or how people respond to discontinuous innovation.

Discontinuous innovations are those products or services that require people to change their behaviour, on the promise that they will gain unimaginable benefits. What this means in practice is that when a new technology becomes available, people adopt it or not depending on how risk-averse they are.

- **Innovators** and **technology enthusiasts** move to the front, wanting to be first to try out the new technology. They take pleasure in mastering its intricacies or just fiddling with it

- Next are the **early adopters** or **visionaries** in organisations. Their expectation is that by exploiting the new technology they will be able to achieve an insurmountable competitive advantage

- The **early majority** or **pragmatists** follow. They believe in 'evolution, not revolution' so they're not visionaries, nor do they like technology for its own sake

- The **late majority** or **conservatives** only buy in when the no-longer-new technology has become a commodity product

- Finally, there are **late adopters**, the **laggards** or **sceptics**. They would rather write with a fountain pen than use a word processor – and, if you ask them, they have a perfectly rational explanation for doing so.

Are *you* an early adopter or late adopter of technology?

In Chapter 10, we asked if you considered yourself a technophile or early adopter, or a late adopter. Many people are early adopters of new technology in some areas of their life, but late adopters in others.

- Which are you?
- In which areas?

12.11 Universal access and 'design for all'

Finally, we looked at different approaches, methods and practices for the design of interactive systems that can be used by anyone, anytime, anywhere.

As we discussed in Chapter 11, the different approaches go by different names. The terms *universal access* or *universal design*, for instance, are more familiar in America. Their European counterparts are known as *design for all* or *inclusive design*.

What they have in common is a concern to ensure that interactive systems can be used by anyone, regardless of their strengths and weaknesses, their level of expertise, disabilities or the environments they find themselves in. In this sense, increased usability or accessibility is a benefit for everyone.

References and further reading

Barnard, P (1987), *Cognitive resources and the learning of human–computer dialogs*. In Carroll, JM (Ed.), *Interfacing Thought: Cognitive Aspects of Human–Computer Interaction*, Cambridge, Mass: MIT Press.

Broadbent, DE (1984), The Maltese Cross: a new simplistic model of memory, *Behavioural and Brain Sciences*, 7, 55-94.

Moore, GA (1998), *Inside the Tornado: Marketing Strategies from Silicon Valley's Cutting Edge*, Oxford: Capstone Publishing.

Moore, GA (1999), *Crossing the Chasm: Marketing and Selling Technology Products to Mainstream Customers*, Oxford: Capstone Publishing.

Norman, DA (1999), *The Invisible Computer*, Cambridge, MA: MIT Press.

Norman, DA (2004), *Emotional Design: Why We Love (or Hate) Everyday Things*, New York: Basic Books.

Glossary of terms

Here are the definitions of some key concepts in this area.

- Accessible: an accessible system design ensures that users with disabilities or working in extreme circumstances can still access system functions
- Adaptable: applied to interactive systems which can be fed the profile of an individual at the start of a work sessions and adapt the system interface to reflect the requirements and preferences contained in that profile. Such systems may also store such profiles on a long-term basis and apply them when each user logs on
- Adaptive: applied to interactive systems that can observe user performance and adapt their interfaces to that performance during the work session. Note that adaptable and an adaptive systems are different: an adaptive system can change on the basis of what the user does or can do, although an adaptable system cannot (see below)
- Adaptable systems: for example, a word-processing package that presents visual information in different ways for users with different visual impairments
- Adaptive systems: can respond to the performance of a user by changing system parameters to enhance user performance. For example, consider a web browser which responds to the errors of a user by changing the appearance of the information on the screen
- Artefact: an artefact is defined as a characteristic product or by-product of human activity, a hand-made or mass-made item representing a particular culture or stage of technological development (*Webster's Ninth New Collegiate Dictionary*)
- Assistive technology: adds to the basic functions of a system so as to support the performance of users with disabilities or who work in extreme environments
- Avatar: a human-like image on a screen which mimics human-like attributes and which is used by a system to interact with individual users
- Customisation: adaptation of an existing system to meet the needs of a specific user. For example, changing the set-up of a mouse for a left-handed person
- Design for all: indicates a design or set of designs so that the system can be used by all users, regardless of their strengths and weaknesses, their level of expertise, disabilities and environments. Design for all includes adherence to design standards to achieve user accessibility. For example, consider a word-processing application with a number of different design versions, for people with different requirements or disabilities. See also *Universal access*
- Human–computer interaction (HCI): the study of the interactions between people and interactive computer systems, including insights into user models and user requirements, as well as the application to the design and evaluation of such systems for usefulness, usability and accessibility

- Natural computation or computing: natural computing is the study of how people process and store information, manipulate symbols, ascribe personal values to events, attribute cultural and emotive judgements etc and how we use interactive artefacts to enhance our lifestyles. Such artefacts include, but are not limited to, computer-based systems as well as other technologies such as interactive television, mobile telephony, embedded processors etc. It also provides an environment within which to consider methods by which designers can build systems which are more useful, usable and accessible

- Self-configurable system: this kind of system is able to observe its own status and change its parameters (hardware or software) accordingly. There are a number of circumstances when this is important. For example, a system working in a remote or dangerous location (e.g. on the sea bed) cannot be accessed easily by a mechanic, or a computer system under attack by a virus, which may need to respond quickly and automatically. In the area of universal access, a system might need to respond quickly to the performance problems of a specific user

- Universal access: this indicates system design that can be used by anyone, anytime, anywhere. It involves both suitable system designs and suitable means of access to the system. For example, consider an adaptive web browser which translates websites into appropriate formats. The basic concept focuses upon providing many paths to a well-designed system. See also *Design for all*

- Usable: usability has been defined by the ISO as ... the effectiveness, efficiency and satisfaction with which specified users achieve specified goals in particular environments. Not to be confused with *Useful*

- Useful: applied to systems which provide or perform functions that users require; not to be confused with *Usable*

- User-centred system design (UCSD) also known as user-centred design (UCD): puts user needs and capabilities at the centre of the design process.

Bibliography

*Titles are shown alphabetically, with an indication **in bold** as to the chapter(s) of this book in which they are encountered.*

Adams, R and Langdon, P (2003, *SIMPLEX: a simple user check-model for Inclusive Design*. In *Universal Access in HCI: Inclusive Design in the Information Society*, Stephanidis, C. (Ed.). 4, 13-17. Mahwah, NJ: Lawrence Erlbaum Associates. **Ch 7**

Adams, R, Langdon, P and Clarkson, PJ (2002), A systematic basis for developing cognitive assessment methods for assistive technology. In: Keates, S, Langdon, P, Clarkson PJ and Robinson, P (eds), Universal Access and Assistive Technology, London: Springer-Verlag **Ch 3**

Anderson JR (1983), The Architecture of Cognition, Cambridge, Mass: Harvard University Press **Ch 3, 7**

Annett, J, & Duncan, KD (1967), Task analysis and training design, *Journal of Occupational Psychology*, 41, 211-221 **Ch 5**

Barnard, P (1987), *Cognitive resources and the learning of human–computer dialogs*. In Carroll, JM (Ed.), *Interfacing Thought: Cognitive Aspects of Human–Computer Interaction*, Cambridge, Mass: MIT Press. **Ch 12**

Barnard, PJ (1985), *Interacting Cognitive Subsystems: A psycholinguistic approach to short term memory*. In A Ellis (Ed.), *Progress in the Psychology of Language*, Vol. 2, London: Lawrence Erlbaum Associates, 197-258. **Ch 7**

Barnard, PJ, May, J, Duke, D and Duce, D (2000), *Systems interactions macro-theory*, Trans. Human Computer Interface, 7, 222-62 **Ch 3**

Bobby (automated toolkit), available at **www.watchfire .com Ch 11**

Broadbent, DE (1984), The Maltese Cross: a new simplistic model of memory, *Behavioural and Brain Sciences*, 7, 55-94 **Ch 3, 7, 12**

Card, SK, Moran, TP, and Newell, A (1983), *The Psychology of Human–Computer Interaction*. Hillsdale, N.J.: Lawrence Erlbaum Associates. **Ch 3, 7**

Carroll, JM (2000), *Making Use: Scenario based design for Human Computer Interaction*, Cambridge, MA: MIT Press **Ch 6**

Cooper A (1999), *The Inmates Are Running the Asylum: Why High Tech Products Drive Us Crazy and How To Restore The Sanity*, SAMS. **Ch 1**

Darnell MJ (2004), *Bad Human Factors Design* **www.baddesigns.com/ranges.html Ch 1**

Dix, A, Finlay, J, Abowd, GD, Beale, R (2004), *Human-Computer Interaction*, third edition, Harlow: Pearson Education; also **www.hcibook.com Ch 3, 5, 9**

Donald Norman: **www.jnd.org/bio-sketch.html Ch 8**

Dourish P (2004). "What We Talk About When We Talk About Context". *Personal and Ubiquitous Computing*, 8(1), 19-30. **Ch 10**

Gibson, JJ (1979), *The Ecological Approach to Visual Perception*, Hillsdale, New Jersey: Lawrence Erlbaum Associates. **Ch 8**

Gould JD, Boies S J, Levy S, Richards JT, Schoonard J (1987), The 1984 Olympic Message System: a test of behavioral principles of system design, *Communications of the ACM* September 1987, Volume 30 , Issue 9. **Ch 2**

Gould, JD, Lewis, CH (1985), Designing for usability: key principles and what designers think, *Communications of the ACM*, 28(3). 300-311 **Ch 6**

Hewitt T (1986), *Iterative evaluation*. In Harrison M D and Monk A F (Eds), *People and Computers: Designing for usability*, Proceedings of the second conference of the BCS HCI Specialist Group. **Ch 9**

Jakob Nielsen's website: **www.useit.com Ch 11**

James Gibson: **www.huwi.org/gibson/index.php Ch 8**

Laird, JE, Newell, A and Rosenbloom, P (1987), SOAR: an architecture for general intelligence, *Artificial Intelligence*, 33, 1-64 **Ch 3**

LaTeX: **www.latex-project.org Ch 6**

McGrenere, J and Ho, W (2000), Affordances: Clarifying and Evolving a Concept, *Proceedings of Graphics Interface*, Montreal: Quebec. **Ch 8**

Moore, GA (1998), *Inside the Tornado: Marketing Strategies from Silicon Valley's Cutting Edge*, Oxford: Capstone Publishing. **Ch 12**

Moore, GA (1999), Crossing the Chasm: Marketing and Selling Technology Products to Mainstream Customers, Oxford: Capstone Publishing. **Ch 12**

Nielsen J (2000), *Designing Web Usability*, Berkley, CA: New Riders. **Ch 9**

Nielsen J, and Mack RL (1994), *Usability inspection methods*, New York: John Wiley & Sons. **Ch 9**

Nielsen, J (1994), *Usability Engineering*, London: Academic Press **Ch 3, 4, 6**

Nielsen, J (2001), *Ten Usability Heuristics*. **www.useit.com/papers/heuristic Ch 3**

Norman D (1999), *The invisible computer*, Cambridge, MA.: MIT Press. **Ch 1, 8, 10, 12**

Norman, DA & Draper, SW (Ed.) (1986). *User-centered system design*. Hillsdale, NJ: Lawrence Erlbaum Associates. **Ch 10**

Norman, DA (1988), *The Design of Everyday Things*. New York, Doubleday **Ch 3, 4, 8**

Norman, DA (2004), *Emotional Design: Why We Love (or Hate) Everyday Things*, New York: Basic Books. **Ch 12**

Norman, DA (1999), *Invisible Computer: Why Good Products Can Fail, the Personal Computer Is So Complex and Information Appliances Are the Solution*, London: MIT Press. **Ch 8**

Norman, DA (1999), Affordances, Conventions, and Design, In *Interactions*, 6 (3) p. 38-41, Hillsdale NJ: Lawrence Erlbaum Associates **Ch 8**

Pinker S (1997), *How the mind works*, London: Penguin. **Ch 1,2**

Preece J, Rogers Y & Sharp H (2002), *Interaction Design: beyond human computer interaction*, Chichester: John Wiley & Sons. **Ch 1,2,4,7, 9**

Procedural Task Analysis: **http://classweb.gmu.edu/ndabbagh/Resources/Resources2/ procedural_analysis.htm Ch 5**

Richard Gregory: **www.richardgregory.org/ Ch 8**

Royal National Institute of the Blind (RNIB): **www.rnib.org.uk Ch 11**

Royce, WW (1970), *Managing the Development of Large Software Systems*, Proceedings of *IEEE WESCON*, August 1970. **Ch 4**

Shneiderman B (2002), *Leonardo's Laptop: Human Needs and the New Computing Technologies*, Cambridge, MA: MIT Press. **Ch 2, 7**

Shneiderman, B (1998), *Designing the User Interface*, 3rd edition, Addison-Wesley, Reading, Massachusetts **Ch 3**

The Center for Universal Design (1997), *The Principles of Universal Design*, Version 2.0, Raleigh, NC: North Carolina State University **Ch 11**

Tognazzini, B, 'Tog' (1992), *Tog on Interface*. Addison-Wesley, Reading, Mass **www.asktog.com/ Ch 3**

University of Leiden, Center for Natural Computing: **www.lcnc.nl Ch 2**

Web Content Accessibility Guidelines 2.0, available at: **www.w3.org   Ch 11**

Weiser M (1991) "The Computer for the 21st Century", *Scientific American*, Vol. 265, No. 3, September, 94-104 **Ch 10**

www.graphicsinterface.org/proceedings/2000/ Ch 8